The European Union in International Affairs

Institute for
European Studies
Vrije Universiteit Brussel

Thanks to consecutive rounds of enlargement and the stepwise broadening and deepening of internal integration, the EU now undeniably plays a key role in international politics, law and economics. At the same time, changes in the international system continue to pose new challenges to the EU. The range of policies implied by the EU's international 'actorness' grows with every summit, and the EU regularly 'imports' and increasingly 'exports' various policies.

Against this backdrop, this book series aims to be a central resource for the growing community of scholars and policymakers interested in understanding the interface between the EU and international affairs. It will provide in-depth, cutting-edge contributions to research on the EU in international affairs by highlighting new developments, insights, challenges and opportunities. It will encompass analyses of the EU's international role, as mediated by its own member states, in international institutions and in its strategic bilateral and regional partnerships. It will further examine the ongoing profusion of EU internal policies with external implications and the ways in which these are both driven by and feed back into international developments. Grounded in political science (and its various sub-disciplines, including international relations and international political economy), law, sociology and history, the series reflects an interdisciplinary commitment.

Titles include:

Frauke Austermann
EUROPEAN UNION DELEGATIONS IN EU FOREIGN POLICY
A Diplomatic Service of Different Speeds

Joachim Koops and Gjovalin Macaj
THE EU AS A DIPLOMATIC ACTOR

Alexander Mattelaer
THE POLITICO-MILITARY DYNAMICS OF EUROPEAN CRISIS RESPONSE
OPERATIONS
Planning, Friction, Strategy

Louise G. van Schaik
EU EFFECTIVENESS AND UNITY IN MULTILATERAL NEGOTIATIONS
More Than the Sum of Its Parts?

Luis Simon
GEOPOLITICAL CHANGE, GRAND STRATEGY AND EUROPEAN SECURITY
The EU-Nato Conundrum

Forthcoming titles include:

Dimitrios Bourantonis, Spyros Blavoukos and Clara Portela (*editors*)
THE EU AND THE NON-PROLIFERATION OF NUCLEAR WEAPONS

*Alex Warleigh-Lack is currently on leave as an editor of the series.

The European Union in International Affairs series
Series standing order ISBN 978–1–137–00500–7 (hardback)
978–1–137–00501–4 (paperback)

You can receive future titles in this series as they are published by placing a standing order. Please contact your bookseller or, in case of difficulty, write to us at the address below with your name and address, the title of the series and one of the ISBNs quoted above.

Customer Services Department, Macmillan Distribution Ltd, Houndmills, Basingstoke, Hampshire RG21 6XS, England

---

The Securitisation of Migration in the EU

Debates since 9/11

Edited by

Gabriella Lazaridis
Senior Lecturer, University of Leicester, UK

and

Khursheed Wadia
Principal Research Fellow, University of Warwick, UK

First published 2015 by
PALGRAVE MACMILLAN

Palgrave Macmillan in the UK is an imprint of Macmillan Publishers Limited,
registered in England, company number 785998, of Houndmills, Basingstoke,
Hampshire RG21 6XS.

Palgrave Macmillan in the US is a division of St Martin's Press LLC,
175 Fifth Avenue, New York, NY 10010.

Palgrave Macmillan is the global academic imprint of the above companies
and has companies and representatives throughout the world.

Palgrave® and Macmillan® are registered trademarks in the United States,
the United Kingdom, Europe and other countries.

ISBN: 978–1–137–48057–6

This book is printed on paper suitable for recycling and made from fully
managed and sustained forest sources. Logging, pulping and manufacturing
processes are expected to conform to the environmental regulations of the
country of origin.

A catalogue record for this book is available from the British Library.

Library of Congress Cataloging-in-Publication Data

The securitisation of migration in the EU : debates since 9/11 / edited by
Gabriella Lazaridis, Senior Lecturer, University of Leicester, UK ; Khursheed Wadia,
Principal Research Fellow, University of Warwick, UK.
    pages cm. — (European Union in international affairs)
    ISBN 978–1–137–48057–6 (hardback)
    1. European Union countries – Emigration and immigration – Government
policy. 2. European Union countries – Emigration and immigration – Social
aspects. 3. National security – European Union countries. 4. Immigrants –
Government policy – European Union countries. 5. Refugees – Government
policy – European Union countries. I. Lazaridis, Gabriella, editor. II. Wadia,
Khursheed, editor. III. Title: Securitization of migration in the EU.

JV7590.S427 2015
325.4—dc23   2015020069

Contents

Acknowledgements

This edited volume of papers is the result of a seminar series entitled 'Whose Security? Migration-(In)Security Dilemmas Ten Years after 9/11' which was funded by the Economic and Social Research Council (ESRC) and which ran from June 2011 to March 2013 at the universities of Leicester and Warwick.[1]

Many people have contributed in various ways to the completion of this book. First, we would like to thank each of the contributing authors for agreeing to share their expertise and knowledge. We have valued the opportunity of working with many new and established scholars and practitioners and to have gained interesting and new insights from their work in the field of migration and (in)security. We would also like to thank all the editorial staff at Palgrave Macmillan who have been involved in the making of this book, in particular Sara Crowley-Vigneau and Jemima Warren. Finally, but not least, our thanks go to the anonymous reviewers to whom the original proposal for this book was sent, for their valuable comments and suggestions, which have been incorporated into the editing of this book.

Note

1. Grant reference (RES-451-26-0944).

Notes on Contributors

Don Flynn is Director of Migrant Rights Network, a network of civil society organisations which supports the rights of migrants. He leads MRN's strategic development and coordinates its policy and project work. He researched and founded MRN after many years' of experience of working with migrant community organisations, through his previous roles as policy officer with the Joint Council for the Welfare of Immigrants, and as an immigration caseworker in London. He also chairs the UK Race and Equality Network (UKREN) and the Platform for International Cooperation on Undocumented Migrants (PICUM). He has written numerous articles for the daily and periodical press, and papers on immigration law and policy in the UK, including 'Immigration controls and citizenship in the political rhetoric of New Labour' in Zureik and Salter (eds) *Global surveillance and policing: border, security, identity* (2005) and Finch and Goodhart (eds) *Immigration under New Labour* (2010), and policy briefs on behalf of MRN and other migrant support organisations.

Lena Karamanidou holds a PhD from the Department of Sociology, City University, London and joined the same department as a lecturer in 2012. Her main research areas are asylum and migration policy and discourse in Europe and the intersections between migration, exclusion and the state. She has worked on immigration discourse and the radical right in Greece. Her recent publications include 'Realising one's rights under the 1951 Convention: a review of practical constraints on accessing protection in Europe through a case study of Greece' (co-authored with L. Schuster), *Journal of Refugee Studies*, 25(2): 169–192, 2012 and 'Refugees, "illegal immigrants" and asylum seekers: use of discursive categories and legitimation of asylum policies in Greek political discourse', *Mediterranean Journal of Human Rights*, 11(2): 17–45, 2007.

Anna-Maria Konsta is Associate Professor of European Politics and Law at the American College of Thessaloniki, a lecturer at the Hellenic National Centre of Public Administration, and a Thessaloniki Bar Association lawyer. She has been a research fellow at the Boalt Hall School of Law and at the University of California, Berkeley, and has worked for both the European Commission in Brussels and the Council of Europe in Strasbourg. She is author of the book *Working time law in*

Japan and the European Union: a comparative approach in the context of legal culture (2003), and has published in the field of European and comparative social law. Her current research project deals with gender and migration in the EU.

Gabriella Lazaridis is a senior lecturer in the Department of Politics and International Relations at the University of Leicester, UK. She is well known in the field of ethnicity, migration, citizenship and gender and has published extensively in the fields of gender, ethnicity and migration in Europe, and the implementation of European policies in southern Europe. Her work has been translated into Greek, Polish, German and Italian. She is the author of *Women's work and lives in rural Greece* (2009) and *International migration in Europe: from subjects to abjects* (Palgrave Macmillan, 2015). She has authored/co-authored over 45 papers in academic journals and has edited/coedited seven books; she is currently working on a monograph on gender and migration and is researching 'Hate speech and populist Othering in Europe: through the race, age, gender looking glass'. This is a €1,200,000 comparative project funded by the EU's DG Justice, 'Fundamental Rights and Citizenship Programme,' where she is the principal investigator and also leads the Leicester team. The project examines 'populist' political discourse and its effect on those Othered by such discourse, particularly in the context of economic austerity and dwindling opportunities for young people. Eight teams, covering nine EU member states (UK, France, Italy, Greece, Bulgaria, Denmark, Austria, Finland and Slovenia), will take a mixed-methods approach to the analysis of populist discourse and its effects.

Mark Maguire is based in the Department of Anthropology at the National University of Ireland, Maynooth. His research focuses on the areas of migration and security and is concerned with exploring international migration through ethnographic research on everyday lives. He has a growing interest in the technologies and processes of securitisation, especially counter-terrorism, biometric security, affective computing and the detection of abnormal behaviour or 'malintent'. He is author of *Differently Irish* (2004), which explores the lives of Vietnamese refugees and their families, and co-author (with Fiona Murphy) of *Integration in Ireland: the everyday lives of African migrants* (2012). He is also co-editor of *The anthropology of security* (2014). He was a visiting assistant professor in Stanford University's anthropology department in 2008 and an associate professor there in 2011. He is editor-in-chief of *Social Anthropology*, Europe's leading anthropology journal and is an ex officio member of the executive committee of the European Association of Social Anthropologists (EASA).

Laura Zahra McDonald is a founder and co-director of ConnectJustice, a social enterprise which works with academics, communities and practitioners to research, train and facilitate for social justice. With a Master's in Social Anthropology with sub-honours in Arabic and Middle Eastern studies from the University of St Andrews, and a PhD from the Centre for Women's Studies, University of York in Gender, Intersectionality and Islam, she contributed to a seven-year research programme at the University of Birmingham on community-state engagement and conflict, with a focus on the impact of terrorism and counter-terrorism on Muslim communities. As part of her role with ConnectJustice, she lectures internationally, while researching, engaging and advising high-impact projects with diverse organisations. Her recent publications include 'Counter-terror as conflict transformation?' in L. Jarvis and M. Lister (eds) *Critical perspectives on counter-terrorism* (2015), 'Predatory others: child sexual exploitation, ethnicity and faith', a report for the Howard League (2013), 'Gender within a counter-terrorism context' and 'Engaging young people within a counter-terrorism context' in B. Spalek (ed) *Counter-terrorism: community-based approaches to preventing terror crime* (Palgrave Macmillan, 2012).

Awale Olad is the public and parliamentary affairs officer at MRN, coordinating the work of the All-Party Parliamentary Group on Migration and supporting parliamentarians and policymakers in establishing a cross-party consensus on immigration policy in the UK. He organises cross-party parliamentary roundtables and political and public meetings related to immigration policy, as well as prepares briefings, comment pieces, parliamentary questions and submissions for parliamentarians and media. He holds an MA in European Studies from King's College, London, and worked for a few years as a parliamentary researcher for the Justice Minister (2007–2010), and then later for a backbench MP. He also works for the Camden BME Alliance. He is a local councillor in the London Borough of Camden and takes part in local decision-making and campaigning.

Vicki Squire is Associate Professor of International Security in the Department of Politics and International Studies at the University of Warwick. Before joining Warwick in 2012, she was a RCUK fellow at the Centre of Citizenship, Identities and Governance at the Open University, and prior to that, an ESRC postdoctoral research fellow in the Department of Political Science and International Studies at the University of Birmingham. Her research cuts across the fields of critical citizenship, migration and security studies, and coalesces around her interest in the emergence, development and contestation of various rationalities or techniques of governing mobility. Specifically, she considers the political implications of different practices of governing mobility, as well as the transformative potential of diverse struggles through which such practices are contested, resisted and/or subverted. She has published widely in this area, and her recent publications include 'The "minor" politics of rightful presence: justice and relationality in City of Sanctuary', *International Political Sociology*, 7(1): 59–74, 2013; 'Politics through a web: citizenship and community unbound', *Environment and Planning D: Society and Space*, 30(3): 551–567, 2012; *The contested politics of mobility: borderzones and irregularity* (2011); 'From community cohesion to mobile solidarities: the City of Sanctuary network and the Strangers into Citizens campaign', *Political Studies*, 59(2), 290–307, 2011; and *The exclusionary politics of asylum* (Palgrave Macmillan, 2009).

Emanuele Toscano is a researcher at the University G. Marconi in Italy and an associate research fellow at the École des Hautes Études en Sciences Sociales (Centre d'Analyse et d'Intervention Sociologique) in Paris. His research interests are focused on extreme right populist movements in Italy and also on alter-global movements in Europe. His recent publications include a monograph, co-authored with D. Di Nunzio, *Dentro e fuori CasaPound. Capire il fascismo del III millennio* (2011) and journal articles, among which are 'The sphere of action of the alterglobal movement: a key of interpretation', *Social Movement Studies*, 11(1): 79–96, 2012 and, with D. Di Nunzio, 'Il Movimento CasaPound: l'affermazione dell'individuo e i limiti per la democrazia', *Rassegna Italiana di Sociologia*, 53(4): 331–360, 2012. He is also a committee member of the International Sociological Association's RC47 section on social classes and social movements and editor of the online European review, *New Cultural Frontiers*.

Vasiliki Tsagkroni has completed her doctorate degree at Queen Mary University London. Her area of research is political communication and, in addition, the use of marketing and branding in politics, in which she is investigating the interaction between communication strategies and political parties with a special interest in the parties of the far right. She has experience working in a wide range of organisational and managerial positions and has developed her teaching skills in an academic environment while working as a teaching associate at Queen Mary University London. She is working as a research associate at the University of Leicester, as part of the RAGE ('Hate speech and populist othering in Europe: through the race, age, gender looking glass') project team. This is a comparative project funded by the EU's DG Justice, Fundamental

Rights and Citizenship Programme and examines populist political discourse and its effects on those Othered by it.

Khursheed Wadia is a principal research fellow at the University of Warwick and an overseas research fellow at the École des Hautes Études en Sciences Sociales (Centre d'Analyse et d'Intervention Sociologique) in Paris. She has written on aspects of gender, ethnicity, politics and policy. She completed (with Danièle Joly) a four-year investigation of Muslim women and politics in Britain and France, funded by the ESRC (Economic and Social Research Council) and is working on a monograph, to be published by Palgrave Macmillan, titled, *Muslim women and power: political and civic engagement in West European societies*. She has also undertaken research on migration, policy and the integration of migrants in EU countries and written several reports for the EU Commission. She has published monographs (co-authored with Gill Allwood) including *Women and politics in France: 1958–2000* (2000), *Gender and policy in France* (Palgrave Macmillan, 2009), and *Refugee women in Britain and France* (2010). She has published journal articles and book chapters on gender, ethnicity, migration and politics. She is currently involved in a large-scale EU-funded study ('Memory, Youth, Political Legacy and Civic Engagement') of young people and political/civic engagement across 14 countries and is working on a co-authored monograph, titled, *Feminist activism and sexual politics in Europe: a new wave?*

Introduction

Gabriella Lazaridis and Khursheed Wadia

The securitisation of migration

During the 1990s and 2000s, the focus within studies of international migration was placed rather strongly on aspects of (cultural) difference, questions of ethnicity, identity and belonging and the way in which these intersected with age, gender and sexuality (for example, Anthias and Lazaridis 2013; Berggren, Brborić and Toksöz 2007; Borooah and Mangan 2009; Düvell 2006; Mingione 1995; Portes and Sensenbrenner 1993; Weiner 1995; Yuval-Davis 2007). Partly due to the obvious and urgent crises and contradictions engendered by neoliberal globalisation, inequalities have resurfaced as a key concern of sociological enquiry as well as within political, economic, migration and European studies over the past few years. Lately, the question of how the interplay between difference and inequalities is structured by political agency and discourses has risen on the agenda of academics and political commentators, and most notably in recent studies on the securitisation of migration (for example, Bigo 2008; Bourbeau 2011; De Genova 2007; Huysmans 2008; Lazaridis and Konsta 2011; Togral 2011). This is unsurprising, given the influence of the work of securitisation theorists (Booth 1991; Buzan, Wæver and De Wilde 1998; Wyn Jones 1995) on the analysis of numerous global issues ranging from climate change, to religious violence, to health.[1]

Security concerns have topped western political agendas since the attacks of 9/11. Given that non-state agents carried out these attacks, governments in the West resurrected the Cold War argument that security should also be about combating non-military threats. Included among the non-military threats to state security is migration, the idea being that liberal migration regimes advance cross-border risks – for example, terrorism, drugs and human trafficking – while more restrictive regimes minimise such threats and improve state/national and societal security. As Lazaridis and Tsagkroni state in Chapter 9 of this volume, 'securitisation then, takes place when political leaders utilise the rhetoric of threat pushing, in this way, an area of normal politics into the security realm'. Hence, while attempting to facilitate the mobility necessary to the global economy, western governments have sought to control, at the same time, that very mobility by integrating securitisation measures within migration regimes; asylum seekers, economic and other migrant categories then come to be seen as agents of social instability or as potential terrorists seeking to exploit immigration systems.

Scholars of the securitisation of migration have posed a number of questions. Among them: Is migration a security issue? If so, in what ways have the discourses and practices of securitisation rendered migration a security issue? And who produces the knowledge used to transform migration into a security issue? These questions are raised and discussed by Squire, Karamanidou and Maguire in Part I of this book.

Whose (in)/security?

The upshot of treating migration as a security threat is the increased insecurity amongst migrant and ethnic minority populations in the West, and particularly among those from Muslim majority countries or long-settled Muslim and ethnic minority communities.

The state is a territorial unit, enclosed within clearly defined borders and possessing its own legal system and bureaucratic apparatus claiming the monopoly on violence and guarding the existing power system, hierarchically organised from the most privileged at its top, through the *gens simples* or *classes modestes*, as Bourdieu called the ordinary people, to the *précariat* at the bottom of the social ladder, who are characterised as insecure, frequently young workers forced into submission due to a lack of collective bargaining power. However, the lowest place in this hierarchy of power is reserved for the informal migrants, excluded from human rights enjoyed by all other groups integrated into majority society. Thus emerge dichotomies between 'natives' and 'newcomers', as well as new forms of identities and distinctions between 'them' and 'us', as expressed in political discourse, in the art and literature of marginality, and in patterns of adaptation and integration. Such dichotomies and distinctions, and the practices generated by them, lead to increased insecurity among migrants and ethnic minorities.

While it has been difficult to prove whether or not new surveillance technologies and strict policing, across and within borders, actually increase national and/or societal security, there is evidence to indicate that these factors construct a topology of 'insiders' and 'outsiders' (vulnerable to detention, deportation and other exclusionary mechanisms), and that the application of surveillance, policing and other measures harms the security of migrants and citizens and can lead to the economic and/or sexual exploitation of certain vulnerable groups. In addition, and more recently, the human insecurity of migrants has increased, as they suffer disproportionately from the effects of the global economic crisis and associated social and political instability. Both scholars and migrant support practitioners have undertaken numerous studies on the production of insecurities among different categories of migrants in Europe (asylum seekers and irregular migrants, labour migrants and family/marriage migrants). These fall into two broad categories: studies which examine insecurities produced by exclusionary practices of immigration control (refusal of entry, detention, deportation, surveillance – De Genova and Peutz 2010; Squire 2009; Jansen, Celikates and De Bloois 2015; Walton-Roberts and Hennebry 2014) and those which consider insecurities which are generated as a result of poor integration regimes and/or social and economic crises in European countries (Anthias, Kontos and Morokvasic 2013; Carmel, Cerami and Papadoupoulos 2012; Lazaridis 2011; Lester 2010; Vonk 2012). Part II of this book makes a valuable addition to the existing literature, considering not only insecurities engendered by restrictive migration control practices, but also those created as a result of poor integration/inclusionary politics in European countries.

Immigration, (in)/security and the far right in Europe

The last decade has seen an increase in the popularity of far right parties across Europe. Popular support for the far right in the EU has been expressed in recent polls not only in individual member states but also in the European parliamentary elections of 2014, which saw the number of far right MEPs increase by 50 per cent (Isal 2014). While a complex set of reasons govern this trend, and while European far right parties do not represent a unified bloc in terms of ideology and political strategies, what they share in common is that they have gathered popular support, mostly over the issues of immigration and (in)security, particularly since the entrenchment of the economic crisis in 2008 and the subsequent launch of budget-slashing austerity programmes in Europe. Whether or not the increased focus on security issues by European governments since 9/11 has given an advantage to the far right is unclear; few studies on far right parties have mapped or analysed individual party fortunes in relation to the increased securitisation of migration or of Islam.

However, far right discourses frame migration as a security issue through the use of some common themes, namely economic and cultural security and national and internal security.

The theme of economic security constitutes an important element of far right discourse whereby migrants are cast as 'job thieves' in a difficult labour market and as undeserving users of a shrinking welfare state. The theme of economic insecurity is used to amplify the fears and vulnerabilities of Europe's medium-, low-, and unskilled workers who have been the principal losers in globalisation's flexible job market-place and who make up high unemployment statistics. Cultural insecurity is exploited by far right parties to appeal to those who have not benefitted from living in a global, cosmopolitan age but have been left behind: in the margins of societies where long-held values, traditions, thinking and knowledge are being constantly challenged, not only through the new technologies of globalisation, but also by migrants, who bring with them different cultures and religions. In this situation, the feeling that migration undermines the perceived uniqueness of western cultures, and that mainstream parties are doing nothing to protect national cultures, values and so on, leads to support for the far right.

The idea of national security, introduced by European governments and accepted widely after 9/11, is a regular element in far right discourses and policies, and parties of the far right are more comfortable than the mainstream parliamentary parties in calling for the cessation of migration, the incarceration and expulsion of asylum seekers, and the restriction of nationality and citizenship rights to 'native' Europeans in the interests of national security. Finally, the internal security theme, in which migrant and ethnic minority populations are linked with various criminal acts – 'home grown' terrorism, drug smuggling/pushing, or grooming young white women for sexual exploitation – is also a common feature of far right politics in Europe. While there exists a vast literature on the emergence of recent far right parties and movements in Europe (Hainsworth 2009; Klandemans and Mayer 2009; Mammone and Godin 2012; Mudde 2014), few works focus specifically on the intersectional field of far right politics, immigration and security.[2] Security themes in far right discourse and practice, as a response to the securitisation of migration, are dealt with in Part III of this book.

Aims and structure of the book

This edited volume brings together contributions from authors (academics and practitioners) who are experts in migration, ethnic and community relations and/or security studies and whose research in these fields is both topical and based on their engagement with the most up-to-date debates and data gathered through fieldwork undertaken firsthand. The authors, working on countries across Europe, tackle the dilemmas outlined above to reach considered and original conclusions.

This book is organised in three distinct parts, which correspond to its principal aims. As a starting point, in Part I, 'Securitisation of Migration', it aims to advance knowledge and understanding of the evolution of migration policy since 9/11 and how it has been governed by security concerns. It does this through the examination of the structures and processes through which the securitisation of migration policy is said to have taken place. In doing so, it refers to different, often conflicting approaches: on the one hand, the securitisation of migration is treated as a given – a completed project – and on the other hand, this presumption is challenged, and the question posed is whether or not migration policy has undergone a process of securitisation, and if so, to what extent and by which means? Second, this book also seeks to explain and analyse the impacts of security measures, formulated and undertaken by European states, on migrant and established ethnic minority populations in the 9/11 era. Existing evidence shows that the impacts have been largely negative and have led to high levels of insecurity among these populations. Not only is it important to consider the impacts of securitisation, but also to give voice to those who experience these impacts most intensely, and to understand how, if at all, these social actors negotiate their differences with the state. In order to do this, specific cases provide a laboratory for observation and analysis. Here they include London's Somali community, and particularly its young people, who have had to contend with UK immigration and community relations policies, Muslims who have come to be regarded as 'suspect' communities in the wake of 9/11, and migrant detainee populations deemed such a threat to social stability that their isolation from the rest of society, prior to expulsion from the EU, is seen by European states as a reasonable solution. This aim is reflected in the chapters which make up Part II – 'Securitisation and Its Impacts on Migrant and Ethnic Minority Communities' – of this book.

Finally, the aim in Part III – 'Populist Responses to Securitisation and Migration in a Crisis Europe' – is to explore emerging populist reactions across Europe to migration, migration policy and societal security in the post-9/11 years. In an era of security politics, populist extremist parties and groups have railed against immigration, arguing that it constitutes the single biggest threat to the security of Europe and that states need to protect their national cultures and communities by halting immigration, if not by returning large numbers to their country of origin. Such populist reactions have become increasingly clamorous as economic and financial crises have gripped European states, and governments have adopted austerity politics. In Part III, the cases of the British National Party, Greece's Golden Dawn Party, Italy's Casa Pound movement, and the parties of the Scandinavian far right (for example, Sweden Democrats) are examined.

In the first chapter of Part I, Vicki Squire poses the question of whether or not migration has been the subject of securitisation post-9/11. She goes further, asking *how far* and *in what ways* migration been has securitised over the past 10 years and more, and *what consequences* there are. Understanding the value of Christina Boswell's (2007) argument that it would not do to simply presume the securitisation of migration post 9/11, nor to automatically assume that 9/11 had led to an intensification of such a process, and noting the different starting points of the analyses of the liberalisation of migration regimes and the analyses of securitising migration, Squire argues for a more nuanced account of securitisation than one which simply focuses on the association of terrorism and migration after 9/11. She claims that what Boswell suggests to be the 'absence' of securitisation would be better understood as an 'absent presence'. Thus, Chapter 1 draws attention to the importance of understanding the coexistence of 'liberalisation' and 'securitisation' processes, particularly in terms which appreciate the important insights which a range of scholars have provided over recent years.

This is followed by Chapter 2, which deals with the mutually reinforcing nature of European Union and domestic securitisation policies. Lena Karamanidou maintains that a securitising approach has dominated migration policy since 9/11, both at the EU and individual state levels, and has been institutionalised through EU and domestic laws and policies and the establishment of agencies such as FRONTEX. In support of her argument, she explores the establishment of FRONTEX as an agency with a central role in managing security risks at the borders of the EU; the expansion and normalisation of detention and deportation regimes across member states and the impact of the Returns Directive; and finally, a range of internal controls such as identity checks, employment sanctions, arrests and limitations to the movements of migrants within the EU. Karamanidou shows that these developments do not always conform to a pure logic of securitisation, insofar as they are not always a fully conscious designation of threats by policymakers, and they do not always produce the desired outcomes in terms of controlling migration and the perceived risks posed by it.

In the last chapter of Part I of the book (Chapter 3), Mark Maguire contends that the attempt by EU governments to both facilitate the movement of human capital, which is necessary to the success of the global economy, and to control migration of people in the name of reducing security risks, has brought into the European policy-making arena a profusion of security experts. Maguire argues that it is therefore vitally important to understand the realm of expert knowledge, how experts shape various *milieux* of threats, and how states are advised to (re)act therein. He considers the alarming visions of the future constructed within the realm of security experts, paying particular attention to the security threats posed by climate change, for instance, and the ways in which 'migrants' have been turned into a part of the threatening masses imbricated by criminality and political dangers. Maguire shows how security expertise can be partial, contingent and mythic.

At the same time, the securitisation of migration policies has had serious implications in eroding the rights of migrants – in particular asylum seekers and irregular migrants – in Europe. This brings us to the second part of the book, which deals with the impacts of securitisation on migrant and ethnic minority communities.

In Chapter 4, Khursheed Wadia focuses on the securitising and practice of detention (and linked to it, that of deportation) which is so extensively deployed by EU states today. The practice of detaining large numbers of migrants is used widely across Europe as a means of 'migratory management', and consequently, numerous reports by human rights experts and academic studies have sought to explain why such measures are used, their significance, and whether or not their increased deployment since 2001 is indicative of an 'insecuritisation' of migration. Until recently, not many have sought to explain and consider the nature of such restrictive practices and the insecurities they generate among different migrant populations. Yet, to do so is important in a context where there is wide public acceptance that migration must be managed within a security framework and where, as a result, questions about daily security practices and their impact on ordinary people, are rarely raised. This chapter therefore aims to do two things. First, it examines the conditions under which migrants are detained, and in a significant proportion of cases, deported from Europe, and second, it considers the types of insecurities produced by detention and deportation. It focuses on migrant women as a particularly vulnerable population among detainees (and eventual deportees) and on gendered forms of insecurity, drawing evidence mainly from Britain and France. It goes beyond the state-centric migration-security nexus to consider the experiences of migrants (ordinary, more often than not marginalised people) in order to open up the study of migration and (in)security to 'voices from below' (Hoogensen and Stuvoy 2006: 217).

Laura Zahra McDonald deals with Muslim communities and securitisation in Chapter 5. She reminds the reader that in the wake of 9/11, 7/7 and subsequent al-Qaeda-influenced attacks, the notion that 'communities defeat terrorism', borrowed from Britain's experiences in Ireland, has been reestablished as a security mantra. McDonald argues that, intended at one level to engender a sense of inclusion and partnership between state-led operations and 'communities' (in this case Muslim communities), the result has often been the effective profiling of an entire population, not only in relation to religion, but also geographical locations, ethnicities, socialities and political affiliations. The direct impact of counter-terrorism policies and practices such as those contained in the 'Prevent and Pursue' counter-terrorism strategies (a theme also touched upon by Don Flynn and Awale Olad in Chapter 6) has been well documented: for example, spikes in police stop and search of young Muslim men, travel disruptions and heavy-handed policing at international borders under Schedule 7 of the Terrorism Act 2000, pre-charge detentions, covert data collection and spying, control orders, and terrorism prevention and investigation measures (TPIMs). This chapter focuses on the indirect and vicarious forms of victimisation on the individual and communal levels, through which forms of physical, verbal, discursive and epistemic violence are committed on migrants and ethnic minority groups. The assertion by the state and within public discourse that Islam and Muslims exist in a binary of 'moderate' and 'extreme', within which a battle of loyalty and civilisation rages, has created internal tension and fuelled outsider perceptions of a communal cognitive dissonance. The impact on human experience, the author argues, is profound, and examples abound of self-censorship in matters of dress, politics, religious expression, processes of communal regulation, and complex negotiation for established and recent Muslim communities in Britain. In particular, the state pathologising of Islamic concepts, including the notion of *ummah* and definitions of *jihad*, define this struggle to 'live Islam' in such challenging contexts.

In Chapter 6, Flynn and Olad deal with securitisation and its impact on the Somali community in London, a community that is by and large

Muslim, which has grown rapidly over the last three decades. Drawing on conversations with prominent Somali community activists, Flynn and Olad review the policy landscape in which Somalis have been received in the UK and consider the factors contributing to the uncertainties and insecurities faced by this community as well as its well being. This chapter looks at the ways in which the immigration and policy framework has set out the options which young ethnic Somalis consider are available to them, and the implications these are likely to have for their future.

Flynn and Olad conclude with a consideration of the question as to whether the post-9/11 policy agenda conferred a security dimension to immigration management, or whether immigration and security are, and remain, distinct modes of approach which, at best, overlap only at the edges; that is, the authors ask whether life for young Somalis could be significantly different if 9/11 had not occurred, or whether the broad determinants of their fate in UK society had already been set by existing immigration and integration policies. They argue that, this fact notwithstanding, it appears to be a misjudgement to view securitisation as a phenomenon which is uniquely oppressive and dangerous to the community. In many ways, community activists regard it as symbolic of the many things which are wrong about the position of Somalis in British society, but the wider frame in which the spectrum of discontent exists has deeper roots in the older and more extensive forms of marginalisation which have marked the experiences of this ethnic group.

After considering the implications of securitisation discourses and practice for human security, which exposes the gap between the protection that migrants and migrant communities in principle enjoy under international laws and the human rights deficit and disproportionate levels of insecurity they experience in the name of securitisation, Part III of this book moves on to deal with populist far right responses to securitisation and migration in a Europe beset with crisis. Immigration ideologies which incorporate strong sentiments of xenophobia are among the most characteristic themes of the far right, with a distinguishing popular appeal within the electorate. Taking advantage of the framing of migration as a threat, not only to state security but also to our ontological security, the far right has managed to launch openly racist and hostile campaigns and attacks which violate the civil liberties, recognised in international treaties on human rights, of vulnerable populations living in Europe.

In Chapter 7, Emanuele Toscano investigates CasaPound, a far right movement in Italy. CasaPound is a cultural and political movement which, since its foundation in Rome in 2003, has spread throughout Italy. Referring directly to fascism, they define themselves as 'fascists of the third millennium'. However, as Toscano explains, Casapound appear to be far removed from the traditional extreme right, dealing with issues such as immigration and civil rights differently from other neo-fascist groups and organisations in Italy and Europe. Nevertheless, CasaPound militants oppose Italian 'multiracial' society from a number of standpoints. As Toscano argues, from a political point of view, the intensification of the migratory phenomenon represents for them the failure of national states to protect their own citizens; from a cultural point of view, 'multiracial' society is considered to be the result of a process of destruction and homogenisation of cultural differences under the push of globalisation; and from a social point of view, the migratory phenomenon is seen as a threat because it leads to a decrease of rights and protection for everybody. Similar to other far right parties and move-ments (see Chapter 8 by Gabriella Lazaridis and Anna-Maria Konsta and Chapter 9 by Gabriella Lazaridis and Vasiliki Tsagkroni, respectively), the presence of irregular migrant workers in the labour market is seen as a form of unfair competition, exploited by unscrupulous businesses. Moreover, immigrants are considered to be the new 'slaves' of global society, useful to the entrepreneurial system, the trade system, and the interests of organised crime. Migration (from the developing South) is perceived as a forced act, undertaken by individuals, a consequence of the impoverishment of their countries, which in turn is often connected to the expropriation of economic resources by northern hemisphere multinational companies. Hence, it is argued by CasaPound that the control of migratory phenomena is only possible through cooperation with non-European countries, in order to promote their own develop-ment, and through the intensification of restrictions on immigration into Italy. Toscano points out that these positions are not followed through by claims of presumed racial superiority over migrant subjects, and that this is where CasaPound's thinking represents a rupture with classic postwar neo-fascism.

As Chapter 8, by Lazaridis and Konsta, shows, the position of Golden Dawn in Greece and the British National Party (BNP) in the UK is very different to that of CasaPound. In this chapter, Lazaridis and Konsta examine what they refer to as 'majority identitarian populist' parties in the UK and Greece: two countries with contrasting historical and politico-economic trajectories, both affected by the current economic crisis, but to different degrees, and dealing with this in different ways. Focusing on the core narratives of two 'identitarian populist' parties, the

BNP in the UK and Golden Dawn in Greece, this chapter shows how populist actions, in the name of security, promote exclusionary practices through the construction of Otherness. Such practices are commonly heralded as answers to the 'soft' security issues which have arisen after 9/11 and the more recent hardships encountered by citizens in their daily lives (to do with changes in the economy, work and social organisation), which range from profound hostility to immigration and multiculturalism in the UK, to covert and overt violence against the Other, in Greece. The otherness of migrants is seen as a threat to the state and also to the social and economic security of 'majority' society in both countries under study. Finally, Lazaridis and Konsta assess the attractiveness of these 'identitarian populist' groups to young people and examine the paths of engagement for young people in these parties.

Finally, in Chapter 9, Lazaridis and Tsagkroni shine the spotlight on the far right in Scandinavian countries. The authors look at the rise and popularity of far right parties in Scandinavia and ways in which they use the securitisation of migration and the alleged threat migrants pose to 'our' state, economic and ontological security and identity, as a conduit through which to justify and legitimise their anti-immigration, racist and xenophobic rhetoric and praxis. As this chapter shows, despite their differences and background, what the Scandinavian parties present is a rhetoric with strong populist elements, in which immigrants are cast as dangerous, and in which states need to be alerted to the threat their countries face. Contributing to the rise in xenophobia and Islamophobia, the securitisation of migration represents more than a theory in the case of the parties under examination. The fear of Islam, in recent years, is a key element of the policy of these far right parties, which seem to have taken an uncompromising position against immigrants. Muslim migrants, seen as agents who are out to subvert 'western' values of free speech and freedom of the individual, are set as particular targets.

We believe that this assembling of several different expert approaches to the theme of securitisation of migration and its impacts on European societies lends this edited volume its particular value and strength. This is further enhanced by the fact that the securitisation of migration and the insecurities which processes of securitisation have generated are analysed here at the regional (EU), national and sub-national levels.

The study of migration and security poses a dilemma: whether to adopt national-societal or human-centric perspectives and whether the divergent and competing approaches to security (national, societal, and human) can or should ever be reconciled. The questions arising from this dilemma are important, not just for academics, but also for current and future policymakers, influencers and the general public so that all of society can make informed choices about migration and its place in contemporary Europe – on the basis that 'human security' is taken into account rather than a narrowly conceived 'state/national security'; and by human security, we mean the security of all people residing in a member state, not just those who hold EU citizenship. The clamour for greater securitisation has not created a safer European society. Rather, it has created a society which permanently lives in fear of real or imaginary threats, on the one hand, and on the other hand, has cohorts of the population scapegoated, marginalised and excluded in a 'fortress Europe', where the recognition of rights is seen as a pull factor, thus encouraging more migrants to come to Europe, who will be seen to further endanger EU citizens' identity, economic opportunities, health and safety. This perceived threat informs the discourses of the rising-in-popularity far right, which opposes immigration and rights of migrants to hold rights – this, despite the presence of international human rights law, or the EU's Charter of Fundamental Rights, or the rights and freedoms enshrined in the European Convention of Human Rights – and renders the opportunity to improve the current situation rather limited.

Directions in future research

A review of the chapters contained in this edited volume suggests a number of future research directions which may be followed. Where the securitisation of migration and human (in)security is concerned, three gaps in academic and policy research may be highlighted, although, of course, there are bound to be many other areas which are also worthy of attention. The first thing which emerges is that both securitisation and human (in)security, as concepts related to migration, are subject to little interdisciplinary conversation. Currently, securitisation tends to be debated extensively within the area of politics and international studies, while human (in)security has been picked up by other social science disciplines, in particular sociology. While Maguire informs us that the production of expertise in security techno-science has been subject to research in anthropology, he is one of the few within the discipline to work on the input of such expert knowledge into the securitisation on migration. He also argues that more useful work could be undertaken within anthropology and psychology on what the erection of walls and borders across Europe and elsewhere signifies, on psychical levels, given that they fail to deliver the intended outcome of resisting undesired populations in material and practical terms. On the whole, only a few anthropologists (De Genova and Peutz among them) have undertaken studies on the intersecting themes of migration and mobilities and (in)security and exclusion. Where other disciplines are concerned, Mountz, Coddington, Catania and Lloyd (2012) argue that there is an urgent need for critical research, in geography, on migration and the processes and practices of mobility and containment, bordering and exclusion, which are undertaken in the name of increased security. They contend that such processes and practices are fundamentally geographic in nature, both empirically and conceptually, given that spatial tactics form an intrinsic part of them.

Second, it can be argued that far more academic and policy research needs to be undertaken, linking the concepts of securitisation and human (in)security in migration, in order to suggest ways in which European states may, if at all, ensure freedom from fear for both national and migrant (and minority) communities. Empirical research on the impacts of the securitisation of migration at local levels may also prove useful in answering questions about what policy initiatives and governance measures are best adopted in addressing the challenges of human (in)security among migrant and ethnic minority populations in Europe. In undertaking such research, it is important that certain assumptions about where (geographically) risk, and hence securitisation and human (in)security matters, are not perpetuated; currently there is a tendency among academics, policy makers and influencers to assume that risk and increased national security is an important issue for western countries, while human (in)security is a matter for countries in the developing South. Such thinking produces a 'politics of pity' *vis-à-vis* the South (Aradau 2004), while obscuring the fact that human (in)security issues arise and should matter in the North.

Third, more critical research needs to be carried out where collective resistance and education is concerned. The resistance discourses and action of civil society organisations and communities against the framing of migration as a security issue, and the perception of people from the most vulnerable cohorts of society as dangerous Others, is currently under-studied. Analyses of 'best practice' action which promotes a humanitarian and inclusive anti-discrimination approach would be welcome. In addition, the role of education (both formal and in the wider cultural sense) in sensitising young people against the dangers of far right, anti-immigrant discourses and policies which de-normalise certain cohorts of the population also requires further examination.

Notes

1. For an overview of the development of different schools of thought in securiti-sation studies and issues to which securitisation theory is applied, see Balzacq (2011) and Williams (2011).
2. As part of its *openSecurity* section, *Open Democracy* recently published a multi-authored dossier entitled 'Security and the far right in Europe' (2012).

References

Anthias, F., Kontos, M. and Morokvasic, M. (eds) (2013) *Paradoxes of integration: female migrants in Europe*, New York: London: Springer.
Anthias, F. and Lazaridis, G. (2013) 'Introduction: women on the move in southern Europe' in F. Anthias and G. Lazaridis (eds) *Gender and migration in southern Europe: women on the move*, Oxford: Berg, pp.1–14.
Aradau, C. (2004) 'The perverse politics of four-letter words: risk and pity in the securitisation of human trafficking', *Millennium: Journal of International Studies*, 33(2): 251–277.
Balzacq, T. (ed) (2011) *Securitization theory: how security problems emerge and dissolve*, London and New York: Routledge.
Berggren, E., Brborić, B. L. and Toksöz, G. (eds) (2007) *Irregular migration, informal labour and community: a challenge for Europe*, Maastricht: Shaker Publishing.
Bigo, D. (2008) 'Globalized (in)security: the-field-and-the-ban-opticon' in D. Bigo and A. Tsoukala (eds) *Terror, insecurity and liberty: illiberal practices of liberal regimes after 9/11*, London: Routledge.
Booth, K. (ed) (1991) *New thinking about strategy and international security*, London: Harper Collins.
Borooah, K. V. and Mangan, J. (2009) 'Multiculturalism versus assimilation: attitudes towards immigrants in western countries', *International Journal of Economic Sciences and Applied Research*, 2(2): 33–50.
Boswell, C. (2007) 'Migration control in Europe after 9/11: explaining the absence of securitization', *Journal of Common Market Studies*, 45(3): 589–610.
Bourbeau, P. (2011) *The securitization of migration. A study of movement and order*, London; New York: Routledge.
Buzan, B., Wæver, O. and De Wilde, J. (1998) *Security: a new framework for analysis*, London: Lynne Rienner.
Carmel, E., Cerami, A. and Papadoupoulos, T. (2012) *Migration and welfare in the new Europe: social protection and the challenges of integration*, Bristol: Policy Press.
De Genova, N. (2007) 'The production of culprits: from deportability to detain-ability in the aftermath of "Homeland Security"', *Citizenship Studies*, 11(5): 421–448.
De Genova, N. and Peutz, N. (2010) *The deportation regime: sovereignty, space, and the freedom of movement*, Durham; London: Duke University Press.
Düvell, F. (ed) (2006), *Illegal immigration in Europe: beyond control?* Houndmills: Palgrave Macmillan.
Hainsworth, P. (2009) *The extreme right in Europe*, London: Routledge.

Hoogensen, G. and Stuvoy, K. (2006) 'Gender, resistance and human security', *Security Dialogue*, 37(2): 207–228.

Huysmans, J. (2008) *The politics of insecurity: fear, migration and asylum in the EU*, New York: Routledge.

Isal, S. (2014) 'Alarming rise in support for far-right European parties', *The Parliament Magazine*, 10 June, https://www.theparliamentmagazine.eu/articles/news/alarming-rise-support-far-right-european-parties, accessed 20 March 2015.

Jansen, Y., Celikates, R. and De Bloois, J. (2015) *The irregularization of migration in contemporary Europe: detention, deportation, drowning*, London: Rowman and Littlefield.

Klandemans, B. and Mayer, N. (eds) (2009) *Extreme right activists in Europe: through the magnifying glass*, London and New York: Routledge.

Lazaridis, G. (ed) (2011) *Security, insecurity and migration in Europe*, Aldershot: Ashgate.

Lazaridis, G. and Konsta, A. M. (2011) 'Plastic citizenship (in)securities and processes of abjectification: the case of Albanian migrant women in Greece' in G. Lazaridis (ed) *Security, insecurity and migration in Europe*, Farnham: Ashgate.

Lester, E. (2010) 'Socio-economic rights, human security and survival migrants: whose rights? Whose security?' in A. Edwards and C. Ferstman (eds) *Human security and non-citizens: law, policy and international affairs*, Cambridge: Cambridge University Press.

Mammone, A. and Godin, E. (2012) *Mapping the extreme right in contemporary Europe: from local to transnational*, London: Routledge.

Mingione, E. (1995) 'Labour market segmentation and informal work in southern Europe', *European Urban and Regional Studies*, 2: 121–143.

Mountz, A., Coddington, K., Catania, R. T. and Lloyd, J. M. (2012) 'Conceptualizing detention, mobility, containment, bordering, and exclusion', *Progress in Human Geography*, 37(4): 522–541.

Mudde, C. (2014) *Youth and the extreme right*, Brussels: IDEA.

openSecurity (2012) 'Security and the far right in Europe' (special dossier), *Open Democracy*, https://www.opendemocracy.net/freeform-tags/security-and-far-right-in-europe, accessed 20 March 2015.

Portes, A. and Sensenbrenner, J. (1993) 'Embeddedness and immigration: notes on the social determinants of economic action', *American Journal of Sociology*, 68(6): 1320–1350.

Squire, V. (2009) *The exclusionary politics of asylum*, Basingstoke: Palgrave Macmillan.

Togral, B. (2011) 'Convergence of securitization of migration and "new racism" in Europe: rise of culturalism and disappearance of politics' in G. Lazaridis (ed) *Security, insecurity and migration in Europe*, Basingstoke: Ashgate.

Vonk, G. (ed) (2012) *Cross-border welfare state, immigration, social security and integration* (Social Europe series), Antwerp: Intersentia.

Walton-Roberts, M. and Hennebry, J. (eds) (2014) *Territoriality and migration in the EU neighbourhood: spilling over the wall*, New York; London: Springer.

Weiner, M. (1995) *The global migration crisis: challenge to states and to human rights*, New York: Harper Collins College Publishers.

Williams, M. C. (2011) 'The continuing evolution of securitization theory' in T. Balzacq (ed) *Securitization theory: how security problems emerge and dissolve*, London and New York: Routledge.

Wyn Jones, R. (1995) '"Message in a bottle"? Theory and practice in critical security studies', *Contemporary Security Policy*, 16: 299–319.

Yuval-Davis, N. (2007) 'Intersectionality, citizenship and contemporary politics of belonging', *Critical Review of International Social and Political Philosophy*, 10(4): 561–574.

Part I
Securitisation of Migration

1
The Securitisation of Migration: An Absent Presence?
Vicki Squire

Introduction

Nearly 15 years after 9/11, whether or not migration is the subject of securitisation appears to be a question worth asking. Is the linkage between migration and security a stable and enduring feature of contemporary society and politics? Or is the assumption of migration's securitisation misplaced and lacking the appropriate evidence? Some scholars have suggested that migration has, indeed, been addressed as a security issue in both the pre- and post-9/11 period (Huysmans 2006; Van Munster 2009). Others, by contrast, question whether it is appropriate to claim that migration has been securitised in a context marked by intensified concerns over terrorism (Boswell 2007a).

Christina Boswell (2007a) suggests that it would not do to simply presume the securitisation of migration, nor would it do to automatically assume that 9/11 led to an intensification of such processes. Rather, she claims that it is important to pay attention to institutional interests and cognitive factors conditioning processes of securitisation (or non-securitisation), if we are to better understand whether or not migration has become articulated and addressed as a security problem in a post-9/11 context. This chapter concurs with Boswell's suggestion regarding the importance of unpacking processes of securitisation, rather than assuming their presence. However, it also suggests that her challenge to the claim that migration has been securitised post-9/11 falls short, because it fails to take on board some of the key insights of scholars in the field of critical security studies.

Rather than simply ask whether migration has or has not been securitised post-9/11, the chapter contends that it is more appropriate to pose this as a question regarding as to how far, in what ways, and with what consequences migration been has securitised over the past 15 years and more. This can facilitate appreciation of the securitisation of migration, which is neither absent nor present in any straightforward way. By contrast with Boswell, this chapter thus argues that raising these broader questions can help us to develop appreciation of securitisation as an *absent presence* in the contemporary European context.

An entrenched divide

A key argument of this chapter is that divergent responses to the question of whether or not migration is securitised not only reflects divergent conceptualisations of securitisation, but also the entrenchment of a disciplinary divide between scholars of migration studies and scholars of critical security studies. In order to develop such an argument, the analysis examines key dimensions of Boswell's argument regarding the absence of securitisation, in order to set out some of the elements of critical security studies that she appears to overlook.

Boswell argues that, although there is evidence of the securitisation of migration in the United States, this is not the case in the European context (2007a: 590). Specifically, she argues that there is no evidence of a direct causal linkage between migration and terrorism at the level of political discourse or rhetoric in the European context, and that at the level of practice, there is evidence of the transportation of migration control instruments into anti-terrorism practice, but not of the transportation of anti-terrorism practices into the field of migration control (Ibid.). Drawing on neo-institutionalism and systems theory, she argues that there is no evidence that 9/11 led to the securitisation of migration. This, she suggests, is a finding that is demonstrative of the deficiencies of scholarship in the field of critical security studies.

We will come back later in this chapter to consider some of the assumptions that Boswell imports through her reading of critical security studies as primarily exploring how 'public discourse can legitimise security practices' (Ibid.). For now, however, it is worthwhile reflecting on the broader academic context within which her intervention is situated. In particular, this chapter will emphasise the significance of a series of differences, which arguably suggest an entrenched divide between scholars of migration policy and critical security studies scholars. This divide can be understood primarily as reflecting the different emphasis or focus of each body of literature, which also reflects a different political orientation and a different account of what serves as an important analytical intervention in the related fields of migration and/or border studies.

For scholars of migration policy, the emphasis has often been orientated toward explaining the development, persistence and/or significance of liberalised immigration policies, particularly in light of the strength of popular anti-immigration sentiment. This reflects an interest in the 'liberal constraints' on government policy, such as liberal institutional norms or interests and the legitimacy of civil or human rights claims (for example, Freeman 1995; Joppke 1998). Such a focus often entails an analytical intervention that explores the relationship between interests or institutional structures/norms and the development of policy and practice (see Boswell 2007b). In the broader literature in this area, liberal im/migration policies appear to stand in a relation of opposition to processes of securitisation (see Gibney 2004).

By contrast, scholars of critical security studies do not assume a distinction between liberalisation and securitisation, but instead focus attention on the illiberal practices of liberal states (Bigo and Tsoukala 2008). A key focus of critical security studies scholarship over recent years has been the development of border controls as manifestations of an (il)liberal rationality or form of governmentality. This includes consideration of the relationship between bordering practices and restrictive migration policies more broadly, as well as consideration of the development of techniques of surveillance and data management in particular. For example, critical scholars have focused on the exclusionary political effects of security discourses and practices in relation to the politics of mobility, particularly, though not exclusively, in the European context (for example, Aradau, Huysmans and Squire 2010; Guild 2003; Jones 2012; Lazaridis 2011; Squire 2009). Others have focused in more detail on the problematic implications of governing migration or mobility through risk-based biometric technologies (for example, Ajana 2013; Amoore 2006; Epstein 2007; Huysmans and Buonfino 2008; Lewis 2005; Lyon 2005; Muller 2005, 2010, 2011) and through digital forms of data management and surveillance (for example, Balzacq 2007; Bellanova and Fuster 2013; Bonditti 2004; Rygiel 2011, 2013; Salter 2008). This reflects a critical orientation toward the ways in which mobility or migration is governed. For some scholars, this is conceived of in terms of an exceptionalist politics marked by sovereign power and the violence of the decision (for example, Salter 2003, 2012). For others, it is seen as the result of the ordinary law and practices of liberal states (see Basaran 2008). The latter in particular contributes to what Didier Bigo (2002) has called the production of a 'generalised unease'.

It is not the aim of this chapter to interrogate how the different strands of critical security studies address the issue of migration (see Huysmans and Squire 2015). Nor is it the aim to pose either liberal migration studies or critical security studies scholarship as more important than the other. Rather, the aim of this chapter is to draw attention to differences in the focus, approach and orientation of migration studies and critical security studies scholarship, in order to emphasise the ways in which these lead to differing assessments of the securitisation of migration. This is developed here as a means to argue for the importance of a more nuanced understanding of the relationship between liberalisation and securitisation, as well as for a critical understanding of securitisation as a much more complex process or set of practices than Boswell assumes it to be. The chapter thus highlights the significance of a critical perspective, without dismissing the important insights that scholars of migration policy such as Boswell develop.

In other words, this chapter seeks to make the case for a more careful consideration of the logic, practices and effects of security practices (or processes of securitisation), as a means to develop a more nuanced appreciation of the securitisation of migration both pre- and post-9/11. This is done by developing three lines of argument. First, the chapter sets out a more nuanced understanding of what it means to analyse the securitisation of migration. Second, it argues for an understanding of what Boswell suggests to be the absence of securitisation as an absent presence. Third, it emphasises the importance of understanding the coexistence of liberalisation and securitisation in terms that do not discount the important insights that a range of critical security studies scholars have developed over recent years. Having set the scene of a disciplinary divide in the context of which these three interventions are developed, the chapter will now set out each argument more fully by engaging in further detail with the various dimensions of Boswell's argument.

The securitisation of migration

The first line of analysis that Boswell develops emerges from her focus on the rhetorical or discursive dimensions of securitisation. She refers to this as the 'non-securitisation of migration control' at the political level (2007a: 598). Here, Boswell argues that migration is not correlated with terrorism in political debate in the European context, and that there are three key cognitive and practical reasons for this. First, she argues that this represents a case of non-securitisation because terrorism and migration present incongruous images, such as that of the destitute asylum seeker versus that of the organised terrorist cell (Ibid.: 598). Second, she claims that migration is not causally related to terrorism because the links between terrorism and migration are not held up by empirical evidence, with many terrorists found to be European nationals (Ibid.: 598–600). Third, she argues that a causal linkage is absent because of a clash between the securitisation of migration control and more liberal policies toward labour migration that have been predominant in Europe in the 2000s. For example, she notes that centre-left governments in the UK and Germany during that period had recently reintroduced schemes for highly skilled migration and were 'loosening access to labour markets for foreign students' (Ibid.: 600).

Boswell clearly highlights some important points here in assessing securitisation understood as a discursive or rhetorical process of articulating migration as a security issue. In particular, her insights are important for an analysis of the securitisation of migration as a 'speech act' (Buzan, Wæver and Wilde 1998), because it facilitates an appreciation of the ways in which the process of securitisation can fail if key audiences do not accept statements regarding migration as a security threat. For example, in a context whereby the links between terrorism and migration are subject to question, or whereby the positing of migration as a security threat lies in conflict with wider discourses regarding the positive contribution of migration, then wider audiences may be unlikely to accept a securitising speech act. This would be understood as a failed securitising move, according to scholars inspired by the Copenhagen School of securitisation theory (see Balzacq, 2005). That Boswell pays attention to the specificity of the institutional context, as well as to the way in which a speech act of security involves cognitive processes that are important to the issue being accepted by an audience, is thus helpful from this perspective.

Nevertheless, questions arise as to whether these insights support the argument that Boswell makes regarding the non-securitisation of migration control. For example, that the asylum seeker and the terrorist represent incongruous images does not necessarily lead to non-securitisation. Even if there is no direct and explicit link made between terrorism and migration, these can still be articulated as mutual threats, and accepted by an audience as such. For example, migration and terrorism were flagged up by the UK rotating presidency of the European Union in 2005 as equivalent challenges in an increasingly 'interconnected' world: 'Many of the issues faced by governments today, such as terrorism, asylum and immigration, and organised crime can be tackled most effectively through increased cooperation between member states' (Council of the European Union 2004: 5). Statements such as this are indicative of a mode of securitisation that does not presuppose the need for a direct or causal link between migration and terrorism, but rather involves the presence of associational links as dimensions of the process of securitisation (see Squire 2009).

It might be argued that it is precisely through such associational links that the securitisation of migration resonates with wider publics. Indeed, links between migration and terrorism are more widely evident in political and popular discourse throughout the 2000s. A notable example here is the 2000 Afghan hijackers case, whereby nine men fleeing the Taliban regime hijacked a domestic Afghan flight and forced the crew to land the airplane at Stansted airport in the UK. This was the subject of widespread debate in the UK media and government, particularly as it went through processes of appeal in the courts in the mid-2000s. The attention that this case gained might itself be understood as indicative of an intensification of the securitisation of migration, rather than as its absence, because of the resonance of the hijacking of an airplane and the terrorists' attacks of 9/11. However, what is important from the perspective developed here is that securitisation involves associational processes through which migrants are constituted as 'culpable' or 'threatening' subjects (see Squire 2009: 72–74). We can thus go further here in drawing on Boswell's analysis to show how, even in the absence of evidence of any direct empirical linkage between migration and terrorism, such associations are precisely indicative of the extent to which securitisation has become a key way of framing migration (or articulating migration as an issue to govern) over recent years. To say that there is an absence of securitisation at a rhetorical or discursive level in this regard would seem to miss processes of securitisation that rest on associative relations. It is precisely through indirect associations between migration and security concerns such as terrorism that some forms of migration have come to be addressed as threatening and have thus become addressed as a question of security.

Moreover, if we move on to the second line of argument developed by Boswell regarding the linkages between migration policy and counter-terrorism at the level of practice, it would appear that her intervention may inadvertently further support the suggestion that securitisation has become key to the framing or governing of migration over recent years. She suggests that, at the level of practice, there is a clearer linkage of migration control and anti-terrorism measures (Ibid.: 600). For Boswell, however, the direction in which these practices travel is posed as indicative of the absence of migration's securitisation, with little change in migration practices post-9/11, but significant use of migration measures in the field of counter-terrorism. For example, she argues that migration measures such as linked databases, passenger record information sharing, and border checks have been used as counter-terrorism measures, but that counter-terrorism measures have not been similarly carried over into migration control (Ibid.: 601). By contrast, I want to suggest that the institutional or practical links that Boswell points to are precisely indicative of the securitisation of migration, regardless of the direction in which such practices travel. That migration was securitised prior to 9/11 (see Huysmans 2006), and that the use of migration control measures in the field of counter-terrorism could be interpreted as indicative of this, is an argument that Boswell would appear to overlook.

As a brief aside, it is interesting to note Boswell's jump here from what she calls the absence of securitisation at the level of discourse/rhetoric or political debate, to the absence of securitisation at the level of practice. Although Boswell couches this in terms of functional systemic or institutional differences between politics and administration (2007a: 591–592), this is also suggestive of an analytical distinction between discourse (or rhetoric) and practice. The latter distinction has been problematised within critical security studies over recent years (see Squire 2009).

The Copenhagen School's conceptualisation of securitisation as a 'speech act' (Buzan, Wæver and Wilde 1998) may lead some to conceive a strong distinction between discourse and practice, such as is evident, for example, in Boswell's analysis. However, many scholars within the field of critical security studies engage discourse more broadly in relation to an appreciation of the constitutive role of knowledge or rationalities of government (see Huysmans 1998). This lies in contrast to what might be defined as 'thinner' constructivist approaches that conceive discourse more narrowly in relation to terms such as rhetoric, narrative or speech. Indeed, scholars of securitisation as a speech act have focused attention on the contextual dimensions that render any separation of discourse and practice problematic, such as through looking to the broader political landscape in the context of which speech acts are assessed by an audience (Balzacq 2005). This clearly has implications for an argument regarding the absence of securitisation that begins with discourse understood simply in terms of speech or political debate. Nevertheless, it is not necessary to dwell on these differences here, but rather we can take from Boswell the invitation to think more carefully about the various dynamics that play into the development of migration policy and practice, taking this as important in understanding how migration is constituted as an issue to govern, and in particular addressing this problematic in relation to the question of securitisation.

As indicated above, Boswell's argument regarding the absence of securitisation at the level of practice hinges on the direction in which control instruments travel between the diverging areas of anti-terrorism and migration policy (2007a: 601). Here, she draws on scholarship focused more on security professionals and institutionalised practices, and in particular on the 'transversal' dimensions of such practices (Bigo 2000; Huysmans 2000). Focusing on data collection and management during the post-9/11 period, she challenges what she interprets to be the assumptions of critical security studies scholars by contending that it is more accurate to understand the interoperability of migration and security tools in terms of the use of migration control instruments for anti-terrorist purposes, rather than the extension of anti-terrorist instruments for migration control, as indicated above (Ibid.: 601–605). She interprets this as corroborating her claim that securitisation has not occurred post-9/11, and out of her analysis produces a range of important insights regarding the divergent goals of security professionals and administrators as these relate to matters of institutional complexity and organisational goals or objectives (Ibid.: 603–605).[1]

When it comes to the question of the securitisation of migration, however, Boswell's analysis potentially lends itself to a divisive reading of the differences between scholars of migration policy and critical security studies scholars. This is because the question remains a reductive one as to whether or not securitisation occurs, rather than the more pressing one of how far and in what ways securitisation occurs, and with what effects. This reflects a limited understanding of securitisation, which Boswell conceives in narrow terms as the correlation of migration to terrorism, or the transfer of counter-terrorism policy to migration control. Such a definition overlooks the broader sense within which securitisation has been interpreted in the critical security studies literature, where this refers to a process of governing through the production of 'threats' or 'unease' (Huysmans 1998; Bigo 2002).

Taking this broader definition as a starting point, we can understand securitisation as part of a wider process of 'threat' production through which migration (or specific forms of migration) are linked with various forms of in/security through processes of association. This contrasts to a narrow understanding of securitisation in terms of a direct correlation of migration and security and/or in terms of a unidirectional relationship between the practices of controlling terrorism and those controlling migration. The securitisation of migration in this regard is not necessarily clearly distinguishable from the criminalisation of migration, since the production of threats entails modes of governing in relation to problems of criminality as well as security. For this reason, I suggest elsewhere that it may be more appropriate at a general conceptual level to address such processes in terms of the broader concept of irregularisation (see Squire 2009, 2011). The analysis in this chapter suggests that this broader conceptualisation may allow for an understanding of the ways in which processes of securitisation feature in the governing of migration, even where a direct or causal linkage of terrorism with migration (or a transfer or anti-terrorist measures to migration control instruments) appears to be absent.

Securitisation as an absent presence

To go back momentarily to the opening question of whether or not migration has been securitised post-9/11, I would agree with Boswell that the impact of 9/11 is less important than it might be (or have been) assumed. The association of migration and terrorism has a much longer and more varied history than an emphasis on 9/11 would imply, going back to the 1980s in the European context with the Trevi Group addressing security and policing concerns in the context of free movement (see Huysmans 2006; Squire 2009). More recently, the interoperability of migration and security instruments to which Boswell points have often been made sense of at the popular or political level through a narrative regarding emergent threats in 'an age of globalisation', as indicated above in relation to the associative links that the chapter argues are integral to processes of securitisation. 9/11 and the subsequent 'war on terror' may have added fuel to the fire of this narrative. Meanwhile, anti-terrorist measures may in more or less identifiable ways have been invested in practices of governing migration that are exceptionalist in their orientation (such as the FRONTEX rapid border intervention teams) and/or in terms that are orientated more toward the more general production of unease (such as intensified surveillance and databases) (see Neal 2009). Even where such developments are carefully evidenced, it is still not clear that 9/11 was a moment of marked change that marks the introduction or intensification of securitisation. As Boswell and others have suggested, the picture is more complex in the European context, which is the focus both of this chapter and of Boswell's work.

Nevertheless, this insight regarding the questionable significance of 9/11 to migration debate, policy and practice does not directly translate to an argument regarding the absence of securitisation following

9/11. Indeed, it seems important to acknowledge that processes of securitisation have continued to play an important role in the governing of migration over recent years. Here, a point that Boswell brushes over rather briefly in her article would appear to be more critical than her analysis suggests. Boswell claims that migration policy debates and practices were primarily framed in three ways prior to 9/11: with reference to the problems of irregular entrance, with reference to social and economic pressures (such as the pressure on welfare, housing and jobs), and with reference to the smuggling and trafficking of peoples (2007a: 594–595). Importantly, Boswell notes that each of these ways of framing the 'problem' of migration conditions the development of exclusive or exclusionary policies. Going further, one might ask whether the presence of these 'problems' in the sphere of migration policy is precisely indicative of the presence of processes of securitisation to contemporary practices of governing mobility, not only prior to but also in a post-9/11 context. To make such a claim rests on a different understanding of securitisation than that developed by Boswell, namely of securitisation as involving a divisive process that governs subjects (here: migrants) with reference to 'threatening' behaviours that are bound up with insecurities of various forms.

The argument developed here is, however, slightly different from one that in any simple sense emphasises the presence of securitisation. Specifically, this chapter considers whether what Boswell interprets as an absence of securitisation might be better understood as an 'absent presence'. In other words, the aim here is to pose an alternative question, as to whether the very 'absence' of the direct or explicit dimensions of securitisation that Boswell highlights may imply that migrations (or particular forms of migration) are *already assumed* to pose a threat or to provoke various insecurities, and are thus governed as such. Far from the absence of securitisation, this might be understood as implying the relative success of securitisation. From the perspective of the 'Copenhagen School' of securitisation theory (Buzan, Wæver and Wilde 1998), one might say that the audience already takes as given the truth of the securitising speech act, and thus, the latter becomes superfluous. From a broader critical perspective, one might say that migration is already understood and governed within a frame of security according to a paradigm of threat (or, one might say, risk), and thus the causal linkage of migration and security need neither to be directly articulated in debate nor to be directly traceable in practice in order for securitisation to be said to occur. Going further, one might say that the successive criminalisation of migrants such as through the increase of workplace raiding and the development of irregular entrance as a criminal offence is indicative of the ways in which criminality has increasingly featured in the governing of migration over recent years. This, in turn, might be understood as indicative of the success of securitisation in the broader sense of governing migration through the production of 'threat'. Nevertheless, rather than simply focus on the presence or success of securitisation, I want to make the case for a more nuanced and multidimensional account of securitisation in order to address the questions of how far, in what ways, and with what consequences migration is securitised. This is an important shift away from Boswell's focus on whether or not migration is securitised.

What the chapter thus argues for is greater appreciation not only of the differences between what Boswell calls political and administrative functions, but also of the intertwinement of policy and practice with public, political and popular debates. The importance of this might be exemplified with reference to the three policy 'problems' of irregular entrance, social and economic pressures, and criminal smuggling and trafficking to which Boswell refers. This is not to refute the importance of the work of migration and critical security studies scholars who engage in the analysis of institutional and practical dynamics, which importantly draw attention to the limitations of an analysis that focuses solely on public or political debate. However, it is to suggest that more work needs to be done to address the ways in which securitisation can become a self-legitimating and self-fulfilling mode of governing migration. This precisely demands an analysis that is sensitive to the ways that debates around migration and its control interrelate with practices in the constitution of migration as a 'threat'. Indeed, what some might conceive of as the absence of securitisation may better be understood as an 'absent presence' if we understand (a) securitising narratives and practices in a relatively broad sense as entailing the production of 'threat' and (b) an absence of direct and causal links between migration and insecurities such as terrorism as indicative both of the success of securitisation as well as the apparent absence of evidence to support such a linkage. A different conceptualisation of securitisation in this regard provides a very different interpretation of how migration is governed than that which Boswell puts forward.

It is therefore worthwhile briefly to unpack the absent presence of securitisation to which I refer here in relation to irregular entrance, social and economic pressures, and the smuggling and trafficking of migrants. I want to suggest that these policy problems can be understood as produced or reproduced through the very practices that are engaged to address them, when viewed from a broader perspective focusing on the intertwinement of discourse and practice. Indeed, I have argued elsewhere that the very problem of irregular entrance is one that needs to be understood as constituted as such through the development of restrictive measures that prevent authorised entrance in the first place, rather than a problem that is simply addressed by policy (Squire 2009; see also Dauvergne 2008). For example, practices of externalised control that are developed in order to prevent entrance to the European Union can be understood as producing 'illegal migrants' deemed as culpable of crossing borders without authorisation (Squire 2009: 93–115). Similarly, I have argued that pressures on housing and services are often provoked through the ways in which policies such as dispersal are put into practice (Squire 2009: 116–141). Other scholars have pointed to the problems or insecurities associated with smuggling and trafficking as provoked by state policies that create certain migrants as vulnerable in the first place (for example, on the migration of sex workers to European Union, see Andrijasevic 2010). The securitisation of migration, in other words, can be understood as bound up with the constitution of policy problems that become self-perpetuating in effect.

Going further, it is important to stress that the ways in which these policy problems are engaged do not only constitute migration (or particular migrations and migrants) as 'threatening', but they also shift the burden of insecurity onto migrants in ways that foreclose different understandings of such issues. For example, irregular entrance might be alternatively conceived of as reflecting a problem whereby political and social arrangements are ill-suited to contemporary migratory dynamics, while social and economic pressures might be conceived of as reflecting a problem of growing global and localised inequalities that serve as conditions under which migration occurs. The association of migration with different problems might in this regard be conceived of as a particularly effective way of constituting migration as a 'threat', because it invokes the presumption of 'guilt' without exposing the limitations of making the direct linkage between migration and a range of wider concerns. At the same time, however, I have suggested that policies and practices that rest on an assumption that such a linkage is founded can produce the very problems that they are purportedly designed to resolve, because in taking for granted the implication that such a link exists, they reproduce such an assumption, and thus recreate this in the practices that they enact. Securitisation in this regard would seem to be present precisely through what Boswell (2007a) refers to as its absence, which in my terms is better understood as an absent presence. In the very absence of its direct articulation, securitisation thus marks its presence, just as in its presence we find an absence of evidence by which to ground any claim to securitisation.

Securitisation and liberalisation

I would now like to return briefly to Boswell's final claim regarding the reason for an absence of the securitisation of migration at the level of political debate, which I suggest reflects her problematic assumption regarding the distinction between processes of liberalisation and processes of securitisation. Boswell argues that a causal linkage between migration and terrorism is absent because of the clash between securitisation and more liberal policies toward labour migration predominant in Europe in the 2000s (2007a: 600). It is here that the political differences between – or differing political diagnosis of – scholars of migration policy and scholars of critical security studies are most evident. Boswell's critique might be understood as suggesting that a focus on securitisation of migration implies a failure to acknowledge the liberalisation of migration policy. Yet this in turn would seem to rest on a misreading (or limited reading) of the critical security studies literature, while at the same time overlooking the critical importance of understanding how liberalisation and securitisation play into one another in the development of 'managed migration' or liberal labour migration policies. In turn, this reflects the limitations of Boswell's opening question of whether or not migration is securitised post-9/11. Not only do the continuities between the pre- and post-9/11 period show this question to be problematic, but so also does the coexistence of liberal and securitised policies suggest that there is more at play here than simply different institutional pressures or aims that render particular organisational units 'incoherent', as Boswell suggests.

For critical scholars such as Didier Bigo and Anastassia Tsoukala (2008), the processes of liberalisation to which Boswell refers are less distant from securitisation than we might assume. Indeed, it could be argued that 'managed migration' has never been simply a project of liberalisation, but rather it rests on the opening of migration routes (such as those within the European Union) as conditional on the closure of others (such as non-European Union routes). Similarly, it can be argued that the acceptance of some migrants (such as the highly skilled) is conditional on the refusal of others (such as asylum seekers) (see Squire 2009). Going further, scholars of critical security studies often challenge the distinction between liberalisation and securitisation that is so central to a liberal perspective. Instead, they focus attention on the ways in which an exceptionalist or exclusionary politics are integral to liberalism, such as with reference to the illiberal practices of liberal states (Bigo and Tsoukala 2008). What Didier Bigo (2002) has called the production of a 'generalised unease' in this regard is inseparable from the liberal dimensions of European policy, which Boswell claims to be a factor that explains the non-securitisation of migration.

Far from evidence of non-securitisation, developments such as 'managed migration' can be interpreted as indicative of the absent presence of a form of securitisation that is difficult to directly evidence, but that nevertheless haunts contemporary migration and border control.

We might conceive managed migration in different ways: whether as an institutionalised mode of 'governing through freedom' as Foucauldian critical security scholars might conceive it (Kalm 2010), or as a compromise solution between liberalism (or neoliberalism) and restrictionism, as an analysis focused on 'liberal constraints' might suggest. Whichever our preferred interpretation, to engage in an analysis of managed migration as refuting the significance of processes of securitisation risks an approach that writes out some of the most pressing political considerations that emerge with regard to questions of governing migration in contemporary Europe. Asking how far, and in what ways, migration is securitised, rather than posing a more liberal question as to whether or not migration is securitised, is thus critical in this context.

Conclusion

This chapter has undertaken a sustained engagement with Christina Boswell's argument regarding the non-securitisation of migration since 9/11, and suggests that the securitisation of migration remains an absent presence in the European context. The argument regarding the absent presence of the securitisation of migration has two key dimensions. First, the chapter has suggested that the association of migration with a series of problems is so well embedded in the European context that migration is successfully constituted (that is, broadly accepted) as a threat (or particular types of migrants are successfully constituted as threatening subjects). Thus we can effectively understand securitisation as conditioning the very assumptions under which migration policy and practice is developed. Second, the chapter has suggested that the very assumption of migration as a 'threat' effectively becomes self-fulfilling in practice, where policies and practices fail to resolve problems associated with migration as a 'threat', and thus in effect *produce* the problems associated with the 'threat' of migration. In order for securitisation to occur, migration (or specific forms of migration) in this regard does not need to be explicitly articulated as a security threat (although it sometimes is), nor does it need to be directly and causally linked to issues such as terrorism (though it sometimes has been). From this perspective, it is not the unidirectional relation between terrorism and migration policy that is relevant in assessing processes of securitisation. Rather, what is of most concern is the process by which migration or specific types of migration become bound up with concerns over in/security, and the effects of such processes in circumventing alternative engagements with migration in terms that escape such processes of securitisation.

The differences between this reading of the securitisation of migration and Boswell's reading of migration's non-securitisation reflect differing political, methodological and analytical concerns. While Boswell seeks to examine divergent institutional and systemic functions within an administrative framework, this chapter seeks to develop a broader political sociological analysis of the governing of migration. Boswell distinguishes discourse from practice, while this chapter does not accept such a division. Moreover, Boswell identifies a difference between processes of securitisation and processes of liberalisation, while the analysis here suggests that the two are less distinct than it is often assumed. Yet the aim of this chapter is not to further entrench existing divides; rather, it is to penetrate more carefully the question of how, in what ways, and with what effects migration is securitised. This is not to assume the securitisation of migration, nor is it to privilege 9/11 in the history of this process. Rather, it is to unpack securitisation more fully, to consider the benefits and limitations of its differing operationalisations of the term, and to open the scope for alternative ways of engaging migration. Such a focus need not divide scholars of migration studies and critical security studies, but can also bring them together as a means to explore how security features in debates and practices around migration and its control.

Note

1. I do not want to go into the details of this here, since it takes us in a somewhat different direction from the one I want to take in this chapter. However, I do want to indicate that the issue of contradictory goals or pressures to which Boswell points in her discussion of organisations or institutions (such as the Home Office in the early-mid-2000s) is important. Indeed, this may be particularly the case when it comes to the issue of the coexistence of securitisation and liberalisation in the field of migration policy, which is a broader issue

with which this paper engages. Boswell's intervention provides some important insights that may allow us to consider further how this coexistence might be understood in relation to what she conceives as 'conflicting' institutional norms and organisational goals. As I suggest later in this chapter, the extent to which the norms of securitisation and liberalisation conflict is questionable from a critical perspective.

References

Ajana, B. (2013) *Governing through biometrics: the biometrics of identity*, Basingstoke: Palgrave Macmillan.

Amoore, L. (2006) 'Biometric borders: governing mobilities in the war on terror', *Political Geography*, 25(3): 336–351.

Andrijasevic, R. (2010) *Agency, migration and citizenship in sex trafficking*, Basingstoke: Palgrave Macmillan.

Aradau, C., Huysmans, J. and Squire, V. (2010) 'Acts of European citizenship: a political sociology of mobility', *Journal of Common Market Studies*, 48(4): 945–965.

Balzacq, T. (2005) 'The three faces of securitisation: political agency, audience and context', *European Journal of International Relations*, 11(2): 171–201.

Balzacq, T. (2007) 'The policy tools of securitization: information, exchange, EU foreign and internal policies', *Journal of Common Market Studies*, 46(1): 75–100.

Basaran, T. (2008) 'Security, law, borders: spaces of exclusion', *International Political Sociology*, 2(4): 339–354.

Bellanova, R. and Fuster, G. G. (2013) 'Politics of disappearance: scanners and (unobserved) bodies as mediators of security practices', *International Political Sociology*, 17(2): 188–209.

Bigo, D. (2000) 'When two become one: internal and external securitisations in Europe' in M. Kelstrup and M. Williams (eds) *International relations theory and the politics of European integration. Power, security and community*, London: Routledge, pp.171–204.

Bigo, D. (2002) 'Security and immigration: toward a critique of the governmentality of unease', *Alternatives*, 27: 63–92.

Bigo, D. and Tsoukala, A. (eds) (2008) *Terror, insecurity and liberty: illiberal practices of liberal regimes after 9/11*, London: Routledge.

Bonditti, P. (2004) 'From territorial space to networks: a Foucaultian approach to the implementation of biopolitics', *Alternatives*, 29: 465–482.

Boswell, C. (2007a) 'Migration control in Europe after 9/11: explaining the absence of securitization', *Journal of Common Market Studies*, 45(3): 589–610.

Boswell, C. (2007b) 'Theorizing migration policy: is there a third way?', *International Migration Review*, 41(1): 75–100.

Buzan, B., Wæver, O. and Wilder, J. D. (1998) *Security: a new framework for analysis*, Boulder, CO: Lynne Rienner.

Council of the European Union (2004) 'Operational programme of the council for 2005, submitted by the incoming Luxembourg and United Kingdom Presidencies' in *POLGEN* 57, http://register.consilium.europa.eu/doc/srv?l=EN&f=ST%2016299%202004%20INIT, accessed 28 June 2011.

Dauvergne, C. (2008) *Making people illegal: what globalisation means for globalisation and law*, Cambridge: Cambridge University Press.

Epstein, C. (2007) 'Guilty bodies, productive bodies, destructive bodies: crossing the biometric borders', *International Political Sociology*, 1(2): 149–164.

Freeman, G. (1995) 'Modes of immigration politics in liberal democratic states', *International Migration Review*, 29(4): 881–902.

Gibney, M. J. (2004) *The ethics and politics of asylum: liberal democracy and the response to refugees*, Cambridge: Cambridge University Press.

Guild, E. (2003) 'International terrorism and EU immigration, asylum and borders policy: the unexpected victims of 11 September 2001', *European Foreign Affairs Review*, 8(3): 331–346.

Huysmans, J. (1998) 'Security! What do you mean? From concept to thick signifier', *European Journal of International Relations*, 4(2): 226–255.

Huysmans, J. (2000) 'The European Union and the securitization of migration', *Journal of Common Market Studies*, 38(5): 751–777.

Huysmans, J. (2006) *The politics of insecurity: fear, migration and asylum in the EU*, London: Routledge.

Huysmans, J. and Buonfino, A. (2008) 'Politics of exception and unease: immigration, asylum and terrorism in parliamentary debates in the UK', *Political Studies*, 56(4): 766–788.

Huysmans, J. and Squire, V. (2015) 'Migration and security' in T. Balzacq, M. Dunn Cavelty and V. Mauer (eds) *The Routledge handbook of security studies* (2nd edition), Abingdon: Routledge.

Jones, R. (2012) *Border walls: security and the war on terror in the United States, India and Israel*, London: Zed Books.

Joppke, C. (1998) 'Why liberal states accept unwanted immigration', *World Politics*, 50(2): 266–293.

Kalm, S. (2010) 'Liberalizing movements? The political rationality of global migration management' in M. Geiger and A. Pecoud (eds) *The Politics of International Migration Management*, Basingstoke: Palgrave Macmillan, pp.21–44.

Lazaridis, G. (ed) (2011) *Security, insecurity and migration in Europe*, Aldershot: Ashgate.

Lewis, N. (2005) 'Expanding surveillance: connecting biometric information systems to international police cooperation' in E. Zureik and M.B. Salter (eds) *Global surveillance and policing: borders, security, identity*, Devon: Willan Publishing, pp.97–112.

Lyon, D. (2005) 'The border is everywhere: ID cards, surveillance and the other' in E. Zureik and M. B. Salter (eds) *Global surveillance and policing: borders, security, identity*, Devon: Willan Publishing, pp.66–82.

Muller, B. (2005) 'Borders, bodies and biometrics: towards identity management' in E. Zureik and M. B. Salter (eds) *Global surveillance and policing: borders, security, identity*, Devon: Willan Publishing, pp.83–96.

Muller, B. J. (2010) *Security, risk and the biometric state*, Abingdon: Routledge.

Muller, B. J. (2011) 'Risking it all at the biometric border: mobility, limits, and the persistence of securitisation', *Geopolitics*, 16(1): 91–106.

Neal, A. (2009) 'Securitization and risk at the EU border: the origins of FRONTEX', *JCMS: Journal of Common Market Studies*, 47(2): 333–356.

Rygiel, K. (2011) 'Governing border zones of mobility through e-borders: the politics of embodied mobility' in V. Squire (ed) *The contested politics of mobility: border zones and irregularity*, Abingdon: Routledge, pp.143–168.

Rygiel, K. (2013) 'Mobile citizens, risky subjects: security knowledge at the border' in S. Ilcan (ed) *Mobilities, knowledge and social justice*, Montreal: McGill-Queen's University Press, pp.152–176.

Salter, M. B. (2003) *Rights of passage. The passport in international relations*, Boulder: Lynne Rienner.

Salter, M. B. (2008) 'Imagining numbers: risk, quantification and aviation security', *Security Dialogue*, 39(2): 243–266.

Salter, M. B. (2012) 'Theory of the / : the suture and critical border studies', *Geopolitics*, 17(4): 734–755.

Squire, V. (2009) *The exclusionary politics of asylum*, Basingstoke: Palgrave Macmillan.

Squire, V. (2011) *The contested politics of mobility: borderzones and irregularity*, Abingdon: Routledge.

Van Munster, R. (2009) *Securitizing immigration: the politics of risk in the EU*, Basingstoke: Palgrave Macmillan.

2
The Securitisation of European Migration Policies: Perceptions of Threat and Management of Risk

Lena Karamanidou

Introduction

Over the last few decades, migration has been constructed as a process that poses threats to the security, identity and wellbeing of European states and societies, and has been the target of policies aimed at reducing the risks posed by it. While securitised discourses, politics and policy responses are often articulated at the national level, the European Union has been the locus of both discourses and practices securitising migration in the European context. As a territorial political entity with defined external borders and political institutions generating binding legal and policy arrangements on behalf of its member states, the European Union has been particularly active in the field of migration control and asylum policies. These policies, as will be demonstrated in this chapter, are not only guided – although not exclusively – by a logic of securitisation, but have had the effect of producing and reproducing migrants as security threats.

The development of asylum and migration policies in the European Union took place over nearly three decades. Initially a matter of intergovernmental co-operation, asylum policy development produced, *inter alia*, non-binding resolutions on safe third countries, manifestly unfounded asylum applications, and minimum standards for asylum procedures (Lavenex 2001). The process of abolishing internal borders engendered policies aimed at controlling migration, incorporated in the Schengen Agreements of 1985 and 1999 (Van Munster 2009). The Amsterdam Treaty Europeanised migration and asylum policies, rendering them a matter of EU policies and actions (Kasparek 2010). In the field of asylum, the recently revised directives on minimum standards on procedures in member states for granting and withdrawing refugee status (2005/85/EC and 2013a/32/EU), on standards for the qualification of third-country nationals or stateless persons as beneficiaries of international protection (2004/83/EC and 2011/95/EU), and on laying down minimum standards for the reception of asylum seekers (2003/9/EC and 2013b/33/EU), as well as the Dublin II and III regulations (EC 343/2003 and EU 604/2013c) reforming the previous Dublin Convention (1990), created common asylum policies and standards across member states.

Policies on irregular migration and border controls were expanded with new instruments such as the Returns directive, the establishment of FRONTEX, and the development of technologies of control such as the Schengen Information System and Eurodac. The external dimension of asylum and migration policies, emphasised in the EU's Global Approach to Migration Management (GAMM) and involving the transposition of EU control instruments to third countries, expanded considerably with both unilateral and multilateral readmission agreements (Geddes 2005). Taken together, policy developments in the field of migration and asylum created a highly diverse and far-reaching legislative framework, and also one that, under the influence of the 9/11 attacks, established migration as a phenomenon that poses risks and needs to be regulated and controlled even more tightly.

Securitisation is seen in this chapter as a social process that involves elements of both discursive designation and social practice. Following the Copenhagen School, it incorporates a process of socially constructing issues as security threats through 'speech acts', a discursive process of 'talking security and insecurity' (Huysmans 2006: 25; see also Wæver 1995), which involves the development of shared, intersubjective understandings among political elites and audiences of what constitutes a security threat (Wæver 1995). The existential threats invoked by securitising speech acts are seen as having 'unprecedented threatening complexion' (Balzacq 2011: 3) and shared understandings impose a 'rationality of security' on social and political beliefs, relations and actions, and justify the undertaking of *exceptional* political action in order to eliminate threats (Buzan, Wæver and Wilder 1998; Huysmans 2006; Squire 2009).

Securitisation entails the construction of opposing identities between existential threats – in this case, migration and migrants – and the object that they are threatening, for example, societies, states or supra-state entities such as the European Union (Huysmans 1995; Squire 2009). Thus securitisation is significant for the reproduction of social and political identities through a process of othering and division of 'us' and 'them' (Huysmans 1995; Squire 2009) and contributes to the exclusionary politics of migration (Squire 2009). The securitisation of migration policy in the EU should be analysed with reference to the liberal political project of establishing the EU as 'an area of freedom, security and justice' (Huysmans 2006; Van Munster 2009). A 'liberal mode of governing' as Van Munster (2009: 9) argues, sees 'freedom as an indispensable element in administering a population'. The principle of freedom underpins the free movement afforded to – and expected from – the citizens of the Union in order to realise the economic aspects of the creation of denationalised and deregulated zone of economic activity (Squire 2009). However, freedom in liberal regimes has to be exercised responsibly by 'autonomous' individuals that can govern themselves (Van Munster 2009; Huysmans 2006). It has to be protected from its 'deviant', irresponsible forms of exercising freedom through the monitoring of populations (Ibid.). From this perspective, forms of unauthorised migration such as asylum-seeking, irregular migration, smuggling and trafficking challenge the regulated exercise of mobility as an expression of freedom (Huysmans 2006; Van Munster 2009). Ensuring security within the European Union, in this respect, guarantees the conditions for the desirable exercise of freedom.

However, securitisation is not only a discursive matter: it encompasses a range of social practices of controlling and governing populations. Securitisation emerges not only from discursive framings of phenomena as security threats but from practices of bureaucratic governance which reflect Foucault's concept of governmentality – a form of governance, associated by Foucault with the modern state, which relies on bureaucratic and technological techniques to govern and control populations (Huysmans 2006; Squire 2009). Bigo (2002) and Huysmans (2006) point to the role of a range of institutions and security agencies – the police, the military, immigration control institutions, private security agencies (Squire 2009). Rather than suggesting a logic of urgent response to an unprecedented threat that transcends the norms of ordinary political conduct, securitising practices might be oriented towards the management of risk in the sense of anticipated dangers (Van Munster 2009; Squire 2009). In this context, the role of knowledge production is crucial, since the designation of threat often draws on bureaucratic and scientific assessments of risk that anticipate security threats (Van Munster 2009; Squire 2009).

It is recognised that policy developments in the EU do not always conform to a pure logic of securitisation. The economic neo-liberal rationale is also reflected in the 'migration management' model which, although sometimes hindered by national interests, underpins support for allowing the migration of third country nationals as labour needed for the economic development of the Union (Squire 2009). Further, human rights and refugee protection norms are significant for the identity of the European Union as a liberal entity characterised by the rule of law, democracy, freedom and security. The development of asylum and refugee policies has been guided, to an extent, by humanitarian imperatives emanating from the Union's normative commitments to human rights and justice (Boswell 2003). However, this chapter maintains that a securitising approach has dominated migration policy since 9/11, both at EU and individual state levels, and has been institutionalised through EU laws and policies and the establishment of agencies such as FRONTEX. It is further argued that the increasingly complex and diffuse network of securitising discourses and practices, despite the existence of opposing discourses, has reproduced and reinforced the perception of migrants and migration as a threat, and justified the perpetuation of securitising measures. At the same time, the securitisation of migration policies has had serious implications in eroding the rights of migrants and refugees in Europe.

The chapter will focus on four aspects of migration policy in the EU in order to trace securitising discourses and practices: the discursive securitisation of migration within policies of the EU; the establishment of FRONTEX as an agency with a central role in managing security risks at the borders of the European Union; the expansion of externalised policies; and the expansion and normalisation of detention and deportation regimes. The analysis is focused both on the discursive enunciation of threats and their securitising effect as practices.

Asylum and migration policies and securitisation

While the securitisation of migration is often associated with policy responses after 9/11, its roots can be traced much earlier. Postwar migration in western European countries was a source of much needed labour to help their economic development, but the economic downturn of the 1970s triggered the intensification of concerns around social conflicts and integration (Van Munster 2009; Huysmans 2006). Rising numbers of asylum applications in the 1980s and 1990s, the collapse of communist regimes in the turn of those decades and the refugee crisis caused by the civil war in Yugoslavia provide the geo-political context in which migration came to be seen as a cause for concern for national governments and in European Union circles (Lavenex 2001; Schuster 2003). In the context of the European Union at the time, in the process of greater integration, the securitisation of migration can be seen as a response to the creation of a zone of free movement and the abolition of internal borders among states joining the Schengen zone (although not among those which did not sign the convention) so as to allow the free movement of 'goods, persons, services and capital' (European Communities 1986: 7) and as a trade-off between internal security and free movement, whereby restrictions to migration were seen as essential in order to guarantee the internal security of the Union (Lavenex 2001). Neo-functionalist explanations, as Van Munster (2009) and Huysmans (2006) have argued, ignore the discontinuities and multiplicity of institutional actors with differing interests involved in the process of securitisation, and run the risk of rendering it a 'natural' response to 'external' threats.

They also ignore the development of securitised responses to migration before the establishment of a zone of free movement and the perceived pressures by new patterns of asylum seeking (Van Munster 2009). Intergovernmental fora, such as the Trevi group in the 1970s and the Ad Hoc Working Group on Immigration in the 1980s, staffed by security experts from the interior ministries of member states, were instrumental in establishing migration as a security issue and promoting agendas that highlighted the perceived intersections between criminal activities and migration movements. Three securitising moves can be discerned in the discourses of such institutions. First, asylum seeking was securitised through discursive construction of 'bogus' asylum seekers and its discursive association with 'illegal migration' (Van Munster 2009; Walters 2010). The 1992 Edinburgh European Council conclusions, for instance, called for 'common endeavours to combat illegal immigration' and preventing 'the misuse of the right to asylum in order to safeguard the principle itself' (European Council 1992: 47). Secondly, 'illegal migration' became the focus of securitised discourses and policies (Walters 2010). The Schengen Agreements of 1985 and 1990 clearly enunciated a link between internal security and threats posed by migration, and highlighted the 'need for effective external border controls' given the 'the risks in the fields of security and illegal immigration' (European Communities 2001: 95). Thirdly, the unauthorised movement of people was linked to criminal activities (Bigo 2002; Lavenex 2001; Van Munster 2009).

While these developments took place largely under an intergovernmental framework, the Treaty of Maastricht institutionalised these arrangements by incorporating them within the Justice and Home Affairs pillar (Van Munster 2009). It can be argued, however, that securitarian discourses and practices were not firmly established at that point and coexisted with humanitarian agendas, driven mainly by the commission, which prioritised addressing the root causes of migration and ensuring a common system of asylum protection (Boswell 2003; Van Munster 2009). The establishment of the European Union as an Area of Freedom, Security and Justice with the Amsterdam Treaty brought to the fore the political significance of security issues (Van Munster 2009; Walters 2010). In the text of the treaty, one of the main aims of the institutions of the European Union is

> to maintain and develop the Union as an area of freedom, security and justice [AFSJ], in which the free movement of persons is assured in conjunction with appropriate measures with respect to external border controls, asylum, immigration and the prevention and combating of crime. (European Communities 1997: 8)

The EU is given a political identity – identified with the values of freedom, security and justice – whose maintenance is conditional upon migration and security policies. Reflecting the securitised language of the Schengen Agreement, they are presented as 'flanking' measures (Ibid.: 28). The juxtaposition between the discursive construction of a secure Europe and threats coming from outside it is reflected in the 1999 Tampere conclusions:

> This freedom should not, however, be regarded as the exclusive preserve of the Union's own citizens. Its very existence acts as a draw to many others world-wide who cannot enjoy the freedom Union citizens take for granted. It would be in contradiction with Europe's traditions to deny such freedom to those whose circumstances lead them justifiably to seek access to our territory. This in turn requires the Union to develop common policies on asylum and immigration, while taking into account the *need for a consistent control of external borders to stop illegal immigration and to combat those who organise it and commit related international crimes* [my italics]. These common policies must be based on principles which are both clear to our own citizens and also offer guarantees to those who seek protection in or access to the European Union. (European Council 1999)

The condition of freedom in the EU, in this extract, is presented as a reason for seeking asylum in its territory. While the statement commits

to principles of providing protection, the preservation of the EU commitment to asylum and refugee protection requires security measures.
Employing the militarised language of 'combating' illegal immigration
and crime (Van Munster 2009) to enunciate security threats, the statement also alludes to shared understandings of threat with the audience
of 'our own citizens' to legitimate policy actions.

This juxtaposition between security and freedom is reiterated in the
Hague programme, this time after the events of 9/11 reignited security
concerns over terrorism and threats to order and democracy:

> The European Council reaffirms the priority it attaches to the devel-
> opment of an area of freedom, security and justice, responding to a
> central concern of the peoples of the States brought together in the
> Union. ... The citizens of Europe rightly expect the European Union,
> while guaranteeing respect for fundamental freedoms and rights,
> to take a more effective, joint approach to cross-border problems
> such as illegal migration, trafficking in and smuggling of human
> beings, terrorism and organised crime, as well as the prevention
> thereof. ... The management of migration flows, including the fight
> against illegal immigration should be strengthened by establishing
> a continuum of security measures that effectively links visa applica-
> tion procedures and entry and exit procedures at external border
> crossings. Such measures are also of importance for the prevention
> and control of crime, in particular terrorism. (European Council
> 2004: 2–3 and 16)

Echoing the shared understanding between the EU and its citizens by
invoking the expectations of the 'citizens of Europe' and commitments
to the maintenance of the Area of Freedom Security and Justice (1999),
the Hague programme (2004) proposed a continuum of measures which
merge migration policies with security objectives of preventing crime
and terrorism. Guild, Carrera and Bigo (2008) argue that the Hague
programme was instrumental in introducing a conceptual shift in the
discourse of European Union where security concerns take priority over
the values of freedom and justice and the protection of human rights,
which are reduced to the level of a disclaimer in the above extract.
Importantly, the Hague programme also transposes the pursuit of
security beyond the territory of the Union, highlighting the interconnected nature of internal and external policies. Subsequent migration
programmes and key documents suggest the same priorities (Hyndman
and Mountz, 2008). The Lisbon Treaty (2007) reasserts the significance of

'appropriate measures with respect to external border controls, asylum, immigration and the prevention and combating of crime' for the maintenance of security and freedom within the territory of the European Union (European Union 2007: 11). In the Stockholm Programme (2010), trafficking and smuggling are treated as internal security threats to be confronted by crime prevention measures. A section entitled 'Access to Europe in a globalised world' focuses extensively on border management and irregular migration and visa policies, which, while it is claimed that 'they should not prevent access to protection systems' (European Council 2010: 26) are repeatedly related to maintaining security and preventing crime.

What the increasing prominence of securitised pronouncements and policies brings into relief is their contradictions with human rights and refugee obligations. The introduction of securitised policies runs parallel with the development of human right frameworks such as the Charter for Fundamental Rights (2000) and the development of binding legal frameworks, such as the asylum directives on minimum standards (2005/85/EC and 2013a/32/EU), refugee status qualification (2004/83/EC and 2011/95/EU), and the reception (2003/9/EC and 2013b/33/EU) whose aim – at least the proclaimed one – is to ensure protection for migrants fleeing insecurity and the respect of their human rights. EU texts, from directives to presidency conclusions to press statements by EU officials, regularly express these principles. The Tampere Conclusions (1999), for example, express the commitment of the EU and its member states 'to absolute respect of the right to seek asylum' (European Council 1999) and the Hague Programme, for example, states that one of its objectives is 'to improve the common capability of the Union and its member states to guarantee fundamental rights, minimum procedural safeguards and access to justice, to provide protection in accordance with the Geneva Convention on Refugees' (European Council 2004: 1). Similarly, the above-mentioned directives clearly state their alignment with the principles of the Geneva Convention relating to the states of refugees. Yet, not only do discourses designate migrants as security threats, but also, securitised practices of migration control prevent migrants from reaching the EU as a self-proclaimed space of security and freedom which affords human rights and refugee protection (Hyndman and Mountz 2008; Guild, Carrera and Bigo 2008).

The remainder of this chapter will illustrate the securitised discourses and practices of the EU migration regime in three areas where migration is securitised and controlled: at the border, focusing especially on the practices of FRONTEX; beyond the border, focusing on the 'external' dimension of migration controls; and within the border, focusing on the policing of migrants through practices of detention and deportation.

Securitisation of the border and the role of FRONTEX

In the process of securitisation of migration, the border is one of the most important sites. EU policies such as border checks and patrols are exercised at the border and aim at preventing the risks and threats posed by migration from entering the territory of the European Union. As mentioned earlier, border controls are an integral part of EU policies articulated in the Schengen regime, and FRONTEX, as an independent agency specifically created for enhancing the border control regime of the EU, is an example of how securitisation practices have become normalised.

FRONTEX was established in 2004 by regulation EC2007/2004, as an independent agency charged with the task of more efficiently protecting the borders of the Union, and amended by two further regulations – EC863/2007 and EU1168/2011 – which provide for the deployment of Rapid Border Intervention Teams (RABITS). Discursively, FRONTEX is placed within the imperative of securing the EU's borders from the external threats of irregular migration. In his inaugural speech of the FRONTEX agency, Commission Vice President Frattini made the following statement:

> The spectre of international terrorism, the human tragedies of victims of trafficking and the equally sad and grave consequences of illegal immigration into the EU, are constant reminders that we need to do even more to combat the many and diverse threats facing this area... The European citizens rightly expect us to find efficient solutions to these security problems. But these solutions must always fully respect human rights and preserve the integrity of the common, free travel area provided by the Schengen cooperation. No member state, however well prepared, can shoulder such a task alone, and this is why we have created the FRONTEX Agency. (European Commission 2005a: 1)

Neal (2009: 334) sees FRONTEX as the failure of securitising logics rather than its outcome, arguing that the 'documents, political processes and rationales relating the construction of FRONTEX do not use overtly securitising language and do not follow the classic logic of securitisation' in that it was not 'the urgent and exceptional policy that the securitisation theory would expect'. The logic of anticipating and managing risk is reflected in the activities of FRONTEX. However, the language and argumentation of the above extract are very similar to the discursive contructions of security and migration in the Hague progamme, which stated that 'the fight against illegal immigration should be strengthened by establishing a continuum of security measures' in order to prevent the 'control of crime, in particular terrorism' (European Council 2004: 16). FRONTEX is clearly constructed as a response to security threats posed by irregular migration, associated here with trafficking and terrorism, and said to have 'grave consequences' for the security of the European Union. As in the Hague programme, Frattini also alludes to the intersubjective understanding essential to securitisation processes: he states that the perception of threat is shared by the citizens of the Union.

FRONTEX presents itself as an organisation that supports member states, rather than one that is a primary instrument of control, and as Neal (2009) argues, an organisation that anticipates risk rather than being guided by a logic of exceptional threats. According to its mission statement, FRONTEX 'promotes, coordinates and develops European border management in line with the EU fundamental rights charter applying the concept of Integrated Border Management' (FRONTEX 2014). The wide range of activities it performs go well beyond standard border controls that are customarily exercised by member states (Kasparek 2010; Leonard 2010). They encompass joint operations of border surveillance and control, personnel training, planning and coordinating joint operations, including deportation flights, and research and risk analysis. Taken together, all of these tasks are central to the securitised management of migration in the European Union (Kasparek 2010; Leonard 2010). Given that securitisation does not only entail exceptional measures but normalised practices (Bigo 2002; Huysmans 2006), the manner in which FRONTEX responds to the 'threats' posed by migration, through planned activities that rely on information gathering, reflects the perception of securitision as routine, normalised governance of security threats (Bigo 2002; Huysmans 2006). For reasons of space, the analysis here will focus on two aspects of FRONTEX's activities – the production of knowledge through risk assessments and practices of border control and surveillance.

Risk assessment – identified by Bigo (2002) as one of the key administrative practices of securitisation – 'is at the core of all activity planned and undertaken by FRONTEX' (Kasparek 2010: 125; see also Leonard 2010). The fact that FRONTEX uses the word intelligence to refer to its risk assessment and research activities is, according to Leonard (2010), a securitising practice in itself, since the term has been employed to refer to threats to national security. The knowledge of risk produced within the auspices of FRONTEX is aimed at establishing the need for action in order to manage risks posed by migration. The knowledge produced by FRONTEX shapes the construction of migration threats and risk and legitimates the power it has to shape the security operations of the EU.

The case of the 2010 deployment of RABIT teams along the Greek-Turkish land border is illustrative of the continuum between knowledge production, discursively designating threats and legitimising action on this basis. In its 2010 risk assessment report, FRONTEX claimed that 90 per cent of irregular migrant entries to Greek territory – and by extension, to the EU space – occurred through Greek borders. The claim was repeated in the announcement of the deployment of RABIT teams:

> Due to the exceptionally high numbers of migrants crossing the Greek-Turkish land border illegally, Greece now accounts for 90 per cent of all detections of illegal border crossings to the EU. In the first half of 2010 a total of 45,000 illegal border crossings were reported by the Greek authorities for all their border sectors. Greece currently estimates that up to 350 migrants attempt to cross the 12,5-km area near the Greek city of Orestiada every day. The situation in Greece is very serious. Acting on the basis of the Regulation 863/2007 of the European Parliament and of the Council, I have decided that FRONTEX will provide assistance to the Greek border authorities by deploying adequate number and composition of Rapid Border Intervention Teams. (FRONTEX 2010a)

The statement by FRONTEX Executive Director Ilkka Laitinen, announcing the deployment of RABITS in Greece, utilises knowledge about risk – such as '90 percent of all detections'; '45,000 illegal border crossings' – to support its assessment of the situation as 'very serious'. It alludes to the exceptionality and urgency of threats posed by patterns of irregular migration originating in the Middle East, Asia and Africa, shifting at the time from the maritime to the land Greek-Turkish border, in order to justify the deployment of RABIT teams in the area. Discursively, the enunciation of threat and the statement of the security issue is followed by the legitimated security action that accompanied it. But as Carrera and Guild (2010) demonstrate, this particular statistic was inaccurate for two reasons. It includes, as acknowledged in the second quarter FRAN 2010 report, interceptions at the Greek Albanian border, which constituted half of the detected unauthorised border crossings (FRONTEX 2010b). The same publication acknowledges that the increase in entries was due to seasonal fluctuations (FRONTEX 2010b). The emphasis placed on the 12.5 kilometre stretch of the Greek Turkish border – the only area where it does not coincide with the River Evros – further illustrates how the securitising practices of FRONTEX can have an impact within member states. Soon after the deployment of RABIT teams, the Greek government announced the construction of a wall along the self-same 12.5 kilometre stretch, a measure which the Greek Citizen Protection minister of the time described as having a highly symbolic as well as a practical deterrence function (Hellenic Parliament 2011).

FRONTEX's border control activities are possibly the best-known aspect of its securitising practices, especially those pertaining to the patrolling of the maritime borders of the EU's southern borders. Operations such as HERA, NAUTILUS and POSEIDON, involving the cooperation of FRONTEX personnel and members states' security agencies, have aimed both at preventing migrants from reaching the territory of the European Union and gathering intelligence on border movements. While the legality of FRONTEX border surveillance operations has been questioned for not fully adhering to international laws and human rights norms (Bigo and Guild 2010; Papastavridis 2010; Leonard 2010), there is little doubt regarding the securitising effect of these practices. FRONTEX's efforts to prevent migrants from arriving in EU territory, regardless of their efficiency, enact their discursive designation as security threats and reproduce unauthorised forms of migration as threat to the internal security of the Union (Weber and Pickering 2011). Equally, operations by FRONTEX associate irregular migration with preventing cross-border crime. In the context of Joint operation EPN Hermes Extension 2011, a team of Europol staff was deployed in Italy to 'help its law enforcement officers identify possible criminals among the irregular migrants having reached the Italian territory' (European Commission 2011a: 1). At a symbolic level, FRONTEX's activities militarise the border through practices of control and deterrence, customarily employed by states in order to prevent threats to state security (Leonard 2010).

While respect for human rights and adherence to asylum and refugee protection norms are included in the EU documents establishing FRONTEX and in other statements by the organisation – such as that of Frattini at the beginning of this section – its practices undermine these principles. By preventing arrival in EU territory and, by extension, access to protection systems, FRONTEX border surveillance and control activities amount to preventive *refoulement* (Marchetti 2010). The activities of

FRONTEX relating to entry prevention and migrant identification have been criticised for undermining access to asylum systems (Bigo and Guild 2010; Carrera and Guild 2010). Research has demonstrated that in the context of FRONTEX activities, ensuring the safety and access to rights of migrants is seen primarily as a responsibility of member states rather than FRONTEX (Bigo 2014; Klepp 2010). The securitising logic of seeing migrants as threats means that the humanitarian logic of ensuring access to refugee and human rights protection takes second place (Kasparek 2010; Leonard 2010).

Securitisation and the external dimension

One feature of the securitised migration regime is that controls are exercised beyond the territory of the EU as well as within it (Lavenex 2006; Paoletti 2010). While 'externalisation' is a rather broadly defined concept that can refer to the process whereby asylum and migration policies become linked with relations with other states (Haddad 2008), it is used here to signify the 'EU's attempt to project its territorial borders onto surrounding states and regions by exporting its migration and asylum policies' (Paoletti 2010: 29). The expansion of externalised policies was motivated by the perception that domestic and EU-level policies were insufficient in dealing with migration pressures and co-operation with other states would enhance the protection-providing and controlling capacities of the EU (Boswell 2003). Externalised policies started being introduced in the intergovernmental phase of European migration policy and have become Europeanised in nature. For instance, visa policies are currently regulated at the level of the EU through the Schengen Visa Regime, and readmission agreements can be signed both by member states and the EU collectively (FRA 2014). Similarly, border controls outside EU territory or territorial workers involving co-operation among member states are often coordinated by FRONTEX (Leonard 2010). They are also increasingly more wide-ranging in nature and scope, encompassing 'pre-frontier' controls: for example, from carrier sanctions and visa regimes to policing measures patrolling international waters so as to prevent migrants reaching EU territories, to policies on readmission (Geddes 2006; Haddad, 2008; Paoletti 2010). 'Externalised' control policies – that is, policies of control exercised outside the territorial jurisdiction of EU member states (McNamara 2013) – such as carrier sanctions, visa requirements and interceptions at international waters, are the most pertinent from the perspective of securitisation.

In official documents of the EU, externalised policies reflect preventionist, economic and securitarian logics. The Edinburgh conclusions (1992) emphasised the prevention of root causes of migration through continuing 'to work for the restoration and preservation of peace, the full respect for human rights and the rule of law' and through 'promoting economic development' (European Council 1992: 48). Addressing root causes by aiding development is reiterated as a part of external migration policies in most key documents to the present (European Council 1999; European Commission 2014). Equally, the logic of managed migration emphasising legal routes for migration is suggested in the Tampere conclusions with the European Council calling for the development, in close co-operation with countries of origin and transit, of information campaigns on the actual possibilities for legal immigration, and for the prevention of all forms of trafficking in human beings (European Council 1999).

The measures suggested in the Tampere conclusions point towards the development of a system for legal migration for third country nationals, reflecting the economic logic of providing a route for forms of migration desirable by EU member states. Under the Global Approach for Migration, one of the key aims of migration policy is to promote 'well-managed labour migration' (European Commission 2011b: 11) through providing information on legal migration routes and mobility partnerships with third countries (European Commission 2011b; also European Commission 2014).

However, externalised policies have been equally aimed at preventing unauthorised migration movements. In this respect, externalised migration policies are part of the continuum of securitised migration policies, which associate migration with threats and risks that must be kept away from the territory of the Union. This association is evident in the discursive construction of externalised policies. Then Edinburgh Conclusions supported the introduction of bilateral and multilateral readmission agreements to 'combat illegal immigration' (European Council 1992: 48). The Tampere Conclusions proposed a

> common active policy on visas and false documents should be further developed, including closer co-operation between EU consulates in third countries and, where necessary, the establishment of common EU visa issuing offices...to tackle at its source illegal immigration, especially by combating those who engage in trafficking in human beings and economic exploitation of migrants. (European Council 1999)

Both documents invoke security threats through references to securitised forms of migration and through the use of the language of 'combat'. Post-2001 documents are more explicit in discursively establishing links between security and externalised policies. The Hague programme, for instance, stated that:

> in the field of security, the coordination and coherence between the internal and the external dimension has been growing in importance and needs to continue to be vigorously pursued. (European Council 2004: 3)

Referring to measures against irregular migration and trafficking, the Hague programme – and, in the same vein, the Stockholm programme – explicitly link internal security with the external dimension requiring cooperation with third states (European Council 2004; European Council 2010).

It is suggested that externalised policies, especially policies of control, are firmly embedded in the securitisation regime, in that they prevent migrants from accessing EU territory and justify such practices by invoking securitised constructions of migration, such as the threats posed to internal security by unauthorised migration, trafficking and smuggling. Such policies have become normalised within the European Union through readmission agreements and mobility partnerships with non-EU countries (European Commission 2014) and display the highly bureaucratised and technological nature of securitised migration regimes. Extra-territorial controls are characterised by the heavy reliance on surveillance and border control technologies – databases like VIS (the European Visa Information System) are used to retain and share information in order to prevent the entry of 'undesirable' migrants (FRA 2014) – and risk-assessment knowledge in cooperation with third countries (Bigo and Guild 2010).

The process of externalisation involves the export of control instruments developed in the EU to other countries, thus imposing their EU security agendas on them (Geddes 2005; Boswell 2003; Lavenex 2006). It creates regimes of 'policing at distance' (Bigo and Guild 2010), whereby controls are exercised beyond the territory of the EU. The prioritisation and expansion of security has significant implications in terms of human rights. Control measures implemented in other countries, such as pre-arrival visa checks and carrier sanctions, can prevent forced migrants from reaching EU territory and accessing protection systems in a safe manner (McNamara 2013; Paoletti 2010). Practices of interception at sea in international waters have been shown to endanger life and violate the principle of *non-refoulement* (Paoletti 2010). Exercised beyond the territory of the EU, externalised controls can also evade democratic scrutiny and compliance with EU human rights instruments (Carrera 2007; McNamara 2013).

The exercise of securitised control agendas might appear at odds with agendas emphasising protection capacities and addressing root causes. For some commentators (Boswell 2003), these policies represented an indication of the commitment of the EU to promote a protection agenda, informed by commitments to human rights norms which are often seen in contrast to the security agendas dominating EU migration policies (Boswell 2003). However, as practice shows, according to Haddad (2008), protection policies on the one hand and control policies on the other, are different sides of the same coin. They are 'exported' in order to maintain security within the Union by keeping migrants away from the territory of the European Union (Haddad 2008; Hyndman and Mountz 2008). Like border controls, externalised protection policies designate migrants as 'undesirables' who should be prevented from entering European territory and regimes of rights that would be activated once within the European Union (Bigo and Guild 2010).

The expansion of detention and deportation regimes

While controls at and beyond the border securitise migrants by not allowing them into the territory of the Union, practices of detention and deportation constitute them as threats within the territory of the Union that need to be removed in order to restore order and security. Detention and deportation have been used historically as instruments for controlling 'undesirable' populations and designating political and social enemies and threatening subjects (Bloch and Schuster 2005; Schuster 2005; Walters 2010). As processes of governance, they are associated with the exercise of sovereignty by the state and the drawing of boundaries around the national community and polity (De Genova 2010; Walters 2010). They are thus powerful instruments in securitising migrants through establishing the desirability of their exclusion from the physical space of the state (De Genova 2010; Walters 2010; Weber and Pickering 2011). Yet, the practices of detention and deportation by liberal states are assumed to be balanced by legal regimes protecting the human and individual rights of a person (Walters 2010).

In the 1980s and the 1990s, regimes of detention and deportation of asylum seekers and irregular migrants were both expanded and normalised in many member states of the European Union (Bloch and

Schuster 2005). However, provision on return and detention did not feature strongly among emerging EU law and policy on migration, since practices of detention and deportation were seen as the responsibility of member states (Wilsher 2011). Even so, deportation and detention are included in 'the adoption of measures to fight illegal immigration' in the Schengen Agreement (Wilsher 2011; European Commission 2003). The detention and deportation regime expanded in the 2000s. In relation to deportation, the Directive on the Mutual Recognitions of Decisions of the Expulsion of Third Country Nationals (2001) enabled the enforcement of a decision of expulsion by one member state in other member states (Karakayali and Rigo 2010). Council Decision 2004/573/EC provided for 'rational repatriation' of third country nationals through organising joint return flights. Readmission agreements with third countries were also proposed as an instrument to enhance migrant returns in the context of managing irregular migration, although in early documents such as the Tampere conclusion, the emphasis was on voluntary returns (European Council 1999). A formal regime regulating detention and deportation was established with the introduction of the Returns Directive (2008/115/EC) in 2008, which provided for common standards and procedures for the removal of 'third country nationals residing illegally on territory of a member state' (European Union 2008: 1). The use of detention is authorised in a number of legal documents. The Receptions Condition Directive (2003/9/EC) – which defines detention as 'confinement of an applicant by a Member State within a particular place, where the applicant is deprived of his or her freedom of movement' (Art. 2h) – determines when asylum seekers can be detained, including because of unauthorised entry (FRA 2014).

Similarly, the Asylum Procedures Directive (2005/85/EC) allows the detention of asylum seekers according to the conditions of the receptions directive. In addition to providing a common framework for the return of irregular third country nationals and failed asylum seekers, the directive also provides for their detention, pending arrangements for their removal, even though it does not define detention (FRA 2014). However, the maximum detention length of 6 months can be extended to 18 months in cases of non-compliance or inability to obtain travel documents (Returns Directive 2008/115/EC, Arts 15(5) and 15(6)).

The word 'deportation' is not a term used in the legal instruments of the EU; rather, the term used is 'return', a neutral term, reflecting the view that securitising measures are often expressed in a bureaucratic rather than 'war-like' language (Van Munster 2009). The link between the EU's return policy and security threats is, however, explicit. A speech commenting on the development of a returns directive states:

> An effective return policy is the necessary corollary of a common policy on legal migration and asylum, and obviously key in the fight against illegal immigration. The Hague Programme called for the establishment of an effective removal and repatriation policy based on common standards for persons to be returned in a humane manner and in full respect for their human rights and dignity. The Commission responded to this call in September this year (2005) by proposing to approximate Member States' procedures for the return of illegally residing Third Country Nationals....It should be noted that the proposal also takes into account special concerns as regards safeguarding public order and security. (European Commission 2005b: 5)

The extract very explicitly links the introduction to the directive, not only with the 'the fight against illegal immigration', which in itself evokes security concerns by employing the language of war, but with maintaining public order and security. The consideration of issues of security in drafting the returns directive (2008/115/EC) was acknowledged by the commission. In fact, 'public' and 'national' security are invoked as reasons to curtail several provisions of the directive: to remove the possibility of voluntary returns (Art. 7.4), to impose entry bans (Art. 11.3), and to not provide information on the reasons for return decisions or entry bans (Art 12.1). Similarly, the revised reception directive (2013b/33/EU) allows the detention of asylum seekers 'when protection of national security or public order so requires' (European Union 2013c, Art. 8.3.e), while the wording of the previous reception directive (2003/9/EC) made reference to reasons of public order only.

The expansion of the use of detention and deportation under EU law is also illustrative of the construction of EU as a political entity with state-like powers 'seeking to assert legal control over its territorial borders' (Wilsher 2011: 185). In a communication by the Commission, an 'effective returns policy' is argued to be 'key in ensuring public support for elements such as legal migration and asylum' (European Commission 2006: 4). The reference to the 'public' reflects the idea that deportation (and similarly detention) can demonstrate the ability to control migration and especially its irregular forms (Cornelisse 2010).

Detention and deportation are often ineffective in terms of migration control (Gibney and Hansen 2003; Schuster 2005), something that is illustrated by the discrepancies between return decisions and effected returns, and the frequent legal challenges to both detention and return (FRA 2014; European Commission 2014). Nevertheless, they have strong symbolic powers that aim to assuage concerns of the public over migration (Gibney and Hansen 2003; Schuster 2005), something alluded to in the European Commission's reference (2006: 4) to garnering public support for other aspects of its migration policy.

The practices of detention and deportation securitise migrants by the same logic that imprisonment securitises citizens: by excluding them from the territorial entity of the EU in the case of removal, or by physically removing them from the 'lawful' population of the state (De Genova 2010). The increasing commonality of these practices is illustrated by the proliferation of detention or 'reception' camps around Europe, where migrants are entirely deprived of their mobility or afforded very little of it, and by the increasing numbers of returns, many with the involvement of FRONTEX (MIGREUROP 2013; European Commission 2014). Detaining and deporting migrants also conforms to a logic of securitisation that places them outside the legal protection afforded to citizens (Weber and Pickering 2011; Wilsher 2012). However, these practices should not be seen as the expression of a logic of exceptional threat, even if this is invoked by national governments and the EU itself to legitimate their use (Andrijasevic 2010). Rather, they have become normalised techniques in the securitised governance of migration.

Invoking national and public security as a justification for return and detention – a clear logic of securitisation – also brings into sharp relief the tensions between security and respecting the human rights of migrants. The returns directive acknowledges the limitations imposed by human rights and refugee protection instruments and by the qualifications (2004/83/EC and 2011/95/EU) and procedures (2005/85/EC and 2013a/32/EU) directives. It also accepts that the use of coercive measures should comply with human rights, be reasonable and proportionate, and be implemented 'in accordance with fundamental rights and with due respect for the dignity and physical integrity of the third-country national concerned' (Art. 8). However, an increasing number of European Court of Human Rights decisions concerning detention and deportation, even after the entry into force of the Returns Directive, demonstrate that states use these governance techniques extensively and in ways which contravene both the procedures and qualifications, directives and human rights provisions in the EU (FRA 2014).

Conclusion

This chapter has explored how EU policies have increasingly securitised migration. From the intergovernmental period of creating a free movement zone to the highly complex present framework, migration has been constructed as a phenomenon posing threats to the internal security of European societies. These threats are not seen here as 'real' but were established through discourses and practices of securitisation. At the discursive level, the framing of migration as 'illegal' and its association with criminal activities and terrorist threats has constituted migrants as the bearers of risk into the territory of the European Union. These constructions, albeit coexisting with other discursive framings emphasising economic benefits and humanitarian obligations, have been constant in official discourses. While securitising discourses articulated within EU institutions do not have as clearly designated an audience as those articulated in national contexts, they create social knowledge that constructs migration as a security 'problem' and a threat to the polity of the European Union, constructed as an area of justice, security and freedom that needs to defend itself against external threats to its security.

The relation between discourse and practice within securitising processes is seen as interdependent, since both discourses and practices have securitising effects. Securitised discourses have also legitimated practices that constitute migrants as the threatening Other. Policies aimed at the surveillance of migrants and at deterring their entry into the European Union have become normalised and enacted in routinised practices of controls within and outside the territory of the Union (Huysmans 2006; Bigo 2002). At a symbolic level, such practices have securitising effects, in that they designate migrants as subjects who should remain outside the territory of the European Union and place them beyond the rule of law and norms (De Genova 2006; Squire 2009). Thus the logic of securitisation, aiming at preserving the internal security of the EU, not only contradicts normative commitment to rights, but also to policies and practices aimed at enhancing protection (Boswell 2003). More significantly, as human tragedies across the Mediterranean have demonstrated, the logic of securitisation underpinning EU policies of control, within, at, and beyond its borders, has exerted a heavy toll on migrants.

References

Andrijasevic, R. (2010) 'From exception to excess: detention and deportations across the Mediterranean space' in N. De Genova and N. Peutz (eds) *The deportation regime: sovereignty, space and the freedom of movement*, Durham: Duke University Press, pp.33–65.

Balzacq, T. (2011) 'A theory of securitization: origins, core assumptions, and variants' in T. Balzacq (ed) *Securitization theory: how security problems emerge and dissolve*, London: Routledge, pp.1–30

Bigo, D. (2002) 'Security and immigration: toward a critique of the governmentality of unease', *Alternatives: Global, Local, Political*, 27(1): 63–92.

Bigo, D. (2014) 'The (in)securitization practices of the three universes of EU border control: military/Navy – border guards/police – database analysts', *Security Dialogue*, 45(3): 209–225.

Bigo, D. and Guild, E. (2010) 'The transformation of European border controls' in B. Ryan and V. Mitsilegas (eds) *Extraterritorial immigration control. Legal challenges*, Leiden: Brill, pp.257–279.

Bloch, A. and Schuster, L. (2005) 'At the extremes of exclusion: deportation, detention and dispersal', *Ethnic and Racial Studies*, 28(3): 491–512.

Boswell, C. (2003) 'The "external" dimension of EU immigration and asylum policies', *International Affairs*, 79(3): 619–638.

Buzan, B., Wæver, O. and Wilder, J. D. (1998) *Security: a new framework for analysis*, Boulder, CO: Lynne Rienner.

Carrera, S. (2007) 'The EU border management strategy: FRONTEX and the challenges of irregular immigration in the Canary Islands', http://www.ceps.eu/book/eu-border-management-strategy-frontex-and-challenges-irregular-immigration-canary-islands, accessed 8 March 2015.

Carrera, S. and Guild, E. (2010) 'Joint Operation RABIT 2010 – FRONTEX assistance to Greece's border with Turkey: revealing the deficiencies of Europe's Dublin asylum system', http://www.ceps.eu/book/%E2%80%98joint-operation-rabit-2010%E2%80%99-%E2%80%93-frontex-assistance-greece%E2%80%99s-border-turkey-revealing-deficiencies, accessed 8 March 2015.

Cornelisse, G. (2010) 'Immigration detention and the territoriality of universal rights' in N. De Genova and N. Peutz (eds) *The deportation regime: sovereignty, space and the freedom of movement*, Durham: Duke University Press, pp.101–122.

De Genova, N. (2010) 'The deportation regime: sovereignty, space and the freedom of movement' in N. de Genova and N. Peutz (eds) *The deportation regime: sovereignty, space and the freedom of movement*, Durham: Duke University Press, pp.33–65.

European Commission (2003) 'Commission communication on the development of a common policy on illegal immigration, smuggling and trafficking of human beings, external borders and the return of illegal residents', http://europa.eu/rapid/press-release_IP-03-794_en.htm?locale=en, accessed 8 March 2015.

European Commission (2005a) 'Franco Frattini and Luc Frieden visit the external borders agency (FRONTEX) in Warsaw', http://europa.eu/rapid/press-release_IP-05-821_en.htm?locale=en, accessed 7 March 2015.

European Commission (2005b) 'Legal migration and the follow-up to the Green paper and on the fight against illegal immigration', 7 November 2007, http://europa.eu/rapid/press-release_SPEECH-05-666en.htm, accessed 7 March 2015.

European Commission (2006) 'Communication from the commission on policy priorities in the fight against illegal immigration of third-country nationals' /* COM/2006/0402 final */, http://eur-lex.europa.eu/legal-content/EN/TXT/PDF/?uri=CELEX:52006DC0402&from=EN, accessed 8 March 2015.

European Commission (2011a) 'Frequently asked questions: addressing the migratory crisis', 4 May 2011, http://europa.eu/rapid/press-release_MEMO-11-273_en.htm?locale=en, accessed 7 March 2015.

European Commission (2011b) 'Thematic programme for cooperation with non-EU countries in the areas of migration and asylum – 2011–2013 multi-annual strategy paper', http://ec.europa.eu/dgs/home-affairs/what-we-do/policies/international-affairs/global-approach-to-migration/index_en.htm, accessed 6 June 2012.

European Commission (2014) 'Report on the implementation of the global approach to migration and mobility', Brussels: European Commission, http://ec.europa.eu/dgs/home-affairs/e-library/documents/policies/international-affairs/general/docs/gamm_implementation_report_2012_2013_en.pdf, accessed 8 March 2015.

European Communities (1986) 'Single European Act', http://ec.europa.eu/archives/emu_history/documents/treaties/singleuropeanact.pdf,   accessed 8 March 2015.

European Communities (1997) 'Treaty of Amsterdam amending the treaty of the European Union, the treaties establishing the European communities and certain related acts', http://www.europarl.europa.eu/topics/treaty/pdf/amst-en.pdf, accessed 3 March 2015.

European Communities (2001) 'The Schengen *aquis*', Brussels, http://consilium.europa.eu/uedocs/cmsUpload/SCH.ACQUIS-EN.pdf, accessed 8 March 2015.

European Council (1992) 'Conclusion of the presidency', Edinburgh, 11–12 December 1992, Brussels, http://www.europarl.europa.eu/summits/edinburgh/a0_en.pdf, accessed 4 March 2015.

European Council (1999) 'Tampere European Council 15 and 16 October 1999: presidency conclusions', Brussels, http://www.europarl.europa.eu/summits/tam_en.htm, accessed 4 March 2015.

European Council (2004) 'The Hague Programme', http://ec.europa.eu/home-affairs/doc_centre/docs/hague_programme_en.pdf, accessed 8 March 2015.

European Council (2010) 'The Stockholm programme – an open and secure Europe serving and protecting citizens', Brussels: Official Journal of the European Union, http://eur-lex.europa.eu/legal-content/EN/TXT/PDF/?uri=CELEX:52010XG0504(01)&from=EN, accessed 8 March 2015. http://ec.europa.eu/home-affairs/doc_centre/docs/hague_programme_en.pdf.

European Union (2001) 'Council directive 2001/40/EC of 28 May 2001 on the mutual recognition of decisions on the expulsion of third country nationals', Brussels: Official Journal of the European Union, http://eur-lex.europa.eu/legal-content/EN/TXT/PDF/?uri=CELEX:32001L0040&from=EN,   accessed 8 March 2015.

European Union (2003) 'Council directive 2003/9/EC laying down minimum standards for the reception of asylum seekers', Brussels: Official Journal of the European Union, http://eur-lex.europa.eu/LexUriServ/LexUriServ.do?uri=OJ:L:2003:031:0018:0025:EN:PDF, accessed 8 March 2015.

European Union (2003) 'Council regulation (EC) No 343/2003 of 18 February 2003 establishing the criteria and mechanisms for determining the member state responsible for examining an asylum application lodged in one of the member states by a third-country national', Brussels: Official Journal of the European Union, http://eur-lex.europa.eu/LexUriServ/LexUriServ.do?uri=OJ:L: 2003:050:0001:0010:EN:PDF, accessed 8 March 2015.

European Union (2004) 'Council directive 2004/83/EC of 29 April 2004 on minimum standards for the qualification and status of third country nationals or stateless persons as refugees or as persons who otherwise need international protection and the content of the protection granted', Brussels: Official Journal of the European Union, http://eur-lex.europa.eu/LexUriServ/LexUriServ.do?uri =OJ:L:2004:304:0012:0023:EN:PDF, accessed 8 March 2015.

European Union (2004) 'Council decision of 29 April 2004 on the organisation of joint flights for removals from the territory of two or more member states, of third-country nationals who are subjects of individual removal orders (2004/573/EC)', Brussels: Official Journal of the European Union, http:// eur-lex.europa.eu/legal-content/EN/TXT/PDF/?uri=CELEX:32004D0573&from =EN, accessed 8 March 2015.

European Union (2005) 'Council Directive 2005/85/EC of 1 December 2005 on minimum standards on procedures in member states for granting and withdrawing refugee status', Brussels: Official Journal of the European Union, http://eur-lex.europa.eu/LexUriServ/LexUriServ.do?uri=OJ:L:2005:326:0013:00 34:EN:PDF, accessed 8 March 2015.

European Union (2007) 'Treaty of Lisbon amending the treaty on European Union and the treaty establishing the European community', Brussels: Official Journal of the European Union, http://eur-lex.europa.eu/LexUriServ/LexUriServ.do?uri =OJ:C:2007:306:FULL:EN:PDF, accessed 6 March 2015.

European Union (2008) 'Directive 2008/115/EU of the European Parliament and of the Council on common standards and procedures in member states for returning illegally staying third-country', Brussels: Official Journal of the European Union, http://eur-lex.europa.eu/LexUriServ/LexUriServ.do?uri=OJ:L: 2008:348:0098:0107:EN:PDF, accessed 7 March 2015.

European Union (2011) 'Directive 2011/95/EU of the European Parliament and of the Council' of 13 December 2011 on standards for the qualification of third-country nationals or stateless persons as beneficiaries of international protection, for a uniform status for refugees or for persons eligible for subsidiary protection, and for the content of the protection granted (recast)', Brussels: Official Journal of the European Union, http://eur-lex.europa.eu/legal-content/EN/TXT/PDF/?uri=CELEX:32011L0095&from=EN, accessed 7 March 2015.

European Union (2013a) 'Directive 2013/32/EU of the European Parliament and of the Council of 26 June 2013 on common procedures for granting and withdrawing international protection (recast)', Brussels: Official Journal of the European Union, http://eur-lex.europa.eu/legal-content/EN/TXT/PDF/?uri=CE LEX:32013L0032&from=EN, accessed 8 March 2015.

European Union (2013b) 'Directive 2013/33/EU of the European Parliament and of the Council laying down standards for the reception of applicants for international protection (recast)', Brussels: Official Journal of the European Union, http://eur-lex.europa.eu/legal-content/EN/TXT/PDF/?uri=CELEX:32013L0033 &from=EN, accessed 7 March 2015.

European Union (2013c) 'Regulation (EU) No 604/2013 of the European Parliament and of the Council of 26 June 2013 establishing the criteria and mechanisms for determining the member state responsible for examining an application for international protection lodged in one of the member states by a third-country national or a stateless person (recast)', Brussels: Official Journal of the European Union, http://eur-lex.europa.eu/legal-content/EN/TXT/PDF/? uri=CELEX:32013R0604&from=EN, accessed 8 March 2015.

FRA (2014) *Handbook on European Law relating to asylum borders and immigration*, Luxemburg: Publications Office for the European Union, http://fra.europa. eu/sites/default/files/handbook-law-asylum-migration-borders-2nded_en.pdf, accessed 8 March 2015.

FRONTEX (2010a) 'FRONTEX deploys rapid border intervention teams to Greece. 25 October 2010', http://frontex.europa.eu/news/frontex-deploys-rap-id-border-intervention-teams-to-greece-PWDQKZ, accessed 8 March 2015.

FRONTEX (2010b) *FRAN*, quarterly issue 2, April–June 2010, http://frontex.europa. eu/assets/Publications/Risk_Analysis/FRAN_Q2_2010.pdf, accessed 8 March 2015.

FRONTEX (2014) 'Mission and tasks', http://frontex.europa.eu/about-frontex/ mission-and-tasks, accessed 8 March 2015.

Geddes, A. (2005) 'Europe's border relationships and international migration relations', *Journal of Common Market Studies*, 43(4): 787–806.

Gibney, M. and Hansen, R. (2003) *Deportation and the liberal state the forcible return of asylum seekers and unlawful migrants in Canada, Germany and the United Kingdom*, Geneva: UNHCR.

Guild, E., Carrera, S. and Bigo, D. (2008) 'The changing dynamics of security in an enlarged European union', *CEPS Challenge Research Paper* 12, http://www. ceps.eu/book/changing-dynamics-security-enlarged-european-union, accessed 8 March 2015.

Haddad, E. (2008) 'The external dimension of EU refugee policy: a new approach to asylum?', *Government and Opposition*, 43(2): 190–205.

Hellenic Parliament (2011) *Government Gazette*, 14 January, pp.3802–3804, http://www.hellenicparliament.gr/UserFiles/a08fc2dd-61a9-4a83-b09a-09f4c564609d/es20110114.pdf.

Huysmans, J. (1995) 'Migrants as a security problem: dangers of "securitizing" migration' in R. Miles and D. Thranhardt (eds) *Migration and European integration: the dynamics of inclusion and exclusion*, London: Pinter, pp.53–72.

Huysmans, J. (2006) *The politics of insecurity: fear, migration and asylum in the EU*, London: Routledge.

Hyndman, J. and Mountz, A. (2008) 'Another brick in the wall? Neo-refoulement and the externalisation of asylum in Australia and Europe', *Government and Opposition*, 43(2): 249–269.

Karakayali, S. and Rigo, E. (2010) 'Mapping the European space of circulation' in N. de Genova and N. Peutz (eds) *The deportation regime: sovereignty, space and the freedom of movement*, Durham: Duke University Press, pp.33–65.

Kasparek, B. (2010) 'Borders and populations in flux: Frontex's place in the European Union's migration management' in M. Geiger and A. Pecoud (eds) *The politics of international migration management*, Basingstoke: Palgrave Macmillan, pp.119–140.

Klepp, S. (2010) 'A contested asylum system: the European Union between refugee protection and border control in the Mediterranean Sea', *European Journal of Migration and Law*, 12(1): 1–21.

Lavenex, S. (2001) *The Europeanisation of refugee policies: between human rights and internal security*, Aldershot: Ashgate.

Lavenex, S. (2006) 'Shifting up and out: the foreign policy of European immigration control', *West European Politics*, 29(2): 329–350.

Leonard, S. (2010) 'EU border security and migration into the European union: FRONTEX and securitisation through practices', *European Security*, 19(2): 231–254.

Marchetti, C. (2010) 'Expanded borders: policies and practices of preventive refoulement' in M. Geiger and A. Pecoud (eds) *The politics of international migration management*, Basingstoke: Palgrave Macmillan, pp.160–183.

McNamara, F. (2013) 'Member state responsibility for migration control within third states: externalisation revisited', *European Journal of Migration and Law*, 15(3): 319–335.

MIGREUROP (2013) *Atlas of migration in Europe*, Oxford: New Internationalist.

Neal, A. W. (2009) 'Securitization and risk at the EU border: the origins of FRONTEX', *Journal of Common Market Studies*, 47(2): 333.

Paoletti, E. (2010) *The migration of power and north-south inequalities*, Basingstoke: Palgrave Macmillan.

Papastavridis, E. (2010) '"Fortress Europe" and FRONTEX: within or without international law?', *Nordic Journal of International Law*, 79(1): 75–111.

Schuster, L. (2003) 'Common sense or racism? The treatment of asylum-seekers in Europe', *Patterns of Prejudice*, 37(3): 233–256.

Schuster, L. (2005) 'A slegdehammer to crack a nut: detention, deportation and dispersal in Europe', *Social Policy and Administration*, 39(6): 606–621.

Squire, V. (2009) *The exclusionary politics of asylum*, Basingstoke: Palgrave Macmillan.

Van Munster (2009) *Securitising migration: the politics of risk in the EU*, Basingstoke: Palgrave Macmillan.

Wæver, O. (1995) 'Securitisation and desecuritisation' in R. Lipschutz (ed) *On security*, New York: Columbia University Press, pp.46–86.

Walters, W. (2010) 'Imagined migration world: the European Union's anti-illegal immigration discourse' in M. Geiger and A. Pecoud (eds) *The politics of international migration management*, Basingstoke: Palgrave Macmillan, pp.160–183.

Weber, L. and Pickering, S. (2011) *Globalization and borders: death at the global frontier*, Basingstoke: Palgrave Macmillan.

Wilsher, D. (2011) *Immigration detention: law, history, politics*, Cambridge: Cambridge University Press.

3
Migrants in the Realm of Experts: The Migration-Crime-Terrorist Nexus after 9/11

Mark Maguire

Introduction

This chapter explores the power of the future in contemporary security thinking. The contemporary moment is marked by the amplification of amorphous processes of (in)securitisation that traverse institutional and organisational boundaries. The problematisation of migration, crime and security in Europe has led to the rise of new techno-scientific assemblages, new forms of expertise, and new engagements with the milieu that is the near, but deep, future. In this chapter, I pay particular attention to foresight and scenarios as ways through which to explore how security and migration is now perceived and conceived by experts. My concern is to explore the stories about the future told by experts and the ways in which those stories elicit preemptive actions.

During the past two decades there has been a growing interdisciplinary focus on cultures of expertise (see Boyer 2008). Anthropologists have been careful to use this label in open-ended ways in order to capture skilled knowledge and vision, together with the roles played by 'specific intellectuals' (Feldman 2013). The work of Holmes and Marcus (2005) is particularly influential, though they question the degree to which the critical social sciences are equipped to research the realms of experts collaboratively, as 'counterparts'. They advocate 'para-ethnography' to gain access to experts' tacit knowledge, their styles of reasoning, and the ways in which they produce and consume evidence, for example.[1] For many scholars, para-ethnography denotes methodological innovations that foreground the intricacies of research in expert realms. For Holmes and Marcus, it also denotes critique, and, as Michel Foucault reminds us,

> A critique is not a matter of saying that things are not right as they are. It is a matter of pointing out on what kinds of assumptions, what kinds of familiar, unchallenged, unconsidered modes of thought the practices that we accept rest. (1988: 155)

Marcus and Holmes have already attended to illicit discourses available within official knowledge production and are especially interested in going beyond the critique of expert knowledge on its own terms by calling out alternative discourses (see Holmes 2001; see also Gusterson 1999: 342). My aim in this chapter is more modest than the proposition of new, alternative discourses. During a variety of para-ethnographic projects on security techno-science (see Maguire 2009, 2011, 2014), I noted the (in)security imaginations of experts and the stories they told about the future; I became increasingly conscious of the relatively small number of key texts and influential ideas that circulate among them (for example, Schwartz 1996; Tetlock 2005; Kahneman 2011) and their often dark, even nightmarish, visions of the future (for instance, Van Creveld 1991; Connolly and Kennedy 1994; Rhodes and Stelter 2011; Ophuls 2012). Here, I wish to explore the assemblage of crime, migration and security and the associated production of an actionable future milieu in the form of security scenarios and foresight. However, because security experts are keen to distinguish practices such as scenarios and foresight exercises from 'prediction', it becomes clear that what is at stake is the production of particular forms of knowledge that are acceptable but debated, relied upon yet questioned. The incitement to discourse in the realm of security expertise, then, suggests shared knowledge that often is expressed in quasi-mythical ways (see Foucault 1980). In short, even though security expertise purports to be 'evidence-based', this discursive community often operates with little or poor quality evidence to support their visions of the future. Indeed, it is capable of maintaining assumptions about the future in spite of evidence pointing in directions other than those accepted by the community. This is because this discursive community acts as a regime of veridiction that determines what counts as evidence and what does not count, often on the simple basis of what fits with their stories.

I am interested, then, in cultural visions, imaginations and their expressions in often rather simple stories. Speaking from a more subaltern perspective, Michael Jackson tells us that stories, 'testify to the very diversity, ambiguity, and interconnectedness of experiences that abstract thought seeks to reduce, tease apart, regulate, and contain in the name of administrative order and control' (2002: 253). In this chapter, however, I explore the kinds of stories told *within* the realm of order and control. I do this by first exploring the culturally constructed nexus of migration, crime and security, especially after 11 September 2001. Thereafter, I review the contributions made to the study of (in)securitisation by Michel Foucault (2007) by returning to some of his early and prescient comments on security and future planning. Finally, I turn to the stories of (in)security told by experts, to key texts that underpin those stories, and to the powerful ideas that animate them.

The residual, the dominant and the emergent

In the wake of the events of 11 September 2001, international migration came to be regarded as an especially notable arena in which security discourses and practices flourished (see UNHCR 2006). The world had changed, apparently, and especially so for migrants. Others, however, found fault with the image of a straight-line securitisation of migration process flowing directly from terrorist threats. For example, Christina Boswell (2007) argued that there was little evidence of terrorist threats being widely used to amplify European migration security. Her critique was aimed at the so-called Copenhagen School scholars and their efforts to track the emergence and legitimisation of security practices in public talk by public actors. Instead, she called attention to the diversity of organisations and actors involved and to the proliferation of mundane but powerful surveillance practices. Boswell's (2007) intervention was timely and cast critical light on overstated theories of securitisation. However, her eventual focus on surveillance – taken to denote a constellation of technologies, ideologies and practices – fails to mark itself off as different from what other scholars describe in terms of broader (in) securitisation processes that predate 9/11 (Bigo and Tsoukala 2008; Bigo 2007; Huysmans 2014).

While it may be reassuring to analytically divide the realm of security into discrete organisations, political actors, technologies and surveillance practices, it is not analytically beneficial to do so. Rather, the key questions for contemporary migration and security scholars relate to the amplification of security such that it crosses divides and disturbs the existing 'division of institutional labour' (Comaroff 2012: 45). In the present moment, to borrow from Raymond Williams (1976), security has become a 'keyword' that emerges from specific historical and social conditions and gathers around it a 'semantic cluster' of other quasi-related words, from risk to preparedness and from safety to resilience. To understand (in)securitisation, then, means to attend to its specific conditions of possibility and to its ramifications in terms of how the world is imagined and acted upon. Again, Williams' elegant formulations are helpful: rather than presuming straight-line historical transformations, he attends to the residual, the dominant and the emergent (1980: 31–49). The utility of this formulation is shown in a brief sketch of the history of security and migration since 9/11 in the United States and in Europe.

The events of 9/11, together with the terrorist attack by Richard Reid soon thereafter, transformed security and migration in the United States profoundly. The US government quickly established the Department of Homeland Security (DHS), which absorbed the Immigration and Naturalization Service. Migration, crime and terrorism were thus affixed to one another in the most significant shakeup of government since World War II.[2] The DHS Science and Technology Directorate invested in centres of excellence in congenial university environments. The Center for Border Control and Immigration in the University of Arizona in Tucson and University of Texas at El Paso is illustrative: there, academics, industry partners and operational security representatives collaborate to produce automated border control technologies. Close connections exist between US security experts and their counterparts in Europe – with FRONTEX, the EU's Schengen border control agency – trialling transnational automated border technology.[3] In 2012, for instance, they tested AVATAR, an automated border agent designed to detect deceit (see Maguire 2015). Travellers are already used to answering questions and having their biometrics checked at borders, and the policing of borders in a context of ever-increasing mobility presents an expensive global problem. Little wonder, then, that the United States, EU and numerous countries around the world are experimenting with automated border control (ABC) technologies to speed up the movement of 'trusted' (read élite) travel and sift for 'bad guys'. AVATAR is at the cutting edge in this regard, promising a future in which travellers will have their facial and other biometrics read alongside their travel documents by an ATM-sized machine. But, while the friendly computer-generated face is posing questions, travellers' facial expressions, eye movements and a host of other markers will be read by so-called second generation biometrics to detect deceit, criminality and potential terrorists. New forms of expertise are shaping new policies and technologies, and are in turn being shaped by them.

Following the Richard Reid attack in late 2001, security experts in Boston-Logan International Airport initiated research in counter-terrorism screening that later mutated into the passenger-screening programme operated by the Transport and Security Administration (TSA) (yet another post-9/11 agency under the broad Homeland Security umbrella). The TSA programme is similar in kind to programmes developed simultaneously in the UK, the Netherlands and Israel. Such programmes involve new actors, experts and, crucially, a new crime-migration-terrorism nexus (see Maguire 2014). What's at stake, then, are emergent but fractured 'securityscapes' (see Albro, Marcus, McNamara and Schoch-Spana 2012: 11); European and North American security-scapes that are now characterised by discourses on 'vital interests', 'critical infrastructures' and threats to life itself emanating from the near future (see Sweijs 2012: 16–17; see also Collier and Lakoff 2008).

But one could argue that the context of the federal United States is significantly different from the European mosaic of member states – an argument that many high-level security experts in Europe make. Thus, one must ask questions about the (in)securitisation of European migration. Since Boswell's (2007) intervention, a number of large-scale European projects set out to explore the dimensions and drivers of the European security apparatus. The picture that emerges is blurred. In an excellent review of European counter-terrorism measures – no less than 239 specific laws and policies since 9/11 – Hayes and Jones conclude that it is next to impossible to quantitatively evaluate the slow process of piecemeal transposition or to review the effects of those measures (see Hayes and Jones 2014: 8 and 33). However, evidence of the direct connections between the threat of terrorism and the securitisation of migration is available at a higher level. Sweijs (2012) examined the security policies of a large sample of member states, together with Russia and the United States, and concluded that we are witnessing the growth of an 'amorphous' concept of security (see Sweijs 2012: 4). He notes that, according to French national security policy, post-9/11 terrorism 'crossed a historical threshold', and beyond that threshold many European governments agree that terrorism and crime are now imbricated with migration and radicalisation (see, for examples, Présidence de la République Française 2008; Ministry of Defence of the Netherlands 2008; Ministero della Difesa 2005).

But what might be learned from specific European-level migration security policies and practices? Hayes and Vermeulen (2012) reviewed the implications of the EU's so-called smart borders programme, specifically the European External Border Surveillance System and the so-called smart borders package of biometric entry-exit recording and the Registered Traveller Programme. These systems bring security risk analysis together with futuristic high-tech approaches. Although the targets are ostensibly to tackle the vague problem of visa 'overstayers', increase efficient mobility and reduce security labour costs, when the European Commission launched the package, Commissioner Franco Frattini claimed, 'It's because of terrorist threats, criminality, paedophile networks' (EUobserver 2008: no pagination; Hayes and Vermeulen 2012: 12). When one looks at the scale and extent of these efforts and the potential societal impact that they will have, one is forced to attend to phenomena beyond mere political talk, policymaking, specific organisations, technologies or even private interests. Frédéric Gros, Monique Castillo and Antoine Garapon (2008: 6–7 passim; see also Deleuze 1997: 182) capture the situation eloquently when they call for attention to new security paradigms:

> that of [humanitarian] protection and the control of flows. [T]he security problem does not arise in terms of the end as in the previous age...but rather in the control and circulation passages. The major places of safety are no longer borders that delimit states, but within the same territory, airports or stations, that is to say, all the nodes of communication and exchange. The major problem is that of 'traceability': to identify each time that one moves, where one comes from, where one goes, what one does to the place where one is, and if one actually has access to the network in which one moves or if the network is prohibited. ... The globalisation of the world leads to the abolition of the old divisions between inside and outside, the criminal and the enemy, the political and the natural. The age of bio-political security is characterised by the large-scale neutralisation of threats and the elevation of the individual living being as vulnerable more than as a bearer of rights or as the citizen. ... Finally, a new philosophical anthropology emerges from these mutations. [my translation]

Much has already been written about the present moment of humanitarian governance and humanitarian reason (see Fassin 2012). Much more needs to be written about the so-called human factors of security technologies that have mushroomed in 'the nodes of communication and exchange' and the capacities of those technologies to render as code particular visions of bio-social humans and to fundamentally alter societal governance (see Maguire 2012). However, here my concern is with the emergent philosophical anthropology that one finds in the realm of security experts, especially discourses and practices that construct and act in a milieu in the near future and often operate, strikingly, in the form of stories. And, importantly, to investigate this milieu and how it is narrated, one needs to seek conceptual tools, rather than all-explaining theories.

Theorising the (in)security apparatus

During the past decade, critical theorists have turned anew to the work of Michel Foucault, inspired by the recent publication of his Collège de France lectures and interventions by key interlocutors (see Agamben 1998). Some commentators even argue that security is a golden thread that passes through all of Foucault's work (see Dillon and Lobo-Guerrero 2008). Indeed, it is now relatively common to read about 'apparatuses of security' or 'security assemblages' (for example, Larrinaga and Doucet 2010). But what precisely are apparatuses of security? Foucault's use of the term 'apparatus' aims to elicit a 'thoroughly heterogeneous ensemble consisting of discourses, institutions, architectural forms, regulatory decisions, laws, administrative measures, scientific statements, philosophical, moral and philanthropic propositions' (1980: 194). An apparatus, therefore, is not a synonym for some all-seeing and negative state-like organism – a 'meta- or trans-historic subject', as Foucault (Ibid.: 195) puts it, or a great big 'cultural critter', as Marshall Sahlins (2002: 66) has it. Instead, the term 'apparatus' signals a methodological intervention that aims to tease out connections, conjunctions and disjunctures. Furthermore, following Paul Rabinow, one may note that between problematisations, such as crime or immigration, and specific apparatuses, such as those of security, one finds emergent assemblages (see Rabinow 2003: 56).[4] It is those assemblages that construct and work in the near, but deep, future of insecurity that concern me here. But beyond conceptual tools, what else might be gained from this contemporary return to Foucault?

Foucault actually wrote very little about security (for example, 1991, 2007: 5–22, 42–45 and 64–65) and ultimately abandoned the field in favour of studies of governmentality and bio-politics. However, many prescient ideas may still be found, especially in his 1978 lectures in the Collège de France, published as *Security, Territory, Population*. He begins with a rather broad question: 'Can we say...that the general economy of power in our societies is becoming a domain of security?' (2007: 10–11). The search for an answer to this broad question motivated

Foucault to consider everything from spaces of security to uncertainty and from normalisation to the government of population (Ibid.: 11; see also 2008: 255–256 and 260 passim).[5] He begins by providing a brief historical survey of early town planning, especially during the 18th century and quickly identifies the problem of circulation. Planners were faced with open towns without walls and with a potentially 'indefinite series' of mobile persons, elements and events. According to Foucault, 'the management of these series ... because they are an open series and can only be controlled by an estimate of probabilities, is pretty much the essential characteristic of the mechanism of security' (Ibid.: 20). Therefore,

> [t]he apparatuses of security work, fabricate, organize, and plan a milieu even before the notion is formed and isolated. ... What one tries to reach through this milieu is precisely the conjunction of a series of events produced by individuals, populations, and groups, and quasi natural events which occur around them ... – the sudden emergence of the problem of the 'naturalness' of the human species within an artificial milieu. (Ibid.: 21–22)[6]

Foucault's work is tentative at best here, but also crystal clear: 'a good town plan,' he tells us, 'takes into account precisely what might happen' (Ibid.: 20).

In later lectures, when he turns to matters such as scarcity in the history of planning and population management, he begins to isolate key features of security apparatuses and the milieu in which they work. The basic function of security apparatuses, he suggests,

> is to rely on details that are not valued as good and evil in themselves, that are taken to be necessary, inevitable processes, as natural proc-esses in the broad sense, and it relies on these details ... in order to obtain something that is considered to be pertinent in itself because situated at the level of the population. (Ibid.: 45)

Rather than focusing in on every detail, like disciplinary mechanisms do, apparatuses of security, he suggests, stand further back in an effort to grasp that which occurs naturally at an exact point 'in reality' and then respond 'in such a way that this response cancels out the reality to which it responds – nullifies it, or limits, check, or regulates it' (Ibid.: 46–47). Later still, he turns to bio-security and the threats of disease from the 18th century onwards in order to isolate the new notions that accompany apparatuses of security, such as risk, danger and crisis. He notes that security interventions at the level of population were understood to pose their own risks (for example, inoculations) and that the play of the normal and abnormal became a key way through which to grasp the population as a whole statistically. These observations are crucial, because Foucault realises that speaking of 'exhaustive surveillance of individuals so that they are all constantly under the eyes of the sovereign in everything they do' is not helpful in elucidating fully the mechanisms and apparatuses of security (cf. Boswell 2007).

Much has changed, of course, since Foucault delivered his lectures in the Collège de France. He did not and could not have foreseen the extent of the current digital-industrial revolution or the rise of specific but impactful biometric technologies and their associated databases. Nonetheless, his ideas are prescient. He calls for attention to transversal security apparatuses and assemblages that are nested in dominant and residual organisations and institutions, but which are also boundary-crossing and emergent. He notes the crucial problematisation of circulation and the ways in which security apparatuses respond by producing milieux in which to act, anticipating also the play of the normal and the abnormal, and the rise of new discourses in the management of life itself.

Today, migration, terrorism and crime are connected and problematised by (in)securitisation apparatuses. Those apparatuses compose milieux – described in one EU report simply as 'a common security space' (Giegerich and Comolli 2009: 38). Those apparatuses involve activities such as planning, forecasting and running scenarios for the near future – because, after all, a good plan 'takes into account precisely what might happen' (Foucault 2007: 20). Hereafter, drawing on Foucault's insights, especially on the 'errors' that lurk within these processes, I turn to the expert production of the migration and security future. I acknowledge that much within Foucault's insights would logically push one to consider probability, prediction, and data-driven visions of the future. However, here I wish to attend to the kinds of qualitative stories and judgements that are made by security experts, which are imbricated with broader governmental practice but are also deserving of specific attention.

Insecure futures

The security expert spoke of the need for enhanced technology on the Mediterranean border and for better cooperation between Member States and agencies. He spoke of his genuine concern for the welfare of migrants who often embarked on dangerous journeys facilitated by debts to traffickers. He spoke of his outrage at media representations of 'illegal' migrants.

'Most of them would easily qualify for asylum protection', he explained.

'But there will always be a few among them who pose a real threat!'

Later, he confided that he had only slowly become aware of the scale of the problem – the flow of poor people from Africa, Asia and the Middle East was growing day by day, month by month, and one day it would overwhelm Europe.

The above is an extract from notes taken while attending a major security event in Europe in early 2014. I listened to the individual's presentation to an expert group and spoke with him at length during the event. Since 2008, as is typical for an anthropologist, I have kept retrospective notes on numerous informal conversations and interactions with security experts. I completed specific ethnographic projects on biometric security and counter-terrorism during that period (see Maguire 2011, 2014), but the above note was more in the style of a diary entry, without identifying details, intended to congeal general observations rather than stand as empirical evidence. Other anthropologists have eloquently reflected on the capacities for action and compassion among security technocrats (see Feldman 2013). Here, rather, I was initially impressed with the seniority and fluid career transitions presented by this individual – he moved from the private sector to a senior position in the US federal government, and from there to a cognate role in the UK, and then back to the private sector. I learned that the character of this person was forged between disciplines and sectors, between policy and technological implementation projects, and also by roles in humanitarian governance. But what impressed itself upon me most forcefully about this person was *their* future, their capacity to instantly call up an active milieu replete with 'real' examples, each of which served to illustrate their coherent vision of a threatening near future. Clifford Geertz (1973: v) once warned that 'there is nothing so coherent as a paranoid delusion', but there is much more at stake here than the musings of one anxious technocrat.

When attempting to unpack security experts' imaginings of the future it is useful, following the work of Ian Hacking (1992), to think in terms of 'styles of reasoning'. Hacking's styles of reasoning is an imprecise term, yet it gestures to important features worthy of further exploration. For example, it elicits the ways in which a particular scientific or techno-scientific style of reasoning includes the generation of new propositions, explanations and objects. It also elicits the particular standards of validity that obtain – what counts as evidence and 'truth'. Hacking's approach also attends to the stabilisation of knowledge, which allows one to apprehend how certain assumptions go without saying, *doxa* in short. Finally, this approach points to the cultural history of keywords and concepts. To all of this, I simply wish to argue that styles of reasoning often congeal in rather simple stories and, in fact, need to be narrated as such within a discursive community in order to make the complex future precisely knowable. Therefore, the question before me was what styles of reasoning were instantiated in this expert's presentation and reflections? The person before me was, to paraphrase John Mayard Keynes, a practical man who did not announce his intellectual influences and, yet, he was clearly shaped by residual ideas and a literature shared with like-minded professionals (see Keynes 1964: 383). It was easy, for example, to detect the influence of Matthew Connolly and Paul Kennedy's infamous essay in *The Atlantic Monthly* titled, 'Must it be the West against the Rest?' Partially disguised in a book review, Connolly and Kennedy argue that by 2025 the world will be divided, racialised and characterised by appalling income inequalities, and in their infamous words, 'the rich will have to fight and the poor will have to die if mass migration is not to overwhelm us all' (1994: 62).

During the mid-1990s, many critics dismissed Connolly and Kennedy's apocalyptic essay as post-Cold War, neo-conservatism scrambling in search of new enemies. But there is something particularly striking about the combination of security-focused and humanitarian styles of reasoning required to render poor migrants as 'helpless yet menacing people' (1994: 60; cf. Fassin 2012). There is also much that is revealing about the mode of reception of Connolly and Kennedy's essay – it was panned by left-leaning critics but it circulated widely nonetheless. Indeed, within the essay they seem to anticipate their own reception by pointing to other similarly controversial pieces. Robert D. Kaplan's apocalyptic essay on the ramification for the West of failed African states also appeared in *The Atlantic Monthly* in 1994 and was later circulated by the US State Department to overseas embassies and missions. Moreover, Connolly and Kennedy also note that just as one could find Kaplan's essay travelling via one technocratic network, one could also find Martin Van Creveld's *The Transformation of War* (1991) moving through military and defence industry circles. One is tempted towards a cultural study of security memes, but what all of these texts have in common is their acceptance by a particular set of discursive communities as 'realistic' efforts to construct and act in a milieu composed in the near future. And, Van

Creveld's near future is especially threatening: soon, he tells us, private security will dominate by necessity in a world of low-intensity conflicts resulting from demographic changes. In the near future, therefore, every man, woman and child will be stopped, searched and identified 'at every turn' (223). Plainly, I am pointing here to a certain post-Cold War inter-textuality, and as Julia Kristeva explains, 'every text is from the outset under the jurisdiction of other discourses which impose a universe on it' (quoted in Culler 1981: 105). In Raymond Williams' terms, what is at stake here is simply the 'flow' that holds together ideas, images, shared sensibilities and subjectivities.

Connolly and Kennedy (1994: 64) draw from Kaplan and Van Creveld and zero in on four trends that will shape the migration and security future. They argue that the preponderance of global population growth during the next decades will be among the poor, and that absolute numbers of the poor will therefore explode. They propose that huge numbers will gravitate to 'shanty-cities' and those slum-worlds will therefore be composed of the young, unemployed and angry. They propose that it is there that one will find the security-crime-migration threat: a future population simultaneously envious of western consumer culture and tempted by radicalism's plausible alternatives. This is a vision of a near future world divided along dangerous fault-lines, such as the Mediterranean migration routes.

Strikingly, this same story about the future is now available largely intact in European migration and security foresight and scenario exercises. Take for example the following summation of the future migration, crime and security milieu in a respected EU report (Langton 2009: 59; see also Maguire 2014: 6):

> By 2050 it is estimated that Lagos will have a population of 25 million. In 'mega-slums' communities grow up outside the societies upon whose fringes they exist. The infrastructure of the host cities cannot cope with the additional quantities of people who then construct their own societies, their own rule of law and their own employments which rely on illicit and non-state activities based on a 'Darwinian survival of the fittest' culture. This culture in its turn is based around and is 'governed' by armed gangs which interact with each other. For Europe...the risk is in importing problems (principally crime) from the 'mega cities' of Latin America, Africa, and Asia.

This scenario was derived for one section (on demographics and security) of an extensive foresight report (see Giegerich and Comolli 2009).

In response to the problematisation of particular threats, from immigration to climate change, the report illustrates the assemblages that are common in the European security apparatus. Even a cursory reading imparts the key doxa and concepts, and it is precisely the assembling together of specific problematisations and responses that is of significance.

The report tells us that the West, and especially Europe, is probably in decline and is beset on all sides by complex, transnational threats. These threats have rendered the Cold War world of nation-states, composed of discrete organisations and institutions, internal and external security, as little more than the residual traces of an *ancien régime*. 'In response', we are told, 'traditional security providers have adopted new roles and new actors have emerged', and 'cross agency cooperation is likely to be the only possible way to address increasing complexity' (Giegerich and Comolli 2009: 7). In response also, we find great emphasis placed on potentially vulnerable 'critical infrastructures'. No longer do we see the security, territory, population triad proposed and then hurriedly transcended by Michel Foucault. No longer do we see like a state that is ostensibly governing its boundaries, interests and population contractually. Instead, we begin to see as the security apparatus sees: energy, water, food, transport, communications, finance, government and health services are all perceived, conceived and lived as more or less resilient critical infrastructures in the milieu of the near future. The conceptual tools that are needed for this milieu are multi-agency and future-oriented research and planning, 'horizon scanning', and the prioritisation of key areas, such as 'the link between migration and insecurity' (Giegerich and Comolli 2009: 11). But what are the conditions of the possibility of this vision, and from where does it acquire its clarity and assurance?

The stories experts tell

It is beyond the scope of this chapter to give a full cultural history of forecasting and scenarios. In any case, it is more useful to take the versions of this history directly from the security experts with whom I interacted during the past several years. Working with experts collaboratively, as 'counterparts' (see Holmes and Marcus 2005), means becoming familiar with their intellectual decisions and accepted narratives, but also pushing against the boundaries of their knowledge critically. In short, I tried, para-ethnographically, to be sufficiently familiar with their literature to speak to them about it.

Many problems inherent in scenarios and forecasting are recognised by security experts, and they often debate methodological issues and display scepticism informally, though broader conceptual issues are generally elided. And, although the field of migration studies has a significant history of forecasting and scenario building, this literature rarely if ever is mentioned among migration and security experts.[7] Rather, many of the large-scale EU projects that I reference in this chapter use these techniques methodologically, not because they are especially respected, but more because they fit with the constraints of research and coordination funding, especially in Europe. Large-scale European projects require collaboration across member states and facilitate the mobility of experts for often very short periods. Scenarios and forecasting are often used, then, because they are methodologically *good enough* to satisfy funders and sufficiently accepted to bring people together for workshops and conferences without trepidation. The importance of this latter point was hammered home to me at the beginning of a closed counter-terrorism workshop in the UK in 2011: the facilitator spoke to me about my expertise before the delegates arrived and asked that I remain quiet if I recognised any 'slips' in his presentations during the day: 'I have to work with these people', he reminded me. Moreover, all of this is important not simply because of the institutional and organisational boundary crossing required of large EU projects, but, rather, because experts, planners, academics and those working in operational security come together in project consortia, and the 'common security space' (Giegerich and Comolli 2009: 38) requires and is peopled by a discursive community with common language and conceptual games. One may be sceptical about the game without questioning its underlying rules.

During numerous informal interactions, security experts expressed reservations but also told relatively consistent stories about the cultural origins of their activities: scenarios, I was told repeatedly, owe their origins, firstly, to the Cold War activities of the Rand Corporation. RAND, perhaps the most significant think tank in the world, pioneered everything from satellites to computer tablets (during the 1960s) and was at the forefront of the development of scenarios in areas such as military spending and strategic missile deployments. Secondly, experts also pointed to the apparently successful uses of scenario-building and foresight by Royal Dutch Shell to guide the company's decisions during the turbulent 1970s. Thus, the approach was understood to be blessed by hardheaded military and strategic studies, and it was a proven success in the Darwinian commercial world – few had much historical curiosity beyond that.

In the academic literature, the emergence of scenario-based security strategies is credited primarily to Herman Kahn in the US Rand
Corporation – he later founded the Hudson Institute and wrote a
number of seminal works on the near future (for example, Kahn 1960,
1962, 1967).[8] During the 1950s and 1960s, Kahn's combining of military strategic thinking, game theory and systems theory was principally
directed towards post-nuclear war survivability and resulted in his minor
celebrity status and immortalisation as the title character in Stanley
Kubrick's *Dr Strangelove*. Even the academic literature on scenarios,
then, shows at one and the same time a hardheaded and probabilistic
style of reasoning, together with the distinct possibility that the taming
chance is little more than faith in what looks like science but is actually
conjurers' tricks.

A significant body of research in the anthropology of the contemporary attends critically to the power of scenarios in the realm of security.
Andrew Lakoff (2008), for example, describes the rise of scenarios at the
intersection of the life sciences and national security expertise, specifically *vis-à-vis* emergencies and bio-security threats.[9] Lakoff notes that
Kahn's probabilistic style of reasoning conditioned the early emergence
of scenario-based planning and exercises, but faced with the unknown
threats or unknowable catastrophes, experts use scenarios in relatively
novel ways: not to predict, *per se*, but for 'imaginative enactment' (2008:
402). Lakoff foregrounds the uses of these enactments by experts to
reflect on vital systems security, but while that is wholly appropriate to
the study of bio-threats, catastrophes and preparedness in the United
States, in the European migration and security context imaginative
enactments via scenarios seems less rigorous and less reflexive but still
expensive and time consuming. And, rather than imaginative enactments providing the basis for anticipatory actions, one sees instead
in Europe fearful stories about complex and unknowable futures. This
trend provoked Margaritis Schinas, a senior EU official and analyst, to
declare:

> When it comes to forward-looking studies in modern European poli-
> tics, doomsayers still dominate the debate, as the intellectual appeal
> of pessimism often seems more attractive and devoid of facts; the
> (few) sober analysts, opting for a more rational (and often optimistic)
> view of things to come, find themselves under tremendous scru-
> tiny to prove their case. Somehow, for someone to say, 'Europe is
> declining, its economy will not recover and Europeans will become
> irrelevant' sounds more convincing than to claim that 'Europe will

rise again and come out stronger from the crisis.' The former assumption is accepted as a fact, while the latter needs to be proved and documented. (Schinas 2012: 2)

But, though critical of scenarios and foresight exercises, Schinas reproduces the crime-migration-security nexus and anticipates the future gathering of the dangerous poor in dangerous 'megacities' outside the EU's borders (Schinas 2012: 3).

What is remarkable, then, in the realm of security and migration scenarios is the relative consistency among the expert discursive community. This also has its origin in the more mundane practices captured under the labels of scenarios and foresight exercises. Strikingly, for example, a significant proportion of the data (as opposed to evidence) used to compose the scenarios I mentioned above (see Langton 2009; Giegerich and Comolli 2009), were generated by surveying security experts in a Delphi study that included phases of opinion formation from 270 EU security experts, together with layered feedback. Views on future trends were isolated among stakeholders. 'Thus, future reality is not predicted or prescribed, but is "made" as a result of the decisions Delphi participants take.... [Its] main social function is to coordinate and structure general lines of thought' (Giegerich and Comolli 2009).

Plainly, considerable critical social-scientific and hermeneutic work is needed to unpack the production of knowledge in the European security apparatus, such as, for example, the production of what counts as evidence, and the genre of reporting. The ForeSec report I evaluate here is by no means unique in terms of style or methodology, with several major EU positioning reports tapping expert opinion to better formulate more expert opinion for policymakers (see ESRIF 2009; FOCUS 2011).[10] It is of crucial importance when surveying these reports and para-ethnographically working with security experts to appreciate – but not overemphasise – the different terms in use. One very senior EU security policymaker gave a keynote presentation at a workshop I attended in 2013, and on three occasions stated, 'Foresight is not prediction!' He would have readily agreed with Michel Foucault's comment that, 'there is no way, short of prophecy, to predict the future' (1994: 12). Indeed, the internal styles of reasoning in European security expertise carefully distinguish between prediction, foresight exercises and scenarios methodologically, despite the fact that all of these activities are generally carried out with predetermined or self-selecting samples of experts. Foresighting, for example, does not necessarily involve scenario building, but the majority of foresight exercises produced in Europe do include them. The European Commission's Joint Research Centre (JRC) provides a definition to encourage consistency:

> A scenario is a 'story' illustrating visions of a possible future or aspects of a possible future. It is perhaps the most emblematic Foresight or future studies method. Scenarios are not predictions about the future but rather similar to simulations of some possible futures. They are used both as an exploratory method or a tool. (For-Learn n.d.)

Importantly, the JRC acknowledges that if scenarios are to be used for planning, then the basis of the scenario must be of the highest standard, but, in another breath, it is acknowledged that this method is borrowed from the dramatic arts, and when it deploys qualitative data, it is quite good at revealing shocks and discontinuities that 'capture the imagination' (Ibid.). I will return to discontinuities and 'errors' below, but here it is also important to acknowledge the exclusivist qualities of the knowledge being generated. Gregory Feldman (2013) notes that the mediated qualities of expert techno-scientific knowledge excludes actual migrants and their voices, on the one hand, but also tends to disqualify contexts and, therefore, other ways of knowing the world.

Here, I have been attempting to zero in on specific styles of reasoning and their underpinnings in the discursive communities of security experts. Following the work of Ian Hacking (1992), one may see EU foresight and scenario-building exercises as generative of new objects – such as the migration-crime-security nexus – propositions and explanations, new standards of validity, and new doxa. But one must go further. Andrew Lakoff (2008) takes an important step by analysing how the experts use scenarios involves 'imaginative enactment' that allows reflection on the security of vital systems (2008: 402). But the picture is more fragmented and blurrier in Europe. In this chapter, I have been arguing that the fragmented discursive community of EU security experts (at least partially) shares in the storytelling qualities of foresight and scenario-building exercises. In those exercises, power/knowledge and the future security space hang together and can be grasped by means of quasi-mythical stories. Stories, Michael Jackson (2002) tells us from the position of the phenomenology of experience, refuse the god's-eye view from the position of order and control in favour of understandings and perspectives situated *within* the world; he also forcefully argues that there is always a *more*: the *penumbral* wherein we experience ourselves and the world and the limits of both.[11] But what happens when we attend to diversity, uncertainty and imaginative disruptions transmitted via stories in the heart of apparatuses directed towards order and control? On the topic of myths of the state, Bruce Kapferer (1988) argues that what is at stake is a 'virtual' plane of emergence and potential action with its own ontology (see also Deleuze and Guattari 1994). I will avoid any premature and potentially overstated anthropological theory of governmental legends, myths or even stories; rather, I aim simply to conclude by excavating the precise questions of emergence and potential action in security fore-sighting and scenarios. I do this by returning, once again, to the work of Michel Foucault on errors.

Future errors

The idea that Europe's future security milieu might emanate from experts' rendering of the views of other experts, then rendered as 'stories', such as in the abovementioned reports, suggests that for all its conceptual vagueness, security and its companion, insecurity, are thoroughly cultural concepts. By focusing on styles of reasoning and notions such as intertextuality, I have been attempting to elicit the rules of the game – the ways in which cultural content is added to the milieu of the near future such that it appears external to culture and therefore as a quasi-independent and 'natural' milieu. Michel Foucault was prescient in attending to this feature of security apparatuses: for all their reliance on inevitable, natural processes – 'details that are not valued as good and evil in themselves' (2007: 45) – and efforts to respond to a near future, security apparatuses are concerned with an open series of probabilities and inevitably involve the imagination, storytelling and *emergence*.

Of course, one might immediately assume that imagination, story-telling and emergence are available in the life experiences of security experts and, thus, are available to ethnographic analysis if sufficient access is granted. But in Foucault's last-ever essay, 'Life: Experience and Science', he warns that phenomenology of 'lived experience' is inadequate to the task of supplying 'the originary meaning of every act of knowledge' (1994: 475). Foucault's essay showcases the importance of Georges Canguilhem's 'discontinuous' history of science (for example, Canguilhem 1989) and culminates with a meditation on the 'error' in life itself.

> For, at that most basic level of life, the process of coding and decoding give way to a chance occurrence that, before becoming a disease, a deficiency, or a monstrosity, is something like a disturbance in the information system, something like a 'mistake'. In this sense,

life – and this is its radical feature – is that which is capable of error. And perhaps it is this datum or perhaps this contingency which must be asked to account for the fact that the question of anomaly permeates the whole of biology. And it must also be asked to account for the mutations and evolutive processes to which they lead. Further, it must be questioned in regard to that singular but hereditary error which explains the fact that, with man [*sic*], life has led to a living being that is never completely in the right place, that is destined to 'err' and be 'wrong'. (Ibid.: 15)

The implications of Foucault's proposition are profound. If human life and thought are 'error', then the bio-political grip that holds 'life' to population or species is loosened, and we confront a research programme that Foucault did not live to realise: one on emergence. I am juxtaposing rather than equating emergence in the life sciences with security foresight and scenarios, but as Louise Amoore writes:

The question of emergence – the heterogeneous and contingent properties of a whole system, network, or assemblage that that exceeds its composite parts (its mistakes, its reversals, its mutations, and so on) – has become critical to a range of debates on the governing of life at the edge of catastrophe or crisis, ... like our security techniques that seek out the emergent threat pre-emptively in the form itself, long before it is actualized. (Amoore 2013: 148–149 passim)

But what does it mean to realise the 'error' in life and the imaginative and emergent processes and expertise that seeks to anticipate and act on human life in the near future? It is important to critically evaluate the weak concepts and contested methodologies in the European security apparatus, to show up the cracks and fissures in the securityscape, but much more can also be achieved (see Marcus 2012). The stories about Europe's near future produced in security experts' foresighting and scenarios produce an actionable near future milieu that ties together crime, terrorist threats and human migration; it supports enormous expenditure on security hardware and software (see Hayes and Vermeulen 2012), from databases to drones, and facilitates the growing cohesion of an (in)security apparatus. If rather simple stories are needed to congeal questionable discursive practices and evidence into something quasi-natural, and if at root those stories are needed because of the emergent and error-filled nature of the milieu, then, indeed, it is precisely alternative discourses and stories that are required to confront experts' rendering of life with complexities and diversity. Franz Kafka ended his short story, 'The Great Wall of China' with a terrible vision: to expose the Great Wall as a cultural project 'would mean undermining not only our consciences, but, what is far worse, our feet' (1988: 65–83 passim). This chapter explored some of the resources to undermine the feet of experts in a realm that has so far refused to recognise the strength of its own foundations.

Conclusion

Over the past number of years, but especially in the wake of the events of 11 September 2001, commentators have tracked the (in)securitisation of migration and borders on the ground. From the sea patrols of Mare Nostrum to the fences separating San Diego from Tijuana, borders are spreading out in terms of processes and technologies and being filled in by people categorised as undocumented or undesirable. Numerous scholars have described that vast amplification of security processes and the proliferation of quasi-military security technologies. But alongside this, we must also note the rash of old-fashioned wall building around the world. And, it is when commenting on this trend that Wendy Brown (2010: 144) captures the research challenge most precisely: the effort to, 'grasp what the new walls psychically address or assuage, even when they cannot deliver on their material promises'. Expert styles of security reasoning and new security technologies construct and act in deeply cultural milieux. And, in these milieux, migrants are rendered as potential criminals or terrorists, but not all migrants. Just over 100,000 people were detected 'illegally' crossing the EU's external borders in 2013, but during that same year, approximately the same number of persons legally immigrated to the Republic of Ireland alone. What's at stake, then, is the forms of expertise and techno-science that govern mobility today by separating, analysing, dividing and valuing, all as a way to attend to people qua populations, and thus manage far more than just migration.

Notes

1. There is no consistent definition of 'para-ethnography' and, perhaps, one should be avoided. Rather, the term denotes a movement or response by ethnographers to the circumstances engendered by research in contexts marked by science, technology and experts. The most obvious shift evident in para-ethnographic writing is in the relations with research participants: gone is the 'informant' to be replaced by the expert practitioner, themselves

engaged in specific intellectual or even scholarly labour, thus opportunities for research with counterparts that is co-developed and co-evolving.

2. One might easily point to key post-9/11 legislation here to confirm the importance of the migration-terrorism crime nexus. In *Governing Immigration through Crime,* Dowling and Inda (2013: 24) contextualise and explore HR 4437, the House of Representatives-sponsored *Border Protection, Antiterrorism, and Illegal Immigration Control Act, 2005,* which aimed to make it a specific felony to be illegally present in the United States and thus criminalise anyone sheltering or otherwise assisting an undocumented migrant. The bill was defeated, due in good part to mobilisation and protest by immigrant activist groups.

3. I have simply pointed to specific areas in which US Homeland Security is connected to and shares a milieu with European (in)securitisation. However, a larger set of research questions are inevitably posed, such as, *inter alia,* is Europe developing a homeland security sector (that is, specific institutions, competencies and 'markets') in ways similar to the United States? This question is dealt with comprehensively by Kaunert, Leonard and Pawlak (2012) who contrast the top-down development of homeland security in the United States with the fragmented but incrementally converging European security apparatus.

4. In the 1984 interview 'Polemics, Politics, and Problematizations' (an interview Foucault gave to Rabinow), Foucault describes problematisation in the following way: 'To one single set of difficulties, several responses can be made. And most of the time different responses actually are proposed. But what must be understood is what makes them simultaneously possible; it is the point in which their simultaneity is rooted; it is the soil that can nourish them all in their diversity and sometimes in spite of their contradictions' (1997: 118).

5. Foucault's initial response to the question involves juxtaposing security with the disciplinary regulation of space and the codification of acts and prohibitions – what one must do and what has to be prohibited – the topics in which he invested so much in *Discipline and Punish* (1995). He does not invoke straight-line historical transformations marked by distinct historical eras but, rather, like Raymond Williams he notes the residual, the dominant and the emergent in the interplay between discipline and security.

6. Here it is important to note that Foucault realises that the first town planners of the 18th century did not use the term milieu, yet it maintains an unattended presence in their pragmatic work. Milieu, he explains, refers to 'action at a distance': 'the medium of action and the element in which it circulates' (2007: 20–21 passim). Foucault is cautious about the use of 'milieu', and in a footnote, he also expresses caution about the 'suddenness' of the problematisation of the human species in the security milieu – 'a political artifice of a power relation' (2007: 22). What is new, he argues, is the recognition of potentially positive dimensions, the capacity for amplification of a biopolitical *nature.*

7. For example, in contrast to the scenario of the western world being devastated by armies of radicalised poor in the near future, many migration studies-based forecasts predict a lessening of south to north migration pressure during the coming decades (see Hatton and Williamson 2002).

8. At the same time, the French philosopher and civil servant Gaston Berger was using scenarios to inform public policy in France under the broad heading of *la prospective*. Even today, acolytes of Berger distance themselves from Herman Kahn's approach. Take, for example, the following remarks by Godet and Roubelat (2003: 7): 'The future is multiple and several potential futures are possible; the path leading to this or that future is not necessarily unique. The description of a potential future and of the progression towards it comprises a "scenario". The word "scenario" was introduced into futurology by Hermann Kahn in his book *The Year 2000*, but the usage there was primarily literary, imagination being used to produce rose-tinted or apocalyptic predictions'.

9. One might also point here to Roberto J. Gonzales' study of security forecasting in Iraq and Afghanistan, in which he argues that the modern and techno-scientific cannot be separated from anything categorised as pre-modern. Thus, 'seen through an anthropological lens, the twenty-first-century technologies appear not so much as scientifically based tools for confronting with knowable, predictable phenomena, but as amulets or talismans for dealing with dangerous, unknowable events by means of sacred formulae (or algorithms)' (2013: 83).

10. The intertextuality is again evident in the 2009 European Security Research and Innovation Forum (ESRIF) report, wherein, for example, we find the following summation of threats and responses: 'The European Union and its Member States are part of a highly interdependent complex world. Failed states, border disputes, environmentally induced migration, resource conflicts: all increasingly have intercontinental, if not global, repercussions. Europe cannot ignore these external risks and threats – or their potential impact – on its domestic security' (ESRIF 2009: 12). And later, specified to the EU's maritime borders, 'Risks and threats related to security (unlawful activities: trafficking in human beings and narcotics, illegal migration, terrorism, piracy, and so on)' (ESRIF 2009: 90). And, again, the FOCUS report of 2011 proposes migration as a 'basic security threat and risk' because 'the increase of immigration towards developed countries is having several consequences, such as human trafficking (again organised crime), and export of religious radicalism to western countries. It is also facilitating the rapid spread of infectious diseases, such as avian flu' (FOCUS 2011: 35).

11. Jackson uses the term 'penumbral' (from the Latin *paene*, almost, and *umbra*, shadow) to denote areas outside of the settled self wherein one experiences limits.

References

Agamben, G. (1998) *Homo sacer: sovereign power and bare life*, Stanford, CA: Stanford University Press.

Albro, R., Marcus, G., McNamara, L. and Schoch-Spana, M. (eds) (2012) *Anthropologists in the securityscape: ethics, practice, and professional identity*, Walnut Creek, CA: Left Coast Press.

Amoore, L. (2013) *The politics of possibility: risk and security beyond probability*, Durham and London: Duke University Press.

Bigo, D. (ed) (2007) *The field of the EU internal security agencies*, Paris: Centre d'études sur les conflits.

Bigo, D. and Tsoukala, A. (eds) (2008) *Terror, insecurity and liberty: illiberal practices of liberal regimes after 9/11*, Oxford and New York: Routledge.

Boswell, C. (2007) 'Migration control in Europe after 9/11: explaining the absence of securitisation', *JCMS: Journal of Common Market Studies*, 45(3): 535–769.

Boyer, D. (2008) 'Thinking through the anthropology of experts', *Anthropology in Action*, 15(2): 38–46.

Brown, W. (2010) *Walled states, waning sovereignty*, New York: Zone Books.

Canguilhem, G. (1989) *The normal and the pathological*, New York: Zone Books.

Collier, S. J. and Lakoff, A. (2008) 'Distributed preparedness: the spatial logic of domestic security in the United States', *Environment and Planning D: Society and Space*, 26(1): 7–28.

Comaroff, J. (2012) 'Pentecostalism, populism, and the politics of affect, in Africa and elsewhere' in D. Freeman (ed) *Pentecostalism and development: churches, NGOs and social change in Africa*, London: Palgrave Macmillan, pp.41–67.

Connolly, M. and Kennedy, P. (1994) 'Must it be the West against the rest?, *The Atlantic Monthly*, 274(6): 61–84.

Culler, J. (1981) *The pursuit of signs: semiotics, literature, deconstruction*, Routledge & Kegan Paul: London.

Deleuze, G. (1997) *Negotiations, 1972–1990*, New York: Columbia University Press.

Deleuze, G. and Guattari, F. (1994) *What is philosophy?*, New York: Columbia University Press.

Dillon, M. and Lobo-Guerrero, L. (2008) 'Biopolitics of security in the 21st Century', *The Review of International Studies*, 34: 265–292.

Dowling, J. and Inda, J. (eds) (2013) *Governing immigration through crime: a reader*, Stanford, CA: Stanford University Press.

ESRIF (European Security Research and Innovation Forum) (2009) *Final report*, Brussels: European Commission.

EUobserver (2008) 'EU unveils plans for biometric border controls', http://euobserver.com/22/25650, accessed 21 July 2014.

Fassin, D. (2012) *Humanitarian reason: a moral history of the present*, Berkeley, Los Angeles, London: University of California Press.

Feldman, G. (2013) 'The specific intellectual's pivotal position: action, compassion and thinking in administrative society, an Arendtian view', *Social Anthropology*, 21(2): 135–164.

FOCUS (2011) *Foresight security scenarios – mapping research to a comprehensive approach to exogenous EU roles: report on alternative future models of comprehensiveness*, Vienna: Centre for European Security Studies, Sigmund Freud Private University.

For-Learn (n.d.) European Commission and Joint Research Centre Online Tools for Foresighting, http://forlearn.jrc.ec.europa.eu/guide/2_scoping/meth_scenario.htm#Definition, accessed 21 July 2014.

Foucault, M. (1980) *Power/knowledge: selected interviews and other writings, 1972–1977*, New York: Pantheon Books.

Foucault, M. (1988) 'Practicing criticism, or is it really important to think? An interview with Didier Eribon, 30–31 May 1981' in L. D. Kritzman (ed) *Foucault: politics, philosophy, culture*, New York and London: Routledge, p.155.

Foucault, M. (1991) 'Governmentality' (translated by R. Braidotti and revised by C. Gordon) in G. Burchell, C. Gordon and P. Miller (eds) *The Foucault effect: studies in governmentality*, Chicago: University of Chicago Press, pp.87–104.

Foucault, M. (1994) 'Life: experience and science' in P. Rabinow and N. Rose (eds) *The essential Foucault: selections from essential works of Foucault, 1954–1984*, New York and London: The New Press, pp.6–18.

Foucault, M. (1995) *Discipline and punish: the birth of the prison*, London: Penguin.

Foucault, M. (1997) 'Polemics, politics, and problematizations' in P. Rabinow (ed) *Ethics: subjectivity and truth: essential works of Foucault, 1954–1984* (Volume 1), New York: The New Press.

Foucault, M. (2007) *Security, territory, population: lectures at the Collège de France, 1977–1978*, Basingstoke: Palgrave Macmillan.

Foucault, M. (2008) *The birth of biopolitics: lectures at the Collège de France, 1978–1979*, London: Palgrave Macmillan.

Geertz, C. (1973) *The Interpretation of cultures: selected essays*, New York: Basic Books.

Giegerich, B. and Comolli, V. (2009) 'Executive summary of FORESEC, deliverable D 4.5 report on European security: trends, drivers, threats' in *FORESEC – Europe's evolving security: drivers, trends and scenarios*, pp.7–10, http://www.cmi.fi/images/stories/publications/reports/2009/FORESEC_report.pdf, accessed 1 July 2014.

Godet, M. and Roubelat, F. (2003) 'Creating the future: the use and misuse of scenarios', *Long Range Planning*, 29(2): 164–171.

Gonzales, R. J. (2013) 'Cybernetic crystal ball: "forecasting" insurgency in Iraq and Afghanistan' in N. L. Whitehead and S. Finnström (eds) *Virtual war and magical death: technologies and imaginaries for terror and killing*, Oxford and New York: Berghahn, pp.65–85.

Gros, F., Castillo, M. and Garapon, A. (2008) 'De la sécurité nationale à la sécurité humaine', *Raisons politiques*, 4(32): 5–7.

Gusterson, H. (1999) 'Missing the end of the Cold War in international security' in J. Weldes, M. Laffey, H. Gusterson and R. Duval (eds) *Cultures of insecurity: states, communities and the production of danger*, Minneapolis: University of Minnesota Press, pp.319–347.

Hacking, I. (1992) '"Style" for historians and philosophers', *Studies in History and Philosophy*, 23: 1–20.

Hatton, T. J. and Williamson, J. G. (2002) *What fundamentals drive world migration?* (NBER Working Papers), Cambridge, MA: National Bureau of Economic Research, Inc.

Hayes, B. and Jones, C. (2014) *Report on the transposition of EU counter-terrorism measures*, Dublin: SECILE (Securing Europe through Counter-Terrorism: Impact, Legitimacy and Effectiveness), http://secile.eu/wp-content/uploads/2013/11/Report-on-the-Transposition-of-EU-Counter-Terrorism-Measures.pdf, accessed 21 July 2014.

Hayes, B. and Vermeulen, M. (2012) *Borderline: the EU's new border surveillance initiatives*, Berlin: Heinrich Böll Foundation.

Holmes, D. (2001) *Integral Europe: fast-capitalism, multiculturalism, neo-fascism*, Princeton, NJ: Princeton University Press.

Holmes, D. and Marcus, G. (2005) 'Cultures of expertise and the management of globalization: toward the re-functioning of ethnography' in A. Ong and S. J. Collier (eds) *Global Assemblages*, Oxford: Blackwell, pp.235–252.

Huysmans, J. (2014) *Security unbound: enacting democratic limits*, London and New York: Routledge.

Jackson, M. (2002) *The politics of storytelling: violence, transgression, and inter-subjectivity*, Copenhagen: Museum Tusculanum Press.

Kafka, F. (1988) *Metamorphosis and other stories*, London and New York: Penguin.

Kahn, H. (1960) *On thermonuclear war*, Princeton, NJ: Princeton University Press.

Kahn, H. (1962) *Thinking about the unthinkable*, New York: Horizon Press.

Kahn, H. (1967) *The Year 2000: a framework for speculation on the next thirty-three years*, London and New York: Macmillan.

Kahneman, D. (2011) *Thinking, fast and slow*, London and New York: Macmillan.

Kapferer, B. (1988) *Legends of people, myths of state: violence, intolerance and political culture in Sri Lanka and Australia*, Washington, DC: Smithsonian Institution Press.

Kaplan, R. D. (1994) 'The coming anarchy: how scarcity, crime, overpopulation, tribalism, and disease are rapidly destroying the social fabric of our planet', *The Atlantic Monthly* (February): 44–76.

Kaunert, C., Leonard, S. and Pawlak, P. (2012) *European homeland security: a European strategy in the making?* London and New York: Routledge.

Keynes, J. M. (1964) *The general theory*, New York: Harcourt Brace and World.

Lakoff, A. (2008) 'The generic biothreat, or, how we became unprepared', *Cultural Anthropology*, 23(3): 399–428.

Langton, C. (2009) 'Demographics and security in Europe' in B. Giegerich and V. Comolli (eds) *FORESEC D4.5 Report on European security, trends, drivers, threats*, pp.53–64, http://www.cmi.fi/images/stories/publications/reports/2009/FORESEC_report.pdf, accessed 21 July 2014.

Larrinaga, M. and Doucet, M. (eds) (2010) *Security and global governmentality: globalization, governance and the state*, London: Routledge.

Maguire, M. (2009) 'The birth of biometric security', *Anthropology Today*, 25(1): 9–14.

Maguire, M. (2011) 'Vanishing borders and biometric citizens' in G. Lazaridis (ed) *Security, insecurity and migration in Europe*, Farnham: Ashgate, pp.31–51.

Maguire, M. (2012) 'Bio-power, racialization and new security technology', *Social Identities*, 18: 36–52.

Maguire, M. (2014) 'Counter-terrorism in European airports' in M. Maguire, C. Frois and N. Zurawski (eds) *The anthropology of security: perspectives from the frontline of policing, counter-terrorism and border control*, London: Pluto Press, pp.86–104.

Maguire, M. (2015) 'Questioned by machines: a cultural perspective on counter-terrorism and lie detection in security zones' in S. Wilmer and A. Zukauskaite (eds) *Performing biopolitics*, Basingstoke: Palgrave Macmillan.

Marcus, G. (2012) '"Be all that you can be…": the anthropological vocation in the securityscape' in R. Albro, G. Marcus, L. McNamara and M. Schoch-Spana (eds) *Anthropologists in the securityscape: ethics, practice, and professional identity*, Walnut Creek, CA: Left Coast Press, pp.245–259.

Ministero della Difesa (2005) 'Concetto strategico del capo di stato maggiore della difesa', http://www.difesa.it/SMD/CaSMD/concetto-strategico-ca-smd-en/, accessed 21 July 2014.

Ministry of Defence of the Netherlands (2008) *Future policy survey: a foundation for the armed forces of 2020*, The Hague: Ministry of Defence.

Ophuls, W. (2012) *Immoderate greatness: why civilizations fail*, North Charleston, South Carolina: CreateSpace Independent Publishing Platform.

Présidence de la République Française (2008) *White paper on defence and national security*, Paris: Présidence de la République Française.

Rabinow, P. (2003) *Anthropos today: reflections on modern equipment*, Princeton, NJ: Princeton University Press.

Rhodes, D. and Stelter, D. (2011) *Back to Mesopotamia? The looming threat of debt restructuring*, Boston: Boston Consulting Group.

Sahlins, M. (2002) *Waiting for Foucault, still*, Chicago: Prickly Paradigm Press.

Schinas, M. (2012) 'The EU in 2030: a long-term view of Europe in a changing world: keeping the values, changing the attitudes', *European View*, http://europa.eu/espas/pdf/article_ms_euin2030.pdf, accessed 12 May 2014.

Schwartz, P. (1996) *The art of the long view*, New York: Doubleday.

Sweijs, T. (2012) 'Conceptual foundations of security', WP1.1 deliverable report for European security trends and threats in society FP7-SEC-2011-1, www.ettis-project.eu, accessed 21 July 2014.

Tetlock, P. E. (2005) *Expert political judgment: how good is it? How can we know?* Princeton, NJ: Princeton University Press.

UNHCR (2006) *State of the world's refugees 2006*, New York: United Nations High Commissioner for Refugees.

Van Creveld, M. (1991) *The transformation of war*, New York: The Free Press.

Williams, R. (1980) *Problems in materialism and culture*, London: Verso.

Williams, R. (1976) *Keywords*, London: Fontana.

Part II

Securitisation and Its Impacts on Migrant and Ethnic Minority Communities

4
Regimes of Insecurity: Women and Immigration Detention in France and Britain

Khursheed Wadia

Introduction

Various political commentators and scholars accept that an accelerated progression of 'securitisation' of migration has taken place since the events of 9/11 and subsequent terror attacks by Islamic groups in Europe. As we have learned from preceding chapters in this volume, scholars within both critical security studies (for example, Bigo 1998; Ceyhan and Tsoukala 2002; Huysmans 2006) and migration studies (for instance, Faist 2004; Fauser 2006) recognise that international migration has been increasingly associated with various forms of insecurity (terrorism, riots and social unrest, criminality) experienced by nation-states and their respective general publics. Thus, migrants have been presented as threatening and/or guilty subjects: a standpoint which has gained popular support, particularly in the western world. However, one of the consequences, intended or not, of constituting migration as a security threat in an age of significant global movements of people, is the creation of greater insecurity among migrant populations. As a process, migration is fraught with insecurity from the moment of the decision to migrate, through to departure from the country of origin, entry into the destination country, and settlement or refusal of entry or settlement. Such insecurity is intensified in the case of forced migration, and particularly in contexts where migrants are stigmatised as potential terrorists, criminals and social troublemakers, and where economic crises have led to severe cuts in public services, rising unemployment and an attendant rise in racism and xenophobia.

The social construction of migration as a high level security issue since September 2001 led European Union (and other western) governments to craft and implement policies of which the primary aim was to reduce the number of migrants – and asylum seekers in particular – entering the EU. Using the framework of secure borders, migration and terrorism, governments across the EU introduced legislation and/or rules to restrict the entry of migrants and reduce the rights of settled migrants in respect of health, welfare and employment provision, while increasing budgets for policing migration, security technologies and apparatuses. For example, within a month of the London 7/7 bombings, British Prime Minister Tony Blair announced a 12-point anti-terror plan (*The Guardian* 2005), of which five points related to the acquisition of and right to retain UK citizenship, migration, deportation and border security. His defence of this plan was summed up as follows:

> coming to Britain is not a right. And even when people have come here, staying here carries with it a duty. That duty is to share and support the values that sustain the British way of life. Those that break that duty and try to incite hatred or engage in violence against our country and its people, have no place here. (Ibid.)

In France, too, four months after 9/11, the Socialist government of Lionel Jospin introduced the *loi de securité quotidienne* 'law on daily security' which was packaged as anti-terror legislation while containing elements aimed at young people from the vast outlying housing estates of France's major cities (*les jeunes de banlieue*), in particular young Muslims of migrant descent who were portrayed as a security threat rather than as casualties of socioeconomic deprivation. In Spain and the Netherlands, which have historically known more liberal immigration regimes than the UK and France, the attacks of 9/11, the Madrid train bombings (March 2004), and the killing of the Dutch film maker Theo Van Gogh (November 2004) in Amsterdam by Islamist radicals, led generally to a stricter immigration regime in both countries; more specifically, in the Netherlands, these events led to the restriction of low-skilled labour migration and family reunification against a background of growing debate on the limits of multiculturalism, and, in Spain, to not just stricter immigration laws, but also the allocation of tens of millions of euros to the fortification of border security, in particular the physical barriers between the Spanish enclaves of Ceuta and Mellila and Morocco.

In the name of securitising states and reducing threats to public safety, an array of restrictive immigration practices are deployed in Europe. These include detention and deportation, which may be regarded as interlocking elements in a continuum of restrictive practices, given that they take place as sequential processes with time spent in detention preceding deportation. European governments use both detention and deportation extensively as a means of 'migratory management'. Migreurop's Open Access Now campaign (2014) estimates that, pending deportation, about 600,000 migrants (men, women and children)[1] are detained each year across EU member states for no reason other than non-compliance with rules pertaining to entry and stay within a particular territory. In accordance with European law, they may be held up to 18 months while they wait to be deported, although it is estimated that just 30–35 per cent of detainees across EU member states are deported each year to their country of origin or to a third country; for example, in 2012, 178,000 out of 484,000 detainees were deported (EU Commission 2014). The widespread use of detention and deportation measures and the rapid rise in the numbers of detainees have attracted the attention of human rights activists and scholars of migration and security studies. Numerous human rights expert reports and academic studies have sought to explain why these measures are used so extensively, their significance, and whether or not their increased deployment since 2001 is indicative of a securitisation of migration. Until recently, not many have sought to explain and consider the nature of the many insecurities created by securitisation as a process of governing through the production of threats and unease. Yet, to do so is important in a context where there has been growing public acceptance that migration must necessarily be managed within a security framework and where, consequently, questions about what securitisation actually means in terms of everyday security practices and its impact on ordinary people, are rarely raised.

This chapter, therefore, aims to do two things: first, it presents an overview of detention practices in the UK and France; second, it examines the conditions in which migrants are detained and in many cases eventually deported from Europe, paying particular attention to the insecurities produced by daily practices of detention. It focuses on migrant women as a particularly vulnerable population among detainees and deportees, and on gendered forms of insecurity, drawing evidence from the UK and France. It goes beyond the state-centric migration-security nexus to consider the experiences of migrants (ordinary, more often than not, marginalised people) in order to contribute to the study of migration and (in)security among generally unheard voices. It highlights the case of women migrants because it has been demonstrated that (along with minors and the medically unwell) women, especially those aged 18–24, are the most vulnerable group among detainees, in countries across Europe: they are given far less information about the reasons for their detention and about asylum procedures than their male counterparts; they experience more discrimination than men as a result of not speaking the language of the country in which they are detained; more women detainees report feeling unsafe as a result of suffering verbal and physical abuse at the hands of other detainees and detention centre staff; more women than men are inactive and feel cut off from the outside world – only 50 per cent in detention receive personal visitors; women, more than men, report the overall negative impacts of detention and looming deportation (Jesuit Refugee Service 2010).

Detention and deportation

An extensive body of literature exists on detention and deportation both generally and in Europe more specifically.[2] This literature may be divided into four broad areas of study. First, there is a literature which considers and analyses the trends and practices of detention and deportation through the study of single countries and/or cross-country comparisons. Hence, studies within this category have examined the extent to which immigration detention is used in European countries and the types of detention centres in operation in different countries (see, for example, Flynn and Cannon 2010; Guild 2005; Merlino 2009; Muchielli and Nevanen 2011; Leerkes and Broeders 2010; Welch and Schuster 2005). This category of work on detention and deportation also comprises studies which examine national and EU legislation which both results from certain trends and practices and feeds them further (Zwaan 2011; Flynn and Cannon 2010; Baldaccini 2009); an emergent body of work, being carried out by scholars and migrant human rights organisations (such as Corporate Watch), which has started to look at how the transformation of detention and deportation into a repressive instrument of immigration control and deterrence, used by the state to draw boundaries around the national community and polity, has given rise to an immigration detention and deportation industry which often operates privately and beyond international and European conventions established to protect the human rights of detainees (see, for example, Bacon 2007; Flynn and Cannon 2009; Lemberg-Pedersen 2011).

Second, there exist a significant number of studies on the functions of detention and deportation. Governments and state agencies present detention and deportation as part of a non-punitive package of immigration enforcement measures, so the increase in detention centres and detainees is explained by pointing to the increase in the numbers of 'unwanted' migrants who constitute some form of risk to society and who need to be identified, 'removed' and 'returned' to their country of origin; or, in the case of certain asylum seekers, to the EU country in which they first arrived to claim asylum[3] (Albrecht 2002). However, given the discrepancy between the large numbers of migrants who are detained in order to be deported, and the actual, rather smaller numbers of deportees – which raises questions about the rationale behind inefficient policy and practice – various scholars have offered alternative explanations about the functions of detention and deportation. Thus discouraging irregular migrants from staying on in the country of arrival, through the threat of confinement, is considered an important function (Leerkes and Broeders 2013). Detention and deportation may be also be seen as a way of managing the effects of poverty; here Leerkes and Broeders (2010, 2013) offer the example of some local authorities in the Netherlands using immigrant detention as a (last resort) means of eliminating the visible effects of poverty (such as petty crime, sleeping rough, begging and so on) from public spaces. The findings of research in the Netherlands reflect those of research carried out in the United States on banishment and spatial exclusion (Beckett and Herbert 2010). A third function attributed to detention and deportation is that of soothing public concern over immigration while allowing the state to assert its authority and demonstrate its capacity to control its territorial and social borders precisely because, on close examination, the reality proves otherwise (De Genova 2010; Weber and Bowling 2008). Finally, applying the concept of 'new penology',[4] some scholars have argued that the function of immigration detention and deportation is to deal with and minimise any threat posed by 'unwanted' migrants, constructed as a collective danger to society (Broeders 2014; Cornelisse 2010; Garcia and Bessa 2011).

Third, a substantial literature explores the impacts of detention and deportation practices on detainees and deportees, and the findings of most studies overwhelmingly show that the impacts are mostly damaging. A number of scholars and human rights organisations and activists have studied the effects of detention and deportation on migrants' human rights, focusing on the flouting of international and European human rights conventions by elected governments and state agents: for instance, European Convention on Human Rights (ECHR) provisions covering the length of time migrants may be detained are regularly breached, as are the use of detention on a case-by-case basis (as opposed to its systematic use against irregular migrants or failed asylum seekers as a group) and the non-abusive treatment of detainees/

deportees (see Cornelisse 2010; Webber 2008; Welch and Schuster 2005). Some of the literature on the impacts of detention and deportation has also examined and analysed the way in which governments and state agencies, in using administrative law in immigration detention, have in fact produced 'counter-law' which blurs state practices, undermines the 'traditional principles, standards, and procedures of criminal law that get in the way of pre-empting imagined sources of harm' (Ericson 2007: 24), and reduces the power of legal contestation by immigration detainees (Becket and Herbert 2010). Finally, some studies have shown that an effect of systematically detaining and deporting irregular migrants, failed asylum seekers and other supposed risk-posing categories is that the idea of migrants as benefits scroungers, criminals and a threat to national security who should be removed from mainstream society becomes entrenched in the public imaginary. It criminalises the act of crossing borders (Rahola 2011). There is little doubt that these impacts on migrants' human rights, traditional principles of criminal and civil law, and on public perceptions of 'bad' migrants generate a state of insecurity among detainees and deportees which is detrimental to their health and wellbeing.

While there exists a significant literature on migrant and refugee women's experiences of arrival, reception, asylum determination and settlement procedures and processes, very little has been written about women migrants in detention and under threat of deportation in Europe. No single academic study on women in detention has been undertaken in Europe. Some works on women migrants and asylum seekers make mention of the impact of detention on women (for example, Allwood and Wadia 2010). Hence, in the case of women held in British detention centres, one has had to rely mainly on NGO reports. NGO studies dealing with women in detention include a study carried out on the detention of pregnant women by Bail for Immigration Detainees and the Maternity Alliance (McLeish, Cutler and Stancer 2002); a 2005 study on women's detention experiences at Yarl's Wood immigration removal centre, undertaken by a collective of women's groups based at the Crossroads Centre in London (namely, Legal Action for Women, Black Women's Rape Action Project, Women Against Rape and the All African Women's Group); and studies on women's experiences in detention by Asylum Aid's women's project (2004) and Women for Refugee Women (2014). In France, neither NGO reports nor academic studies focus on women in detention. The annual reports of the five NGOs (La Cimade, France Terre d'Asile, Ordre de Malte, Forum Réfugiés and Association Service Social Familial Migrants) permitted access to detention centres and holding areas in France, contain frequent but brief and unsystematic references to women detainees.

Detention and deportation in the UK and France

In both the UK and France, immigration detention and deportation have become commonplace instruments of procedure, rather than measures of last resort. This accounts for the sharp increase in the number of immigration detainees and the rapid expansion of the number of detention places and deportations in both countries.[5] In both countries, asylum seekers and irregular migrants may be detained on arrival at a port, while their claim is being processed or case investigated, or when their claim has been refused. While the purpose of detention centres is to hold migrants just prior to their deportation, in Britain, and to a lesser extent in France, detainees have found increasingly that they are not at the end of the asylum process or investigation of their case and hence 'awaiting imminent removal' but at the start of the process or at an appeal stage. This means that detainees are often held for long periods of time in prison-like conditions, although they have committed no crime or even contravened immigration rules.

France

The number of places in French detention centres has almost doubled over the last decade as the number of detainees increased from 20,488 in 2004 to 35,000 in 2009 before falling again to 26,441 in 2013 (Cinq Associations 2010: 9, 2014: 13). In addition, it is estimated that approximately 25,000 people were deported each year between the early 2000s and 2007 (Bernardot 2008; Amnesty International 2007), while by 2013, that figure had reached 28,209 (Cinq Associations 2014: 13).[6]

There are two main types of detention facilities within the national immigration and asylum framework (*dispositif national d'accueil*) in France: the LRAs (*locaux de rétention administrative*), in which detainees may be kept up to five days and of which there are 24, and the CRAs (*centres de rétention administrative*), where detainees may be held up to 45 days, after which time they must be released or deported, though exceptionally (as in the case of individuals charged with or suspected of terrorist offences) detainees may be held for up to six months. In all, there are 22 CRAs across mainland France.[7] In addition to the CRAs and LRAs, there are also 57 holding areas (*zones d'attente*) at airports (36), seaports (16) and other places, including railway stations (5) (OEE 2014: 70–72). The *zones d'attente* are used to detain non-citizens refused entry into France when they reach a port of entry. The number of people detained in these holding areas has dropped substantially over the past five years due to the fall in asylum applications lodged at border ports. In recent years, almost all *zones d'attente* detainees have been held at the two main Paris airports, Charles De Gaulle and Orly, before being sent back within four days, or a maximum of eight days, subject to approval from a high court judge. However, very exceptionally, a person may be held for a maximum of 26 days in these most basic of facilities.[8] All detention and deportation facilities are state-run, with responsibility shared between different government departments, namely the interior ministry (deportations); ministry of defence (provision of deportation escorts and security guards); ministry of justice (management of accommodation and catering); ministry of health (health services). Critics see this fragmentation of functions as being responsible, in part, for the poor organisation and management of detention and deportation facilities, which have highly deleterious impacts on detainees/deportees.

Historically, the majority of CRA and LRA detainees have been failed asylum seekers. In addition, detainees have included those refused a temporary residence permit by a prefecture office, those who enter France with incomplete or no travel and entry documentation, those who are from so-called safe countries and who can therefore be sent back, and those suspected of or charged with having committed a crime. However, since 2007, when Romania and Bulgaria joined the EU, a significant part of the detainee/deportee population came to be constituted by Roma people, of whom an estimated 400,000 had lived in France over many years, and 12,000 of whom were recent arrivals (BBC News 2010). As new EU citizens from 2007, they should have enjoyed freedom of movement and employment within EU borders, but under special terms of the EU accession treaties, Bulgarian and Romanian citizens were required, during the first seven years of their respective country's EU membership, to have a residence permit if they wished to remain in France for longer than three months. The acquisition of a residence permit proved difficult, if not impossible, for those from Roma communities under the terms of the 2006 Immigration and Integration Act (*Loi du 24 juillet relative à l'immigration et à l'intégration*), which was passed under the Interior Ministry of Nicolas Sarkozy.[9] The combination of the visibility of Roma populations in the run up to the accession of Romania and Bulgaria to the EU and the passing of the 2006 Immigration and Integration Act meant that dozens of Roma camp sites in France (deemed illegal by the authorities) were dismantled while thousands of Roma were rounded up, detained and deported. In 2006, over 4,000 Romanian Roma were detained and deported (Cinq Associations 2014: 19). Although the numbers decreased in the following four years, government campaigns to close Roma campsites and to detain and deport members of Roma communities in France were renewed in 2010–2012. The government's hand was strengthened by new legislation contained in the hard-line Immigration, Integration and Nationality Act of 2011.[10] Despite an outcry from international human rights and migrant support organisations, the UNHCR and the European Commission figures from 2013 indicate that Romanian Roma continued to be targeted by the Socialist government for detention and deportation.[11]

UK

Until the 1990s, there were no permanent detention centres in the UK given the exceptionality of detention; Welch and Schuster note that in 1993, 250 people were held in detention at any one time (2005: 402). Since then, the detention estate has expanded significantly – tripling between 1997 and 2007 (Weber 2008: 14) – to represent one of the largest in Europe. The expansion of the UK detention estate reflects the rise in detainee numbers. So, whereas Home Office figures put the number of persons in detention facilities at 741 in January 1999 (Home Office 2001: 11), this number had risen to 2,595 and 3,378 by December 2009 and September 2014 respectively.[12] Until 2010, the overwhelming majority of detainees were failed asylum seekers (and their dependents) and/or asylum applicants whose identity and asylum application authenticity were being established. However, as the use of criminal law in immigration enforcement has become more widespread (see Aliverti 2012) and the spotlight has fallen on 'illegal migrants', so the numbers of those detained on the basis of having committed immigration offences has grown. In addition to asylum seekers and those who have fallen foul of the law, other detainee groups include visa overstayers, those who have acquired papers that allow them to remain in the UK through deceptive means, and undocumented migrants.

The UK is unique among EU countries in that the detention of migrants is not subject to a maximum time limit. While the EU Returns Directive (2008/115/EC on 'Common standards and procedures for returning illegal immigrants') limits detention to 18 months, and many countries (for example, France – see above) have adopted shorter limits, the UK has refused to apply the directive and thus stands alone in being condemned for opting into the most coercive of EU measures while systematically opting out of those designed to protect migrants' rights (Geddes 2005: 734).

UK detention facilities are made up of 11 IRCs (immigration removal centres – thus renamed by the New Labour government in 2001 in order to underline the primary purpose of detention), four RSTHFs (residential short-term holding facilities), one NRSTHF (non-residential short-term holding facilities), one pre-departure facility for families, and 19 holding areas found at or near border ports and reporting centres. In addition, 600 places for 'foreign national offenders' are held at prison establishments across the UK (Silverman and Hajela 2015: 3). The greater part of detention facilities (seven of the IRCs, the NRSTHF, two of the RSTHFs and all the holding areas at or near border ports) have been outsourced by the UK government and are now run by private companies involved in the 'security business'. The privatisation of the state's functions in the area of migration has drawn criticism from a number of quarters, notably migrant support organisations (such as Migrants' Rights Network), organisations which monitor the activities of large corporations (Corporate Watch, for instance) and human rights NGOs (Amnesty International). Such criticism hinges upon a number of arguments: even though the government can terminate its contract with a private company running a detention facility when things go wrong, this does not happen in reality because there are few alternative companies in the private sector to replace the one that is dismissed; all the private companies running detention facilities have poor records in respect to abuse of detainees, the supply of welfare services and the maintenance of safety standards; the use of private companies is not more cost-effective; there is a lack of transparency in the way that private companies manage detention sites. These deficiencies are put down to the profit motive of these companies, and crucially, the impact of such deficiencies is the undermining of detainees' welfare and rights (see Siegfried 2014; Medical Justice/National Coalition of Anti-Deportation Campaigns/Birnberg, Peirce & Partners 2008).

As one would expect, and in line with the rising trend of detention figures, deportation numbers also rose rapidly in the 2000s. In 1999, 8,980 deportations took place, including those of port applicants (5,440) and those who agreed to leave as part of voluntary assisted returns programmes (550) (Home Office 2001: 11). All categories included asylum applicants (about 3,000) whose claims, in-country, had failed or were deemed unfounded when they arrived at a UK port of entry. Ten years later, by 2009, the number of deportations had multiplied many times over to reach 67,215.[13] Of this total, 43 per cent was made up by migrants refused entry at port and subsequently deported (29,160), 29 per cent by enforced removals and notified voluntary departures (19,570), 20 per cent by voluntary departures outside specified programmes such as the VARP (voluntary assisted returns programme run by the International Organisation for Migration), and 7 per cent by VARP deportees. As in 1999 and since, asylum seekers (55,580) constituted the largest proportion of all categories of deportees (Home Office 2010: 31). The years 2008 and 2009 mark a peak in deportation rates, unmatched either before or since that time. In 2014, deportation numbers stood at around 52,500. Whereas the deportation of migrants refused entry at port had increased by 15 per cent (to 15,943) compared with the previous year, the number of migrants facing enforced removal decreased by 6 per cent (to 12,460), and the overall number of voluntary departures at 24,001 represented the largest proportion of those deported from the UK (Home Office 2015). As with the running of detention facilities, much of the organisation of deportation has also been outsourced to private companies.

Women in detention: how many women are detained and deported?

Gender-disaggregated statistics in relation to migration are hard to come by in most EU member states despite recommendations over many years for such data to be made available publicly. Migrant support organisations have argued in favour of gender statistics on the grounds that they can be used to demonstrate that certain policies and laws may place migrants of one sex at a particular disadvantage and that such evidence can then enable political decision makers and those implementing policy to address and even out differential outcomes. In 2007, under pressure from migrant and human rights NGOs and groups of MEPs to collect, record and analyse gender-related statistics on immigration, a European Parliament and Council regulation (number 862/2007) on migration and international protection was adopted. It required member states to supply the Commission with data on asylum claimants disaggregated according to sex, age and nationality. Disaggregated data also had to be produced in relation to first-instance asylum decision granting or withholding refugee status or subsidiary protection, and final decisions on the granting of refugee status or subsidiary protection as a result of appeal or review. This regulation was applicable and legally binding on all member states. Despite these moves, gender disaggregated statistics are not provided by many member states, particularly in relation to stages of the asylum determination process after the first instance decision is taken.

Both the UK and French authorities provide gender statistics on asylum claims lodged and on first decisions. In addition, the UK authorities make public gender disaggregated data on decisions reached as a result of appeals and reviews. UK statistics from 2000 onwards indicate the numbers of men, women and dependents placed in detention (therefore facing expulsion in principle), including the method of expulsion (administrative, voluntary and what is termed 'deportation'). In France, data relating to detainees, including those facing expulsion, is not made public in the annual reports of the Office français de protection des réfugiés et apatrides (OFPRA). The only data available on women in detention and facing deportation come from the NGOs which are permitted to enter and monitor detention centres and holding areas. However, the NGOs are not in a position each year to gather and record all data systematically; hence, for example, gender data on deportations can be very sketchy or unavailable altogether.

Historically, women have constituted a significant proportion of migrant inflows to France, due to the emphasis placed by governments, at least in their articulation of the issue, upon the role of immigration as a demographic regulator, rather than a means of responding to the immediate needs of the economy. Thus, a gender balance was reached in 1999 and has been maintained throughout the 2000s (INSEE n.d.; Allwood and Wadia 2010: 58–61). However, women form a smaller proportion of asylum seekers (about one-third) (Ibid.: 67) and figures, even estimated, for women among categories of irregular migrants are unavailable. While women account for half the migrant population in France, they form a small part of those placed in immigration detention and eventually deported. Various reasons explain their relatively small numbers in detention and deportation. Women asylum seekers are more likely than men to be given refugee status or some form of subsidiary protection; in the 2000s, women have accounted for 40–42 per cent of the total number of refugees or persons given protection in France (Ibid.: 70). Also, undocumented women are less likely than men to be stopped, checked for ID and taken into detention. The majority – over 80 per cent – of 'stop and checks' take place in public places (in the street and in railway and coach stations, on public transport, in the workplace and at border control posts) where women are not as present as men (Cinq Associations 2011). Thus, since the early 2000s, women have constituted between 6 and just over 10 per cent of immigration detainees – see Table 4.1.

There is very little if any gender and age or gender and nationality disaggregated data available in the NGO reports. For example, only the

Table 4.1   Women in detention in France

	2003	2005	2007	2009	2011	2013
Number of women detainees	1,524	3,236	2,511	1,761	2,059	Data unavailable
Total number of detainees	22,304	30,474	34,235	27,252	Data unavailable	Data unavailable
Per cent of women detainees of total	6.83	10.62	7.33	6.07	8.10	6.00

Source: Cinq Associations (2007, 2008, 2010, 2012, 2014) *Centres et locaux de rétention administrative* (annual reports for the years 2006, 2007, 2009, 2011, and 2013).

reports for 2006 and 2008 give a breakdown of figures by gender and nationality, showing that there is a high level of diversity among women detainees, with Romanian Roma accounting for almost one-third of female detainees in 2006 (Cinq Associations 2007: 28) and Chinese, Algerian and Moroccan women topping the numbers in 2008 (Cinq Associations 2009: 40). None of the reports present an age breakdown of female detainees, although all the reports consulted (2006–2013) show that the detainee population on the whole is overwhelmingly young; 80–83 per cent of detainees are aged between 18 and 39. As far as deportation is concerned, the reports give no information on the proportion of women among deportees. Given that the NGOs gathering data during visits to detention centres and holding areas do not see all detainees, especially where deportation orders are acted upon very quickly, it is impossible for them to provide statistics which are wholly reliable. It is therefore unwise to speculate on the proportion of women within total deportee numbers.

Until the mid-1970s, women did not make up large proportions of migratory flows to Britain, as historically, British governments had supported a labour migration regime, drawing on European migrant labour before 1945 and on migrant labour from British ex-colonies after the Second World War. It was only with the introduction of family migration in the 1970s that the number of women migrants arriving in the UK increased to reach almost 48 per cent of inflows in 1975 and 60 per cent in 1985 (Dobson et al. 2001: 43). As in France, in more recent refugee migration to Britain, women have comprised about one-third of primary asylum claimants (Allwood and Wadia 2010: 64–65).[14] Also, as in the French situation, asylum claimants have constituted a sizeable proportion of detainees – the majority until 2010. Since then their numbers in

Table 4.2   Women in detention in the UK

	2000*	2002*	2004*	2009	2010	2014
Number of women detainees	35	115	215	4,860	4,340	4,637
Total number of detainees	741	1145	1950	26,880	25,530	30,266
Per cent of women detainees of total	4.72	10.04	11.03	18.08	16.99	15.32

Note: *Figures in Table 4.2 relating to the years 2002, 2003 and 2004 are snapshots taken on a particular day of the year, in this case 4 January 2000, 28 December 2002 and 25 December 2004, respectively. Those relating to 2009, 2010 and 2014 are annual figures.

Source: Home Office *Asylum statistics* (2001, 2003, 2005) and *Control of immigration statistics* (2010, 2011, 2015).

detention centres and holding areas have fallen. Although France and Britain detain comparable numbers of migrants overall, Table 4.2 shows that women are far more likely to be detained in the UK; for example, in 2009, women accounted for 18.08 per cent of detainees in the UK compared with 6.07 per cent in France. Finally, while the Home Office makes public a fairly detailed breakdown of removals in relation to types of departure, category and nationality of migrants deported, it does not disaggregate removals in terms of gender. The proportion of women among deportees each year is therefore unknown.

Immigration detention, looming deportation and the insecuritisation of daily life

There is a clear consensus among migrant support and human rights organisations, and among public authorities responsible for monitoring immigration services, that detention (and with it, deportation) in Europe has expanded needlessly and too rapidly in the 2000s without requisite systems of safety, scrutiny and checks being created. The unfettered development of immigration detention, itself the result of political desires to contain populations seen too often as morally and economically feckless, has led to a system where, in the words of the Nick Hardwick, Chief Inspector of Prisons (UK), 'a sense of humanity was lost' (HM Chief Inspector of Prisons 2013). It is within such a system that hundreds of thousands of migrants across Europe are held, against their will, each year. Among these migrant populations, many have fled political persecution, torture and other harms rendering them vulnerable. International and European conventions and rules recognise vulnerable categories in detention. Thus, both the UNHCR's 1999 'Revised guidelines on applicable criteria and standards relating to the detention of asylum seekers' and the EU's Reception Conditions Directive include among vulnerable categories minors (unaccompanied or not), disabled people, the elderly, pregnant women, single parents with minor children and those who have been subjected to torture, rape and other forms of serious psychological, physical and sexual violence. The preexisting vulnerabilities of forced and/or irregular migrants are compounded when they are placed in detention, recognised as a space where further insecurities and harm are produced.

Women migrants (whether asylum seekers, victims of trafficking or those in an irregular situation) are recognised as a vulnerable category whose experiences in immigration detention are worth examination in order to change the conditions of detention, if it is to be used at all, in favour of reducing insecurities and increasing detainees' wellbeing. Women are deemed vulnerable because studies have shown that the majority have had traumatic experiences prior to leaving their country of origin; for example, a study by Women for Refugee Women, in Britain, found that 80 per cent of asylum-seeking women in detention had been raped or tortured by state and/or non-state agents. Moreover, the majority of them stated that they had been harmed in this way precisely because they were women, in addition to any other factors, such as sexual orientation, or opposing the authorities, practising a certain religion, or belonging to a particular ethnic group. Such experiences mean that many women who enter detention suffer already from anxiety, stress and other mental and/or physical disorders. They are people who, in ordinary circumstances, would require medical attention from a specialist. Women, especially those from highly patriarchal societies, are deemed additionally vulnerable because, as a category, and compared with their male counterparts, they possess less of the social and cultural capital that would undoubtedly help them to negotiate detention procedures and experiences with greater confidence.

Numerous factors account individually or in intersecting ways to create insecurities on a day-to-day basis in detention. These factors may be categorised as environmental or social (see Jesuit Refugee Service 2010: 91). Environmental factors include the location and architecture of the detention centre, the living conditions within the detention centre, the attitudes of detention centre staff, detention centre rules, and the length of the detention period. Among the social factors are relations between co-detainees, relations between detainees and staff (security guards, doctors nurses, and so on), contact with the outside world, the presence of friends and/or family within the detention centre, and information relayed to detainees. Given the constraints of space, some of the most salient factors that create insecurity among detainees are location, architecture and material conditions of detention, the length of detention, deportation, and relations among detainees, and among detainees and staff.

Environmental factors

One of the factors which produces insecurity among detainees is the location and architecture of detention centres. The majority of detention centres in the UK are located in areas which are away from town centres and normal residential areas and are served by poor public transport networks. For instance, women tend to be placed at the IRCs at Yarl's Wood (in rural Bedfordshire), Dungavel (in rural south Lanarkshire), or Tinsley House (on one of Gatwick airport's perimeter roads), or at residential short-term holding facilities based at Manchester airport, Colnbrook (on the A4 by-pass near Heathrow airport) and Larne (County Antrim, Northern Ireland). None of these facilities are easy to reach, and therefore they create a sense among detainees of being in a remote place, cut off from potential visitors and the infrastructures of advocacy. In France also, a number of CRAs are located in geographically remote areas (for example, Rouen-Oissel is at the edge of a forest, at the national police college and miles away from the nearest mainline station). Although many detention centres are located in the very centre of towns and cities (for example, at Paris-Palais de Justice or Bordeaux, at the city's central police station) and are generally well-served by public transport, the sense of inaccessibility is created by physically daunting barriers; the lack of windows and natural light are described by French NGO representatives as highly 'anxiogenic'. The stark, prison-like architecture of most detention centres frightens female detainees, forcing some to relive past experiences of persecution; one woman described her detention as

> Oh God, it was like a prison again, I saw prison again, my memories came back and it was like too much, and I kept on remembering what happened to me in prison, what it was like and it was all too much (...) I kept on saying it, and they [security guards] kept saying we're not going to rape you (...) it's not like that here, we won't stab you, but inside I did not feel comfortable at all. (Cited by Bennett 2014: 153)

For others, being housed in such detention areas, in former industrial or prison buildings, made them simply feel criminalised, punished unjustly, stigmatised but without the safeguards and prisoner rights of the 'normal' justice system: 'When you are in detention it is like you are in a different country without human rights' (cited in Women for Refugee Women 2014: 20). For women in a particularly vulnerable position – those suffering mental or physical illness, pregnant women, and young women with little experience of life generally – the sense of isolation created by the location and carceral architecture of detention centres, the insecuritisation of their life is more acutely felt.

The material and daily living conditions in detention centres in France and the UK have been described time and again by monitoring agencies as generally poor, and they are considered to intensify the negative effects of a carceral environment. The most common criticisms of detention centres in both countries are overcrowding in sleeping and living areas, unhygienic facilities, poor quality food, the lack of intellectual stimulation and educational and recreational activities, and poor communication facilities (telephones and Internet). Poor living conditions not only affect the negative self-perceptions of detainees but also lead to enforced idleness, which increases stress and anxiety.

In the UK, throughout the 2000s, conditions for women held in immigration detention have been subject to a number of harsh criticisms. In 2006, then-HM Chief Inspector of Prisons reported that the provision of facilities generally, and of healthcare more specifically, in the Yarl's Wood removal centre, reserved for women and families, was severely failing detainees. She was echoing concerns raised in previous reports, including Asylum Aid's women's project, *They took me away* (Cutler and Cenada 2004) and the 2005 report, *A 'Bleak House' for our times: an investigation into women's rights violations at Yarl's Wood removal centre*.

In France, monitoring NGOs have reported on the squalid conditions of detention centres each year (see also Chuberre and Simmonot 2008: 87–90; Bernardot 2008). La Cimade, reporting in 2013 on the CRA at Marseille, painted a portrait of the material conditions found across the French detention estate:

> The material conditions of detention at the centre at Marseille are difficult if not disgraceful …. Despite its recent construction in 2006, a number of defects are evident in the building which lead to the same things going wrong: leaking water whenever it rains as well as freezing temperatures in winter, in the common living and other areas of the centre. (Cinq Associations 2014: 82, my translation)

In addition to the squalid conditions of detention prevalent in French detention centres, because women form a small proportion of detainees (6 per cent in 2013), the facilities provided in most centres are not geared towards women. For example, French centres are equipped with meagre recreational and sports equipment – most commonly, they only have television. However, TV areas are more often than not monopolised by male detainees, as is table football and ping-pong. Moreover, women are not inclined to venture into outside courtyards either, as male detainees also occupy these. There are no longer any women-only detention facilities in France. Consequently, women in French detention centres suffer long periods of inactivity and are prone to the negative effects of enforced idleness.

Another important environmental factor which causes increased insecurity among women is the length of the detention period, and more so the lack of information about when it will end and whether or not deportation will follow. According to Women for Refugee Women's 2014 report, among the women they interviewed, the shortest stay in detention was three days, the longest was 11 months, and the average was almost three months. They also found that the longer the period of detention and lack of information about its duration, the deeper the levels of uncertainty and stress suffered, leading to negative health impacts. One woman explained, 'The most depressing thing is that you don't know how long you're going to be here or if you'll still be here tomorrow' (cited in Women for Refugee Women 2014: 24). While a fast-track detention system (detained fast track, or DFT) was introduced in 2003, for the processing of what were deemed 'uncomplicated' asylum claims, with the aim of keeping migrants in detention for the shortest time possible, it became a source of added insecurity, as it became a tool of automatic detention of migrants at ports of entry, regardless of the complexity of their case. The impact of DFT was severe on certain women (Cutler 2007). Suitability for DFT is determined at the asylum screening interview and is based solely on the judgement of one assessor, who decides whether or not the claim can be dealt with 'quickly'. The total time – from arrival at a detention centre, consultation with a legal representative, the asylum interview, and the initial decision – was supposed to be a couple of days, significantly faster than the processing of asylum claims in the community, even under the accelerated non-detained process. However, such a short processing period meant that it became particularly difficult for women whose claims were based on gender persecution, who needed time to recount their experiences to migrant support workers and legal representatives to put together a case to remain in the country.

While there exists a time limit of 45 days for the detention of migrants in France and detention processing times are quicker than in the UK, nevertheless, French migrant support organisations also report on the negative effects of prolonged detention, especially on pregnant women, women with children, and those already suffering trauma or physical illness upon their placement in a detention centre. In 2013, of the 49 per cent of migrants deported, the vast majority left within the first five days. Although this appears to be good practice, it meant that most detainees were unable to put forward a legal case because police and detention centre officials are not obliged to refer detainees to a judge unless they are kept beyond five days. As in the case of DFT in the UK, women detainees who wish to put forward an asylum claim based on gender persecution are particularly disadvantaged, given that gender persecution cases are complex and may therefore require time for the gathering of evidence.

Deportation, as the end stage of the detention process, is a final environmental factor that causes daily insecurity. For forced migrants who have fled serious violence and persecution, deportation back to that same situation is unthinkable and has led many to take drastic action as a result of the insecurity experienced (for example, hunger strikes, attempts at suicide, self-harming, barricading oneself in one's room, and so on). It has led those deemed 'illegal' to resist at the point of identification, on the journey to the airport, or on the aircraft, leading police or security guards to apply extreme restraint, which in some cases has led to death (for example, Joy Gardner in the UK in 1993 or Semira Adamu, while being forcibly deported from France to Nigeria, in 1998). For the majority, the threat of deportation has meant the fear of leaving family, friends, and a life in a new country in which much has been invested, behind. Because deportation procedures in both France and the UK are shrouded in secrecy, many detainees are not notified of their deportation. This leads to permanent anxiety about when deportation will be effected. The insecurity produced by the threat of deportation holds very negative consequences for the mental and physical health of detainees.

Social factors of insecurity

An important social factor in the production of insecurity among women migrants concerns detainees' relations with their peers and also with detention centre staff. One of the most common criticisms raised by migrant support organisations and other monitoring agencies concerns the violence in which women are caught up within detention centres. Evidence of gender-based violence in detention centres in the UK and France has been presented over the last decade or so in various reports. For example, the 2005 *Bleak House* report by Legal Action for Women and other partner organisations which investigated conditions at Yarl's Wood detention centre, based on interviews with 130 women detained there, revealed allegations of sexual intimidation, racism and brutality in detention. The perpetrators were mainly male staff. The vast majority of the women concerned (70 per cent) had fled their countries of origin having experienced rape or other sexual violence. Half of the remaining interviewees had suffered other forms of torture. Many arrived in detention already suffering trauma, then compounded by the regime of brutality encountered in some centres. A 2015 investigation by Channel 4 News into allegations of violence at Yarl's Wood revealed that women continued to be subjected to dehumanising treatment at the hands of male security guards. They were frequently referred to as 'animals', 'bitches' and 'beasties'. Guards were filmed making comments such as 'Headbutt the bitch', and 'They're all animals. Caged animals. Take a stick with you and beat them up' (Long 2015).

Although an HM Inspector of Prisons report had recommended in 2011 that there should be a much higher proportion of female guards at Yarl's Wood in order to improve detainee-guard relations, there is no evidence that Serco, the company which runs the detention centre, had followed it up. The report stated that a considerably higher proportion of female staff at Yarl's Wood was needed because 'the proportion of male-to-female residential staff was too high for a predominantly female establishment, at around 50/50'. And 'for a largely female population, the proportion of male residential staff was too high. Staffing levels were low, particularly at night, and sometimes male officers were left to manage units alone' (HM Chief Inspector of Prisons 2011: para. 2.20–2.22).

In France, an aspect of detention centres which is condemned by refugee support NGOs is the prevalence of violence perpetrated not only by staff but also by co-occupants and by police in the case of border waiting zones, which sometimes double as detention centres or act as relay belts to nearby CRAs/LRAs. Violence in detention centres flares up between detainees as a result of overcrowding and the struggle for scant resources but also because detainees are often thrown together without much thought being given to political differences between certain groups, which can reflect the background of conflict from which they originate. A high level of violence is also displayed by detention centre staff and the police, who have been accused of using Tasers and dog patrols, and even of calling in riot police in a bid to scare occupants into keeping quiet about their slum-like living conditions and the tensions that exist. The threat of violence, including sexual violence, from fellow occupants means that many women feel twice as 'locked in' as they fear for their own and their children's safety (OMCT 2003: 25–26). Women are also vulnerable to sexual abuse and violence from security staff. Although there have been cases of police officers being investigated, placed under probation or, rarely, imprisoned for sexual abuse and violence, the majority of such incidents go unreported because of the culture of secrecy in which such centres are enveloped (Ibid.). Although CRAs/LRAs with 'family zones' are reserved particularly for single women with children, in reality there is little guarantee that such women and their children will be placed there because of chronic overcrowding. Furthermore, women-only rooms or wings are often given over to men in order to ease overcrowding or because of repair works on men's wings, while women are placed in makeshift rooms not designed for sleeping. La Cimade's 2007 annual report on detention centres notes the following about the CRA Coquelles, in the Calais region:

> the situation of the women [at this centre] remains of concern. They are systematically placed in the family wing. In the absence of families this protected zone becomes a mixed one where both men and women are housed. Normally, a few women find themselves among a large number of men. Even where the women are placed in non-mixed bedrooms... their vulnerability in this situation worries us... [because] for security reasons it is impossible for them to lock their own rooms; also there is no CCTV in the rooms for reasons of privacy. (Cinq Associations 2007: 49, my translation)

More recent reports have indicated that the situation at Coquelles and other centres has not improved. Just one example of staff treatment of detainees is presented above. Women in detention centres in both countries also put forward evidence of staff (both security and medical) making it difficult for them to access health services, hindering contact with the outside world (friends, family, advocacy organisations and legal representatives), and ignoring the vulnerability of pregnant women. While not all aspects of staff-detainee relations can be covered here, what is clear from the example presented above is that as a result of their situation, detainees are dependent on detention centre staff to help them meet their needs, and when this does not happen, social relations break down and increase the day-to-day insecurity detainees feel.

Conclusion

This chapter has provided an overview of detention practices aimed at the eventual deportation of detainees from the UK and France. It has also explored the conditions under which migrants are detained in the two countries under study, in order to highlight the day-to-day insecurities faced by detainees. It focuses in particular on women migrants as they are seen to constitute a vulnerable category among detainees. It concludes that practices of detention (and deportation) do not fulfil their stated aims: immigration control and reducing the number of undesired migrants in the two countries. Instead, they form part of the twin processes of securitisation of migration and insecuritisation of migrant lives which have been taking place at a more accelerated pace since 9/11. It also demonstrates that securitisation processes have filtered through to the intimacies of the daily lives of migrants and therefore represent one more aspect of the counteraction to the perceived threat of immigration from the developing South into western Europe. It shows that the study of the securitisation of migration has tended to focus on the national security of states at the expense of the insecuritisation of populations being constantly chased from the space of the European nation state.

Notes

1. Detainee populations may include asylum applicants, failed asylum seekers, migrants whose right to remain has expired, or those who may never have possessed that right but who may have remained in a country for many years. They also include people who have been refused entry at a border port from which they are likely to be deported within hours or days of their arrival.
2. For a useful overview see Parkin (2013).
3. The return of asylum seekers to the EU country of their first entry is managed through the 'Dublin system' of regulations. See European Council on Refugees and Exiles (ECRE) for an overview of the Dublin regulations, http://www.ecre.org/topics/areas-of-work/protection-in-europe/10-dublin-regulation.html.
4. The logic of 'new penology' accepts that because it is impossible to eradicate crime, the state must focus instead on the identification of groups actuarially calculated to pose a risk to social stability and cohesion. Those who make up such groups (for example, young black men, Muslims, irregular migrants)

must be contained or incarcerated, not because of any crime or bad behaviour they may commit as individuals, but because of their membership of a group that is deemed a security risk (Feeley and Simon 1992).

5. Deportation is also framed by states as an administrative procedure aimed at the 'removal' of non-citizens from their territory. In this chapter, deportation covers the expulsion of those non-citizens whose presence is deemed by the authorities to be unconducive to the public good or because, having been found guilty of a crime, their expulsion is recommended by a court of law; the removal of those deemed to be in an irregular situation: that is, they have entered a country without the requisite legal papers, stayed past the expiry of their visa, or in some way violated the conditions of they stay; the enforced removal of non-citizens who have nevertheless agreed to the time and method of their departure – these are known as 'voluntary departures' (or *aides au retours* in France); those refused entry at a border port (including asylum seekers) and subsequently removed – they will not have actually entered the UK through immigration control. In this chapter, 'to deport' and 'deportation' are used to cover all categories of 'removals'.

6. It should be noted that these figures relate to metropolitan France only. They do not include French overseas departments and territories (DOM-TOM), which also host detention centres.

7. There are five CRAs in the French overseas departments of Guadeloupe, Guyane, La Réunion and Mayotte. In 2013, these centres received 42 per cent of all detainees in French overseas departments and metropolitan France combined (Cinq Associations 2013: 13).

8. The figures presented in this chapter relate to the number of detainees in CRAs and LRAs only.

9. To obtain a residence permit, Bulgarians, Romanians and third country nationals are required to demonstrate respect for the principles underpinning the French Republic, competency in the French language, and the capacity to contribute skills and personal character to the economic development and 'intellectual, scientific, cultural, humanitarian and sporting reputation' of France [my translation] (*Journal Officiel* 2006).

10. The 2011 act extended the initial period of detention from 48 hours to five days without the detaining authority having to seek legal approval. This means that faster deportation (within five days) may be effected without detainees being able to contest, before a judge, the decision to detain them, or being able to lodge a complaint, should their rights have been contravened during the first five days of detention. Moreover, the maximum period of detention was increased from 32 days to 45, and detainees can be served an order banning their reentry to French territory.

11. Romanian Roma were the fourth most detained nationality in 2013 (Cinq associations 2014: 19). They constituted a third of all expulsions.

12. These are 'snapshot' figures taken on certain days.

13. It should be noted that post-2005 Home Office figures are not *directly* comparable with pre-2005 figures, due to a change in the data collection methodology. Some increases will therefore be attributable to this change: for example, those categorised under voluntary departures who left the UK without notifying the UK Border Agency (UKBA).

14. This data does not include women who arrive as dependants of male principal asylum claimants and who therefore do not claim asylum in their own right.

References

Albrecht, H. J. (2002) 'Fortress Europe? Controlling illegal immigration', *European Journal of Crime, Criminal Law and Criminal Justice*, 10(1): 1–22.

Aliverti, A. (2012) 'Making people criminal: the role of the criminal law in immigration enforcement', *Theoretical Criminology*, 16(4): 417–434.

Allwood, A. and Wadia, K. (2010) *Refugee women in Britain and France*, Manchester: Manchester University Press.

Amnesty International (2007) *Amnesty International Report 2007 – France* (UNHCR Refworld), http://www.unhcr.org/refworld/docid/46558ec925.html, accessed 14 March 2015.

Bacon, C. (2007) 'The Evolution of immigration detention in the UK: the involvement of private prison companies', *Refugee Studies Centre Working Papers*, 27, Oxford: University of Oxford.

Baldaccini, A. (2009) 'The return and removal of irregular migrants under EU Law: an analysis of the returns directive', *European Journal of Migration and Law*, 11(1): 1–17.

BBC News (2010) 'Q&A: France Roman expulsions', *BBC News*, 19 October, http://www.bbc.co.uk/news/world-europe-11027288, accessed 15 March 2015.

Beckett, K. and Herbert, S. (2010) 'Penal boundaries: banishment and the expansion of punishment', *Law & Social Inquiry*, 35(1): 1–38.

Bennett, C. (2014) *Sexuality and the asylum process: the perspectives of lesbians seeking asylum in the UK*, DPhil thesis, Brighton and Hove: University of Sussex, http://sro.sussex.ac.uk/51595/1/Bennett,_Claire_Marie.pdf, accessed 10 March 2015.

Bernardot, M. (2008) 'Une tempête sous un CRA. Violences et protestations dans les centres de rétention administrative français en 2008', *Collections Esquisses* (Terra) 2, http://www.reseau-terra.eu/article820.html, accessed 2 March 2015.

Bigo, D. (1998) 'Europe passoire et Europe forteresse: la sécuritisation/humanitarisation de l'immigration' in A. Rea (ed) *Immigration et racisme en Europe*, Brussels: Les Éditions Complexe, pp.203–241.

Birnberg, Peirce & Partners (2008) 'Outsourcing abuse', Medical Justice and National Coalition of Anti-Deportation Campaigns, http://www.medicaljustice.org.uk/images/stories/reports/outsourcing%20abuse.pdf, accessed 10 March 2015.

Broeders, D. (2014) *Breaking down anonymity: digital surveillance of irregular migrants in Germany and the Netherlands*, Amsterdam: Amsterdam University Press.

Ceyhan, A. and Tsoukala, A. (2002) 'The securitization of migration in western societies: ambivalent discourses and policies', *Alternatives: Global, Local, Political*, 27(1): 21–39.

Chuberre, M. and Simmonot, C. (eds) (2008) *Conditions des ressortissants de pays tiers retenus dans des centres (camps de détention, centres ouverts, ainsi que des zones de transit), avec une attention particulière portée aux services et moyens en faveurs*

des personnes aux besoins spécifiques au sein des 25 Etats Membres de l'Union Européenne, Report IP/C/LIBE/IC/2006-181, Strasbourg: European Parliament.
Cinq Associations (présent dans les CRA) (2007) *Centres et locaux deretention rapport 2006*, http://www.lacimade.org/publications/5, accessed 10 March 2015.
Cinq Associations (présent dans les CRA) (2008) *Centres et locaux deretention rapport 2007*, http://www.lacimade.org/publications/16, accessed 10 March 2015.
Cinq Associations (présent dans les CRA) (2009) *Centres et locaux deretention rapport 2008*, http://cimade-production.s3.amazonaws.com/publications/documents/38/original/rapportRetention_2008.pdf?1385634716, accessed 10 March 2015.
Cinq Associations (présent dans les CRA) (2010) *Centres et locaux deretention rapport 2009*, http://www.lacimade.org/publications/43, accessed 10 March 2015.
Cinq Associations (présent dans les CRA) (2011) *Centres et locaux deretention rapport 2010*, http://cimade-production.s3.amazonaws.com/publications/documents/57/original/RAPPORT_R%C3%A9tention_2010_OK.versionlegere.pdf?1385634442, accessed 10 March 2015.
Cinq Associations (présent dans les CRA) (2012) *Centres et locaux deretention rapport 2011*, http://cimade-production.s3.amazonaws.com/publications/documents/70/original/Rapport_retention_2011.pdf?1353516787, accessed 10 March 2015.
Cinq Associations (présent dans les CRA) (2013) *Centres et locaux deretention rapport 2012*, http://cimade-production.s3.amazonaws.com/publications/documents/83/original/Rapport_Retention_2012_bdef.pdf?1386155347, accessed 10 March 2015.
Cinq Associations (présent dans les CRA) (2014) *Centres et locaux deretention rapport 2013*, http://cimade-production.s3.amazonaws.com/publications/documents/95/original/Rapport_Retention_2013.pdf?1418986330, accessed 10 March 2015.
Cornelisse, G. (2010) *Immigration detention and human rights: rethinking territorial sovereignty*, Leiden: Martinus Nijhoff Publishers.
Cutler, S. (2007) *'Refusal factory': women's experiences of the detained fast track asylum process at Yarl's Wood immigration removal centre*, London: Bail for Immigration Detainees.
Cutler, S. and Cenada, S. (2004) '"They took me away": women's experiences of immigration detention in the UK', London: Refugee Women's Resource Project (Asylum Aid).
De Genova, N. (2010) 'The deportation regime: sovereignty, space and the freedom of movement' in N. De Genova and N. Peutz (eds) *The deportation regime: sovereignty, space and the freedom of movement*, Durham: Duke University Press, pp.33–65.
Dobson, J., Koser, K., McLaughlan, G. and Salt, J. (2001) 'International migration and the United Kingdom: recent patterns and trends', *RDS Occasional Paper*, 75, London: Home Office.
Ericson, R. (2007) *Crime in an insecure world*, Cambridge: Polity Press.
EU Commission (2014) 'How to ensure fair, humane and effective return procedures?' (press release), http://europa.eu/rapid/press-release_IP-14-340_en.htm, accessed 20 March 2015.
Faist, T. (2004) 'The migration-security nexus: international migration and security before and after 9/11', *Willy Brandt working papers in international migration*

and ethnic relations, 4(3), http://dspace.mah.se/bitstream/handle/2043/686/?sequence=1, accessed 25 March 2015.

Fauser, M. (2006) 'Transnational migration? A national security risk? Securitization of migration policies in Germany, Spain and the United Kingdom', *Reports and Analyses* (Centre for International Relations, Warsaw), 2(6), http://pdc.ceu.hu/archive/00004804/01/rap_i_an_0206a.pdf, accessed 25 March 2015.

Feeley, M. M. and Simon, J. (1992) 'The new penology: notes on the emerging strategy of corrections and its implications', *Criminology*, 30(4): 449–474.

Flynn, M. and Cannon, C. (2009) 'The privatization if immigration detention: towards a global view', Geneva: Graduate Institute of International and Development Studies, http://ssrn.com/abstract=2344196 or http://dx.doi.org/10.2139/ssrn.2344196, accessed 15 March 2015.

Flynn, M. and Cannon, C. (2010) *Detention at the borders of Europe: report on the Joint Global Detention Project*, Geneva: Graduate Institute of International and Development Studies, http://www.globaldetentionproject.org/fileadmin/publications/GDP_Workshop_Report_2010.pdf, accessed 15 March 2015.

Garcia B. J. and Bessa, F. C. (2011) 'The construction of migrants as a risk category in the Spanish penal system' in S. Palidda (ed) *Racial criminalization of migrants in the 21st century*, Farnham: Ashgate.

Geddes A. (2005) 'Getting the best of both worlds? Britain, the EU and migration policy', *International Affairs*, 81(4): 723–740.

The Guardian (2005) 'Full text@ the prime minister's statement on anti-terror measures', *The Guardian*, http://www.theguardian.com/politics/2005/aug/05/uksecurity.terrorism1, accessed 25 March 2015.

Guild, E. (2005) 'A typology of different types of centres in Europe' (Report for the European Parliament, Directorate-General Internal Policies of the Union), IP/C/LIBE/FWC/2005-22, http://www.europarl.europa.eu/RegData/etudes/note/join/2006/378268/IPOL-LIBE_NT%282006%29378268_EN.pdf, accessed 15 March 2015.

HM Chief Inspector of Prisons (2011) *Report on an announced inspection of Yarl's Wood Immigration Removal Centre*, London: HM Inspectorate of Prisons, http://webarchive.nationalarchives.gov.uk/20130128112038/http://www.justice.gov.uk/downloads/publications/inspectorate-reports/hmipris/immigration-removal-centre-inspections/yarls-wood/yarls-wood-2011.pdf, accessed 15 March 2015.

HM Chief Inspector of Prisons (2013) *Report on an unannounced inspection of Harmondsworth immigration removal centre*, London: HM Inspectorate of Prisons, http://webarchive.nationalarchives.gov.uk/20130128112038/http://www.justice.gov.uk/downloads/publications/inspectorate-reports/hmipris/immigration-removal-centre-inspections/harmondsworth/harmondsworth-2014.pdf, accessed 15 March 2015.

Home Office (2001) *Asylum statistics United Kingdom 2000*, London: Home Office (RDS).

Home Office (2003) *Asylum statistics United Kingdom 2002*, London: Home Office (RDS).

Home Office (2005) *Asylum statistics United Kingdom 2004*, London: Home Office (RDS).

Home Office (2010) *Control of immigration statistics United Kingdom 2009*, London: Home Office (RDS).

Home Office (2011) *Control of immigration: quarterly statistical summary, United Kingdom quarter 4 2010* (October to December), London: Home Office (RDS).

Home Office (2015) 'Immigration statistics, October to December 2014', 26 February, https://www.gov.uk/government/publications/immigration-statistics-october-to-december-2014/immigration-statistics-october-to-december-2014, accessed 10 April 2015.

Huysmans, J. (2006) *The politics of insecurity: fear, migration and asylum in the EU*, London: Routledge.

INSEE (n.d.) 'Trente ans d'immigration féminine pour arriver à l'équilibre hommes-femmes' (enquêtes annuelles de recensement 2004–2006), http://www.insee.fr/fr/themes/document.asp?ref_id=ip1098&reg_id=0#inter3, accessed 15 March 2015.

JRS (Jesuit Refugee Service) (2010) *Becoming vulnerable in detention: civil society report on the detention of vulnerable asylum seekers and irregular migrants in the European Union* (The DEVAS project), Brussels: JRS, http://www.detention-in-europe.org/images/stories/DEVAS/jrs-europe_becoming%20vulnerable%20in%20detention_june%202010_public_updated%20on%2012july10.pdf, accessed 10 March 2015.

Journal Officiel (2006) 'Loi n° 2006-911 du 24 juillet 2006 relative à l'immigration et à l'intégration', *Journal Officiel de la République Française*, 170 (Article 15, Chapter 5), http://legifrance.gouv.fr/affichTexte.do?cidTexte=JORFTEXT000000266495&dateTexte=&categorieLien=id, accessed 15 March 2015.

Leerkes, A. and Broeders, D. (2010) 'A case of mixed motives? Formal and informal functions of administrative immigration detention', *British Journal of Criminology*, 50(5): 830–850.

Leerkes, A. and Broeders, D. (2013) 'Deportable and not so deportable: formal and informal functions of administrative immigration detention' in B. Anderson, M. J. Gibney and E. Paoletti (eds) *The social, political and historical contours of deportation: immigrants and minorities, politics and policy*, New York: Springer, pp.79–104.

Legal Action for Women (LAW), Black Women's Rape Action Project (BWRAP), Women Against Rape (WAR) and All African Women's Group (2005) *A 'Bleak House' for our times: an investigation into women's rights violations at Yarl's Wood removal centre*, London: Crossroad Books.

Lemberg-Pedersen, M (2011) 'Private security companies and the European borderscapes' in T. Gammeltoft-Hansen and N. Nyberg Sorensen (eds) *The migration industry and the commercialization of international migration*, London: Routledge.

Long, J. (2015) '"Headbutt the bitch" Serco guard, Yarl's Wood, a UK immigration detention centre', *OurKingdom/OpenDemocracy*, 2 March, https://www.opendemocracy.net/ourkingdom/jackie-long/%27headbutt-bitch%27-serco-guard-yarl%E2%80%99s-wood-uk-immigration-detention-centre, accessed 15 March 2015.

McLeish, J. Cutler, S. and Stancer, C. (2002) *A crying shame: pregnant asylum seekers and their babies in detention*, London: The Maternity Alliance and Bail for Immigration Detainees.

Merlino, M. (2009) 'The Italian (in)security package security vs. rule of law and fundamental rights in the EU', *CHALLENGE Research Paper 14*, Brussels: Centre for European Policy Studies, http://www.ceps.eu/publications/italian-insecurity-package-security-vs-rule-law-and-fundamental-rights-eu,   accessed 15 March 2015.

Muchielli, L. and Nevanen, S. (2011) 'Delinquency, victimisation, criminalisation and penal treatment of foreigners in France' in S. Palidda (ed), *Racial criminalisation of migrants in the 21st century*, Farnham: Ashgate, pp.147–176.

Observatoire de l'Enfermement des Etrangers (OEE) (2014) *Une procédure en trompe l'oeil*, http://www.fasti.org/images/stories/oee/OEE_rapport_acces_recours_2014.pdf, accessed 20 March 2015.

Open Access Now (2014) *The hidden face of immigration detention camps in Europe*, Paris: Migreurop, http://www.migreurop.org/IMG/pdf/hiddenfaceimmigrationcamps-okweb.pdf, accessed 20 March 2015.

Parkin, J. (2013) 'The criminalisation of migration in Europe: state-of-the-art of the academic literature and research', *Ceps Papers in Liberty and Security in Europe*, 61, http://www.ceps.eu/system/files/Criminalisation%20of%20Migration%20in%20Europe%20J%20Parkin%20FIDUCIA%20final.pdf, accessed 12 March 2015.

Rahola, F. (2011) 'The detention machine' in S. Palidda (ed) *Racial criminalisation of migrants in the 21st century*, Farnham: Ashgate, pp.95–106.

Siegfried, K. (2014) 'Private security firms prosper as more migrants detained', Corporate Watch, 27 March, http://www.corporatewatch.org/guest-articles/kristy-siegfried/private-security-firms-prosper-more-migrants-detained, accessed 10 March 2015.

Silverman, S. J. and Hajela, R. (2015) 'Immigration detention in the UK', Migration Observatory, http://migrationobservatory.ox.ac.uk/briefings/immigration-detention-uk, accessed 10 March 2015.

Weber, L. and Bowling, B. (2008) 'Valiant beggars and global vagabonds: select, eject, immobilize', *Theoretical Criminology*, 12: 355–375. Webber, F. (2008) *Border wars and asylum crimes*, London: Statewatch, http://www.statewatch.org/analyses/border-wars-and-asylum-crimes.pdf, accessed 15 March 2015.Welch, M. and Schuster, L. (2005) 'Detention of asylum seekers in the United States, UK, France, Germany and Italy: a critical view of the globalizing culture of control', *Criminal Justice*, 5(4): 331–355.

Women for Refugee Women (2014) *Detained: women asylum seekers locked up in the UK*, London: Women for Refugee Women.

World Organisation Against Torture (OMCT) (2003) *Violence against women in France*, Geneva: OMCT, 15 July, http://www.refworld.org/publisher,OMCT,CO UNTRYREP,FRA,46c190670,0.html, accessed 15 March 2015.

Zwaan, K. (2011) *The returns directive: central themes, problem issues and implementation in selected member states*, Nijmegen: Wolf Legal Publishers.

5
Impact and Insecurity: The Securitisation of State Relations with British Muslim Communities

Laura Zahra McDonald

Introduction

In the wake of 9/11, London 7/7, and subsequent al-Qaeda influenced attacks, the notion that 'communities defeat terrorism' – borrowed from Britain's experiences in Ireland – has been reestablished and embedded as a security mantra in which Muslim communities are the overwhelming focus (Spalek, El Awa and McDonald 2008; Spalek, Lambert and Baker 2009; McDonald and Spalek 2010; Spalek, McDonald and El Awa 2011; McDonald 2011). Although intended at one level to engender a sense of inclusion and partnership between state-led operations and communities, the result has often been the effective profiling of an entire faith group, not only in relation to religion, but geographical locations, ethnicities, socialites and political affiliations (McDonald and Spalek 2010). The direct impact of these counter-terrorism policies and practices, including government-led preventative and pursuit tactics, has been well documented (spikes in police stop-and-search of young Muslim men, travel disruptions and heavy-handed policing at international borders under Schedule 7 of the Terrorism Act 2000,[1] pre-charge and pre-trial detentions, covert data collection and spying, control orders and Terrorism Prevention and Investigation Measures, or TPIMs),[2] as has evidence that such tactics are actually counterproductive in terms of preventative action (Kundnani 2009, 2014; McGovern and Tobin 2010; Weeks 2013). But beyond the implications for state security and its practices, the impact on human life and experience of 'belonging' is deep and long lasting, and as this chapter argues, responsible for shaping social relations in the UK far more broadly.

This chapter therefore focuses on the consequences – intended or not – that counter-terrorism has on British Muslims/ Muslims in Britain,[3] both on the individual and communal levels, and particularly in relation to the broad spectrum of victimisation. The impact on human experience is profound, and examples abound of self-censorship in matters of dress, politics, religious expression, processes of communal regulation and complex negotiation for established and recent Muslim communities in Britain, many of whom may have direct or familial experience of migration and diasporic identity. In particular, the state pathologising of Islamic concepts as inherently dangerous and 'un-British', including the notion of *ummah*[4] and definitions of *jihad*,[5] define this struggle to 'live Islam' in such challenging contexts (Spalek and McDonald 2009). Alongside this analysis of impact, the chapter draws out and explores ways in which the lens of security appears to have magnified and shifted discourse connected to more deeply rooted social and political dynamics, through which that same spectrum of physical, verbal, discursive and epistemic violence are committed: on migration, 'race relations', faith, citizenship and belonging – issues that are connected and referenced implicitly and often explicitly within security discourse itself.

The chapter draws upon academic research carried out within Muslim communities since 2000, in which a range of studies have been undertaken by the author alongside wider community activism (including McDonald 2002, 2006; Spalek, El Awa and McDonald 2008; Spalek, McDonald and El Awa 2011; Spalek and McDonald 2011; Hewitt, Spalek and McDonald 2012; McDonald, Spalek, Silk, Limbada and Da Silva, 2012; McDonald, 2012a, 2012b, 2012c, 2014). The research was carried out nationally in the UK, and was qualitative in method, drawing upon in-depth, semi-structured and unstructured interviews based upon themes of study, as well as participant and non-participant observation. Analyses within the studies used grounded theory and thematic coding, alongside narrative analysis. Participants' self-defined and declared ethnicities, ages, genders, sexualities, class and economic situations, religiosities and understandings of Islam were all diverse, with effort made to include young people, women, community activists, and the 'hard to reach' regular population, to avoid overrepresentation of community 'gatekeepers'. This was important in every study, in order to elicit samples that would provide snapshots of diverse and fluid communities, as well as take into account the power dynamics of research and communities themselves. As throughout this chapter, the definition of Muslim was always self-defined, and therefore broad in range, and reflected the diverse nature of affiliation to Islam. Similarly, the ethnicities of Muslims and migration status or heritage reflected the complex nature of Muslim communities in Britain – from new migrants and new communities, including refugees, asylum seekers, and secondary migrants from Scandinavia and Northern Europe, for example, Somali heritage Danes, or French Muslims seeking more religious freedom in the UK, to long-established minority ethnic communities from pre-war and postwar migration, including communities with Yemeni and Somali heritage in cities such as Cardiff and Sunderland, and from Pakistan and India, as well as from East and South Africa, for whom migration may be a viewed as either or both an historical or a continuing experience, with second, third, fourth and more generations. Similarly, the samples included born Muslims and converts, of whom many had migrant backgrounds, such as Eastern European, Irish and African Caribbean, and also those with white British heritage who did not identify with migration or diasporic experiences, and whose 'Muslim-ness' was experienced as heightening 'Britishness' and belonging, although often in the face of outsider doubt (McDonald 2006). Furthermore, the increased mixing of ethnicities in second and later generations has created new identities, with further complex links to migration and minority identities. These methodological considerations and observations connect with a key point of this chapter: the transectional and intersectional nature of communities in the UK, including those we may categorise, amongst other elements, as Muslim, creates a highly complex confluence of identities and experiences that is rarely reflected in the portrayal of communities within the media or by the political classes and policies. Furthermore, the complex experience and influence of migration is also rarely considered within public discourse: the racialisation, racism and homogenisation of individuals and communities defined as 'migrant' from the outside deletes the complexities and difference, to create monolithic images of minority ethnic and religious communities, as well as far-reaching stigma and marginalisation through the current (and historical) discourse on migration and migrants, viewed as anathema to the 'real Britishness' of popular imagination.

Direct quotes have been used throughout, to explore the individual experiences, perceptions and insights, and to provide participants access to articulate directly to the reader. The research has explored repeating themes, particularly around the intersections of faith, belonging, identities – ascribed and self-declared – and peoples' lived realities at the individual and communal level. This period of time has been particularly pertinent, as it includes the dynamic impact of British discourse around community cohesion after the 'Northern Disturbances' of summer 2001 (Bagguley and Hussain 2008),[6] the attacks of 9/11 with their birthing of the War on Terror, and the British policy response to 7/7 through the CONTEST strategy and its incorporation of both Prevent and Pursue strands (DCLG 2007):[7] historical events that have very clearly brought out the challenges of 'being British Muslim' (Abbas 2005). But it is worth beginning with an acknowledgement of the deeper context, one that locates recent history and current experience in the longer story of migration and community relations in Britain.

Integrating the Other

> You see the thing is that the biggest mistake we do is only think that history started from 9/11. And we forget what happened before. We forget where we were before. We forget we had problems unsolved before. And that those problems are still unsolved. Whether they be social, economic or otherwise. And now it seems that we've said listen, let's brush everything under the carpet, and let's start with terrorism. It doesn't work like that. You know, you have to relate to what happened before, you have to see the continuum of where we were and what we used to have and exactly where does this fit in the whole context of things. (Director of organisation involved in political and social representation of Muslims, male, Egyptian heritage, London, June 2008)

A rich body of literature has explored the creation and sustaining of the image of the Other (Said 2003), in which the colonisation of non-Europeans was achieved via systematic brutalisation: physical, structural and epistemic. The resulting impact affected both the perpetrators and the victims, explored by seminal works such as Fanon's analysis of the psychological internalisation of violence and disempowerment inflicted on colonial subjects (Fanon 2001, 2008), and Taussig's vivid recollection of the blood thirsty paranoia of the colonial actor, whose fear of the Other's imagined savagery and violence was instead enacted by the colonial project itself (Taussig 1987). The relevance of such history to this chapter's discussion is distinct and clear in the dynamics of discourse and power, in which the fear and sense of Other has been sustained and replanted in the context of post-colonial migration to Europe. For the UK, the postwar migration, which saw subjects become citizens, was accompanied by a deeply held racism towards the Other. These normative attitudes incorporated the imperial sense of natural superiority, the fear of invading Others, and a sense – borne out through concepts such as assimilation and integration – that 'race relations' was (and arguably still is) a project to do to the Others, in which, to paraphrase Macaulay (1835, quoted by Bhabha 1997: 194) that 'class of persons' is finally turned 'English in tastes, in opinions, in morals and in intellect'.

For black and minority ethnic groups living from this postwar period onwards, the lived reality has been, in many cases and often, one of violence and intimidation (Gilroy 1982, 1987). This includes the British Muslim population, which long before Islam and its 'Muslim-ness' became recognised in public discourse, was part of the 'non-White Other' subjected to racism and discrimination (Gilroy 2004; Modood 2005, 2010; Abbas 2011). Thus, many British Muslims growing up in such a context, as well as the subsequent generations whose experience is still coloured in parallel ways, have long been subject to abuse as 'lesser' citizens by both state and the public:

> We were getting a lot of things happening with the police and seeing the police beat up and stitch other people .... We began to think, how can we protect the people from police?

> If I tell you that when I was at school when I was about 14–15 years old, a coach load of adult men, skinheads, came with crash helmets on, baseball bats and dustbin lids and piled out of a coach – this is in Birmingham...where my school used to be. So, right in the middle of Birmingham, not in the middle of nowhere – right in the middle of Birmingham, a coach load of men come; skinheads, with baseball bats, pile out of the coach right in front of a school and start attacking us. Can anybody picture that happening today? It's impossible. That's what used to happen in the 70s and the early 80s.

> That's how we lived. When we used to go to school, we used to have to run the gauntlet because all these – the White people – they would come out, they'd have their dogs, they'd be abusing us and whatever and we had to run [the] gauntlet to go to school. This is how we used to go to school. (Male, Pakistani heritage, Birmingham, December 2014)

And continuing with this Muslim part of the story, history did not pause or change its course. As Modood (2010), Abbas (2011) and others have argued, the entry of Muslim identity into the public consciousness over a more generalised political Blackness or Asian identity, may be traced back to the Salman Rushdie Affair in 1989. In this one moment, as protests grew, the Orientalist gaze was reinvigourated. A previously unnoticed minority was suddenly headline news in a media whose reaction to 'Muslim Rage'[8] was neatly tied to a range of fears relating to Islam in the broader context, in particular the bogeyman Khomeini, and the perceived militancy of the Iranian Revolution more generally, as the antithesis of western civilisation, free speech and, at least for black and ethnic minority populations in the UK, the quiet existence expected of them.

So it is not surprising, in the lead up to the shift from race relations to security as the lens through which British Muslims were to be viewed and defined, that the 'Northern Disturbances' of summer 2001 were understood as an integration problem. With bubbling inter-communal tensions rooted in economic deterioration in former industrial, mainly mill towns, of Northern England, and in response to ongoing racist harassment, young Muslim men took to the streets. The scenes of burning cars and violence towards the police were treated in much the same way as black and minority ethnic rioting had been in the past, from the Notting Hill riots in 1958 to Handsworth in 1985: not as symptoms of inequality, frustration and political and social disenfranchisement, but as an expression of the nature of unruly, unintegrated Others, whose Britishness remained questionable, and for whom a new government race relations policy was required. Cantle's government-commissioned report (2001), and subsequent policy of community cohesion, skirted over issues of economics and racism, and instead redefined the 'race relations problem', claiming that a laissez faire multiculturalism had allowed communities of Others, including white working class communities, to remain too different (Modood 2007, 2010; Abbas 2011; Beider 2011). In the case of Muslim youths involved in the Disturbances, this problematic difference was identified as their faith identity: Islam, with it, was once more debated as a limitation on 'true' integration and loyalty to Britain (McDonald 2011).

The final moments of crucial import to this overview of history are that the aforementioned shift, in which Muslim integration – or perceived lack of – was to be fused not just to communal harmony, but to state security. The shockwave of the 9/11 attacks and subsequent launch of the war on terror not only heightened the sense of Muslims as dangerous Others, but reasserted old binaries of West/East, democratic freedom/barbarian totalitarianism, civilised/uncivilised, and reestablished the fragility of Muslim belonging in the west, including the UK. So when the suicide bombings of 7 July 2005 were perpetrated by young

British men, the anxiety over Britain's 'Muslim problem' appeared to be justified, with race relations experts such as Trevor Phillips stating that the attacks were proof that Britain was 'sleep walking into segregation' (Phillips 2005), The loyalty to Others, the sense of detachment from Britain and its peoples, the vengeful and disaffected voice of Mohammad Sidique Khan[9] made the point clearly (Wikisource 2005):

> I and thousands like me are forsaking everything for what we believe. Our drive and motivation doesn't come from tangible commodities that this world has to offer. Our religion is Islam, obedience to the one true God Allah and following the footsteps of the final prophet messenger.
>
> This is how our ethical stances are dictated.
>
> Your democratically elected governments continuously perpetuate atrocities against my people all over the world. And your support of them makes you directly responsible, just as I am directly responsible for protecting and avenging my Muslim brothers and sisters.
>
> Until we feel security you will be our targets and until you stop the bombing, gassing, imprisonment and torture of my people we will not stop this fight. We are at war and I am a soldier. Now you too will taste the reality of this situation.

The policy response was clear in its question and answer: how could young British men commit terrorist murder, and how could such an act be prevented in the future? Counter-terrorism practices were not only to improve the pursue elements in thwarting terrorist plots, but a preventative strand was also imperative, to counteract the attraction of young, British Muslims to a violent and radical religio-polictical ideology that divided them from the majority. And through this reaction, accompanied by media scrutiny, public horror and fear, the 'Muslim community' was at once identified as both the problem and the solution (Spalek and McDonald 2009; McDonald 2011):

> I think there's certain negativities around the media which the Muslim community are not going to be able to get away in a hurry. And a lot of it is very painful and is very unfair.
>
> I do understand, you [the British general public and media] are uncomfortable, you don't know, it's fear of what you don't understand. But don't you understand that we can feel really hurt with what you're doing? And we're feeling really marginalised, and you're

saying Muslims don't integrate. (Community activist, female, African Caribbean heritage, involved in community and police engagement, London, September 2009)

In the phases of the Prevent policy since that moment, the strategy has been developed with varying foci. Preventing Extremism Together (PET 2006), followed by the Preventing Violent Extremism Pathfinder phase (2007–2009) for example, focussed on the assumption that a lack of integration was a fundamental cause of vulnerability to violent extremism. Led by the Department for Communities and Local Government (DCLG), city councils and local government in areas deemed 'high risk' – based on high Muslim /migrant/ working class demographics – funded local projects that intimately, albeit unintentionally, connected cohesion with security (HMG 2006, 2008, 2009). Cricket and football clubs, women's computer literacy, and youth leadership programmes were funded under Prevent, often taken on by community groups whose interest was not only in preventing violence, but also in sustaining grassroots projects at a local level, including youth services that had previously been marginalised or underfunded.[10] The unintended consequences were many: competition for funding drove up rivalries and divisive community politics, and non-Muslim groups felt marginalised and angry that Muslims were being 'rewarded' for violence. However, most insidiously and not instantly realised, the impact on state and community relations – the only language of community development or capacity building, and the relationship with all members of those Muslim communities – was now articulated as in the interest of state security.

Furthermore, the idea that the 'Muslim community' was assumed homogenous and encompassing, began to create a sense of stigma, as the other activities of the state – increased stop and search, draconian anti-terror laws, and police raids, alongside Islamophobic media attention – cast all Muslims as 'potentials', that is, potentially vulnerable to violent extremism (McDonald 2011). Reviewed after controversy surrounding elements of the programme's efficacy, the Home Office took over responsibility for Prevent from the DCLG, and under the Conservative-Liberal Democrat Coalition government, later versions of the policy, such as the Prevent Review in 2011, distanced the strategy from cohesion, focusing more on challenging the ideologies underpinning violent extremisms. This shift did not reduce stigma and concern about spying, and the sustaining of a binary between Muslims considered by Government to be 'moderate' versus 'extremists' – including 'non-violent extremists', continue to create fear at the grassroots (Spalek and McDonald 2009; Kundnani 2014):

> We will take action against those who defend terrorism and violent extremism. We will also continue to challenge views which fall short of supporting violence and are within the law, but which reject and undermine our shared values and jeopardise community cohesion. Some of these views can create a climate in which people may be drawn into violent activity. (HMG, 2009: 13)

Yet the connection with integration has persisted in the Prevent Review 2011:

> 3.6 There is evidence to indicate that support for terrorism is associated with rejection of a cohesive, integrated, multi-faith society and of parliamentary democracy. Work to deal with radicalisation will depend on developing a sense of belonging to this country and support for our core values.
>
> Prevent depends on a successful integration strategy. But integration alone will not meet Prevent objectives. (Ibid. 2011: 23)

Additionally, the state-led nature of the strategy has created an underlying issue, wherein the sensitive and complex nature of preventing violent extremism is yet another example of 'doing to' the Other:

> Security didn't have anything to do with the community before. And then once the Prevent was set up the community felt that they were being targeted first and foremost. And they also felt that because of the Prevent agenda focused on the community, they were being criminalised more so in the wider society. And they thought the more the Prevent focused on them the more it gives rise to the BNP and the extreme right activities and so forth. So they became...in fact they felt that they became a target from both sides – on the Government side as well and now suddenly the (side of Muslim) communities that had existed in for years and years and years and had no problem with, suddenly they found they were a problem. (Muslim community activist and board member of Muslim grassroots organisation, female, Pakistani heritage, Manchester 2013)

Disquiet has been reinforced by a number of more recent incidents that do not directly relate to Prevent policy, yet clearly indicate the level of community securitisation experienced in contemporary Britain by Muslims in particular. The first, which is of direct interest to security practices, was Project Champion in 2010, which was a police and city council-led project to install covert automatic number plate reader (APNR) cameras in predominantly Muslim areas of Birmingham. Instigated without public consultation, the story broke in *The Guardian* newspaper, significantly undermining public trust and confidence and highlighting the apparent mistrust by the State in local communities, while increasing the sense of stigma and fear felt by Muslims who had long claimed they were 'being watched' (see, for example, Spalek, El Awa and McDonald 2008). Shortly afterwards, in 2011, Ahmed Faraz, a bookseller from Birmingham, was convicted of terrorism offences for selling texts that had not been clearly censored in the legal sense, while the legal argument in court included debate over 'correct' theological interpretation in Islam. He was later released on appeal in 2013. Although not all elements of the conviction were overturned, the case once more raised concerns over the apparent blurred lines between owning and selling books (which, while legal, could still be used as proof of terrorism under British anti-terror legislation) which appeared to be targeting Muslims more readily than other groups.

The issue of Muslim ownership of books has returned a number of times, including the case of Moazzam Begg, a former Guantanamo detainee who was arrested and charged for alleged terrorist activities in Syria and held between February and October 2014 in Belmarsh, a British Category A prison. Begg has claimed that the terrorism raid on his home included confiscation of a copy of the popular biography of Malcolm X, as evidence against him (Begg 2014). But the more pressing concern at the grassroots level, both at the time of his arrest when a demonstration was held outside West Midlands Police headquarters (1 March 2014), and at his release, when charges were dropped one week before trial (1 October 2014), centred around state harassment of a man known to be critical of British foreign policy and security practices. His work in Syria and the State's response once more highlighted Muslim community insecurity in relation to humanitarian and military aid work that was explicitly legal at the time Begg had visited Syria, having met and discussed the travel with the British security services (Cobain and Ramesh 2014).

A final example is the recent furore known as 'Trojan Horse' in which a hoax letter triggered government-led (by ex-counter-terrorism police chief Peter Clarke), Ofsted and council investigations into an alleged 'Islamist takeover' of a number of state schools in Birmingham. While bad governance and a range of malpractices were uncovered in some schools, no report found evidence of violent extremism, yet much of the commentary reiterated a connection between the lack of diversity teaching, the effect on children's integration in British society, and vulnerability to violent extremism:

> I neither specifically looked for nor found evidence of terrorism, radicalisation or violent extremism in the schools of concern in Birmingham. However, by reference to the definition of extremism in the Prevent strand of the Government's counter terrorist strategy, CONTEST, and the spectrum of extremism described by the Prime Minister in his Munich speech in February 2011, I found clear evidence that there is a plain number of people, associated with each other and in positions of influence in schools and governing bodies, who espouse, endorse or fail to challenge extremist views. (Clarke 2014: 12)

Furthermore, Clarke stated,

> Young people ... are not being equipped to flourish in the inevitably diverse environments of further education, the workplace or indeed any environment outside predominantly Muslim communities. They are thus potentially denied the opportunity to enjoy and exploit to the full the opportunities of a modern multi-cultural Britain. (Ibid.: 13)

In contrast, community voices, aired at a public meeting (18.00, 26 June 2014, Bordesley Centre, Birmingham), included concern that the religious beliefs of local Muslim parents and their communities was being conflated with extremism. The accompanying politicisation of issues once more inhibited debate and important discussion, about issues such as the limits of cultural and religious sensitivity and inclusion in schools and governance structures in state education, and instead focussed negatively on local communities as 'plotting Islamists'.

This continued erosion of trust between communities and state, and the application of anti-terror laws in ways that increase community insecurity, are further illustrated by current interest in psychological operations – psyops – a military tactic normatively used against enemy populations either to win hearts and minds or strike fear. Examples include Ministry of Defence contracts to explore 'how emerging technologies such as social media and psychological techniques can be harnessed by the military to influence people's beliefs' in a covert manner (Quinn 2014) and Home Office interest in anonymous online counter-messaging, as a way to influence young Muslims away from violent extremism (Home Affairs Committee 2014: 125–126). The covert nature and use of anonymity again lend a sense of mistrust and lack of transparency that erodes state-community relations, the sense of British Muslims as equal, and as the following section explores, the ways in which British Muslims may experience life in this context, personally and communally.

Impact and insecurity

The previous section provided an historical overview, connecting the framework of British race relations with the post 9/11 securitisation of state relations with British Muslims. This second part is thus intended to explore the deeper implications, not on a conceptual level, but in the lived realities of individuals and communities – examples of the internal responses to events that include the individual and collective psychological, emotional, social, economic impacts. Quotes illustrate the challenges, in the words of individuals themselves.

Self-awareness, self-censorship

It is particularly important to note that a young generation has grown up in the shadow of 9/11, and their experience of media and public perceptions of Islam have projected upon them personally:

> It's really not that easy to grow up knowing that everyone thinks you and your family and your community are somehow dangerous, or deviant, or irrational, like we support terrorism. I know my friends are the same – when we meet non-Muslims we make a bigger effort, because we are being judged as Muslims, and Muslims are being judged as us. (Student, female, Algerian heritage, Birmingham, November 2014)

> The Muslims feel that they are being scrutinised, you know, to their little fingertip, and everyone is more sensitive and aware of everything you do. So the work we do, we have to make sure that, you know, we're going the extra mile, if not more, to make sure people understand what we're saying. Everyone is now very suspicious of Muslims and when people like myself who have very different dress, we have to do a lot more to just achieve basic stuff, like even at work. You know, people just don't know how to respond to you, you know,

or sometimes they think oh, she's a Muslim and she can't speak or she's just that way, it's like this. So there's' all these assumptions and you have to work ten times harder than other communities would have to do or even a person who's not dressed in that very visible Muslim way, er, they wouldn't be expected to do certain things that I would be. (Student, female, Bangladeshi heritage, volunteering at mosque for community outreach, London, March 2009)

Such collective responsibility for terrorist attacks, and interacting with or attempting to change negative ascriptions and assumptions, may be felt by individuals as social pressure, affecting personal, professional and communal relationships, and highlights the level of stigma experienced. This is further emphasised by testimony on self-censorship, in which the political or religious standpoints are either not freely discussed, or modified according to perceived 'audience needs':

Of course I don't say what I think! It's not like I have weird or very radical ideas, just that I know I won't get away with views that someone else might. I never talk about Palestine, my religion or even my reaction to a random event, because I know I will be viewed as extreme, because I am Muslim. (Community activist, female, Iraqi heritage, Birmingham)

This self-censorship as a response to perceived and actual policing of Muslim beliefs and individual ideas not only illustrates a lack of freedom that much of the wider population takes for granted, but is also linked to the shutting down of important intra-community debate and conversation. For example, the need to air grievance and discuss theological and political ideas amongst young people, including the concept of jihad, has been well documented in security literature, including the Government's own Prevent policy (2011) and a Home Affairs Committee report (2014). Yet, in this climate of fear, self-censorship and practitioner concern (amongst youth and mosque workers, for example) are not conducive to in-depth, frank and open conversation of the kind needed to engage people (McDonald 2011).

Fear and stigma

The personal impact of public perception is also experienced in interactions with state actors, especially police. Young people, most often young men, continue to refer to abrasive or disrespectful treatment by police officers, as well as levels of stop and search that until recently, on orders to cease from the Home Secretary, confirmed active and prolific profiling of Muslims:

> in one day he was stopped and searched, he was stopped seven times, just in one day. In one day. (Mother of a young man, mixed Pakistani-white British heritage, London, November 2008)

The sense of intimidation is also reported widely at borders under Schedule 7 stops, which are viewed as disproportionately aimed at British Muslims and migrants from Muslim majority countries, giving a sense that the use of profiling is indeed in use:

> The other day I had a flight, a one-hour flight to Paris. I spent two hours just being searched. Standing in a line and being stripped. And it was ridiculous. It was ridiculous. (Director of national Muslim organisation, male)

The website Schedule 7 Stories, a project of CAGE (cageprisoners.com), an organisation campaigning on rights issues in the security arena, reports the stories of individuals' experiences of Schedule 7 stops, of which there are high numbers: for example, 61,145 people in the year 2012–2013, with 2,277 stopped for over an hour in 2012 (Rozenberg 2013). The physical and psychological impact of fear and insecurity is acute, and further exacerbated by the increase in Islamophobic attacks on Muslim – or perceived Muslim – members of the public, which spike at times of counter-terrorist activity (Feldman and Littler 2014), as well as the use of Islamophobic discourse in the recruiting language of the far right (Faith Matters 2014).

Negotiating ascribed identities

The focus on integration and the difference of Muslims, set against a history of discrimination and Othering, and in a contemporary context of the stigma engendered by state counter-terrorism, has created a sense amongst many research participants that their identity as Muslims, as British citizens, as legally resident migrants, and as persons, is increasingly questioned. This may affect not only the sense of self, especially for young people, but also the feeling that as assumptions are made about identity from the outside, there is little choice but to engage and negotiate in the public space:

> We know that when someone meets us, you know, someone who isn't Muslim, they're going to assume things, and think they know

what we'll be like. You know, you can see them thinking 'some Muslim Pakistani Taliban'. And yes, I suppose that makes us interact in a certain way. It's not a good feeling. (Young man, Birmingham, January 2012)

I was born in Britain, in England; I'm not English. I'm not British, we're told that from day one. But when I go to Pakistan. I'm actually treated as English. I'm not English. So where do I belong? (Young man, Bradford, February 2012)

I think the space for identity has been – it's, it's, securitised, it's making people uncertain about themselves. I mean isn't identity about globalisation as well? But we don't really talk about it through a globalisation kind of prism. Now it's all about Muslims, so you can look at migration, oh my god yes it seems Muslims were taking over the world. (Community activist, female, London, September 2011)

Ironically, the political and media commentators, whose voices are often heard espousing better Muslim integration, appear to have the very opposite effect, with participants articulating a sense of being cornered, their identities hardened in response and more neatly expressed in faith terms than anything else:

Identity's important and it's something that we can hold on to, because our Britishness is only ever two questions away from being challenged. Where are you from? Birmingham. Where are you from? You know, it's gone, you've lost it. So your Islamic identity is something that you can't be challenged on. I'm a Muslim. Really? Yeah. Okay. Fine. So that is something that they do hold on to because it, it's secure. (Youth worker, Somali heritage, male, Birmingham, June 2014)

The hardening of identities in response to attack is a useful example of defensiveness, more broadly described in response to a sense of victimisation. The inter and intra community dialogue, open interaction, and 'shared values' talked up by politicians thus becomes less and less likely:

People can be very passionate about what they believe in, yeah. And that personal belief is being attacked. You don't see it like the police through the prism of crime and terrorism. You think actually, my belief is being attacked. My religion is attacked. My community is attacked. So immediately you're on the defensive. (Young man, Manchester, November 2014)

We are trying to get, get the community to come out of the shell they are in, in a way of just being amongst themselves, or you know, going out, because one of the ways post 9/11 it seems like a one way route, you know, the Muslims are always thinking about themselves as being always under attack, always thinking of themselves that every community, or every other person is against the Muslims, so we are trying to open up doors and barriers for other people to come in, to help the Muslims, our community, and not only that, but to have them understand Islam better, help them to understand what we are really about, and not how we are portrayed in the media, or anywhere else. (Imam, male, Birmingham, July 2009)

'Ruining people'

While many of the experiences articulated through research relate to indirect forms of victimisation and a sense of communal hurt, for those individuals caught up directly in security practices, the impact can be ruinous and counterproductive. A number of case studies of people arrested and released without charge under anti-terrorism law have highlighted the destruction at an individual and familial level, and the creation of higher levels of grievance, not only in the individuals involved, but for communities acutely aware of such cases:

You see we forget the names, the names don't matter anymore. We know the names when they're picked up and they're taken to Paddington Green. We see their images when we are reading about all their 'shady lifestyles' in the Sun. But then they're released and we hear nothing about them. Nothing at all. That's it. That is where our attention span ends, that is where it comes to its time... so for the public who followed the story, the story's ended. But those people have to go back to broken homes. Their communities, people who look to them with an incredible amount of mistrust. To, you know, their children not having any friends on the street anymore. Or at school anymore. Not having any careers anymore. You see this is where our interest in the story has stopped. But their lives go on and their lives are invariably broken and some of them broken forever. That's besides any kind of mental or emotional impact that has been delivered onto them and will affect them for the rest of their lives. We don't count that. These people, and this is the problem I was just talking to a friend of mine, I know someone who was picked up and he was kept, detained, for something like seven days. Nothing, nothing. Seven days now in comparison with the 42 days the government wanted at one point, absolutely nothing. Seven days. He came back, his wife now wants a divorce. His in-laws don't want him coming into their house anymore. His children, no one will play with them anymore. He was kicked out of his job. His car was taken away. He was refused credit for his mortgage. He's gone back to a broken house. And now that guy who was admired and was a professional working in IT, was a tax paying citizen, doesn't give a damn about what happens to this country or its people. (Community activist, Iraqi heritage, male, London, June 2009)

Distrust and disenfranchisement

The impact of the history explored throughout this chapter, culminating in the contemporary securitisation of state and Muslim community relations, has without doubt increased levels of mistrust, not only socially but also politically, rendering many, especially young people with a deep sense of disenfranchisement. The frustration is clear that the prioritising of state security over community security stems in part from a cynical politicisation of issues relating to violent radicalisation and associated terrorist acts, in much the same way as migration has been politicised, particularly at times of economic austerity. Many participants articulated this, summarised well in the following:

Unfortunately, we are dealing with symptoms. And we're trying to solve the symptoms by coming down like a ton of bricks because politicians think they have to seem tough, that they're coming down hard on crime, on terrorism, on migration whatever the issue. But for someone to actually say 'hang on, hang on, let's think about this again.' Why is terrorism happening? Why is it that since we declared this global war on terrorism now that everyone has become part of it, everyone around the world has... but terrorism has actually risen. Why is that? Are we doing things ...? I mean the thing is not one, not one single politician who has any aspiration of continuing in office can actually ask that question. Never mind do anything about it. Or say hang on, maybe we're doing it wrong. Maybe we need to start talking to some of the people that we think are on the other side. Maybe we need to extend certain bridges to people who we've burnt our bridges with in the past. Maybe, maybe it's what they have to say.

Let's just see what they have to say. The thing is if you say something like that the Sun, the *Daily Mail*, *Daily Express*, they all come out all gun blazing the next day. And they will have you kicked out of office, you know, the next round of elections. And no one is brave enough to say 'listen, I want to really solve this problem here, I don't care about my career, I really want to solve the problem.' No one is saying that. (Community activist, male, Cardiff, November 2012)

Future resistance

Yet despondency is not the inevitable result. As well as negative impact, a more engaged, politically aware, and activated grassroots may be observed. While disengagement has occurred in the case of some community organisations, especially in relation to direct partnerships with security practitioners and the Prevent policy, there is also a sense of pragmatism and determination not to be marginalised, to resist:

The communities have been polarised, alienated, um, stigmatised, pigeonholed, um, the focus, as a Muslim I don't want to be opening up the newspapers and seeing headlines, we just want to get on with our lives, be part of a wider community, benefit a wider community and not be so insular where we are almost being forced to become, if you like, um, inward looking and worrying about ourselves and looking over our shoulders. (Islamic teacher, male, Pakistani heritage, Leeds, June 2009)

In order to defend ourselves and in order to feel like it's like almost pushing the whole of the Muslim community against the wall and then they say we've got nowhere else to go now that we've got to fight back. And in fighting back it is the younger generation who takes the lead. And obviously they come out with their own background of being born here, being trained here, and they know how to respond to these. Where the older generation would sit back and be apologetic and be probably be more docile and calm, and take it in their stride. Whereas the younger generation now will not take anything sitting down, will not take (anything) quietly. (Young community activist, female, Iranian heritage, London, July 2011)

Perhaps, then, lessons have been learned from the past, when the creation of fear and invocation of 'civilisation' was allowed to justify victimisation of whole peoples. As illustrated by government interest in the phenomenon, the exponential growth of social media and networking has created a new space for the activist voices. Despite the challenges, it seems that securitisation is being called into question at the grassroots, by traditional organising, media engagement and the consciousness raising that this has allowed.

Conclusion

Attitudes to migration in the UK have remained stubbornly reflective of historical prejudice, resulting in a constant negation of the complex, dynamic and varied realities of black and minority ethnic communities. The example of Muslim communities within this chapter is a pertinent example – heterogeneous, trans- and inter-sectional – Muslims as an imagined singular community have been reduced within public and policy discourse to a series of stereotypes, conflating migration, Otherness and danger. Securitisation since 9/11 appears to have magnified the strength and reach of these narratives, creating stigma and suspicion, whilst simultaneously demanding undefined and indefinable assertions of British values and loyalty. The impact on the individual and community levels is profound and disturbing, victimising individuals and sacrificing the human security of ethnic and religious minority communities for state security that claims to protect the British people.

Notes

1. Schedule 7 of the Terrorism Act 2000 allows UK police to stop, examine and search passengers at UK (air and international rail and sea) ports of entry. Unlike other police 'stop and search' powers, Schedule 7 allows police officers to stop passengers, even though there may be no 'reasonable suspicion' that a person is involved in terrorism. Passengers may be held for up to nine hours, are legally obliged to answer questions, and must give up laptops, mobile phones and other electronic data and communication devices for examination and data download if required. Non-cooperation by passengers can lead to criminal charges and up to three months imprisonment and/or hefty fines. Schedule 7 has been the subject of significant controversy.
2. TPIMs are imposed by the Home Secretary on terror suspects who cannot be charged or deported due to lack of concrete evidence. TPIMs, which last for a maximum of two years unless new suspicions of involvement in terrorist activity emerge, include electronic tagging, regular reporting by terror suspects to the police, the obligation to stay at one's permanent home address and not move even temporarily, and limited use of mobile phones and the Internet. Breaching TPIMs can lead to imprisonment.
3. This discussion includes all those resident in Britain, whether or not they are technically British citizens in the legal sense.

4. The Arabic term *ummah* may be understood as (the universal) 'nation' or 'community' of Muslims, and has historically also referred to community at large including other faith groups.
5. The Arabic word *jihad* may be defined broadly as struggling or striving to live by the principles of Islam.
6. The 'Northern disturbances' refer to explosions of social unrest which took place in the northern English towns of Oldham, Burnley and Bradford in the summer of 2001. Young men, mainly of Pakistani descent, expressed feelings of anger and frustration over the unremitting social deprivation they endured, an exclusionary political system in which they were hardly represented, and racism, institutional and individual, which they faced in daily life (Bagguley and Hussain 2008).
7. CONTEST is the UK's counter-terrorism strategy, originally developed in 2003, but considerably revised following the London 7/7 attacks. It consists of four strands: Prevent, Pursue, Protect and Prepare. The Prevent strand was aimed at preventing terrorism against British publics and interests in the UK and abroad; Pursue was about identifying and isolating those involved in extremist activity, while Protect aimed at protecting the public from terrorist attacks, and Prepare at developing public resilience to the negative impacts of terrorism. CONTEST underwent further revisions in 2011, following the accession to power of the Coalition government.
8. The phrase 'Muslim Rage' has become shorthand, typified by the front cover of *Newsweek* magazine and its accompanying article by Ayaan Hirsi Ali (17 September 2012), which reflected fearful discourse around Islam and Muslims, but also sparked criticism for its reductionism and Isamophobia. A Twitter hashtag, #muslimrage trended, populated with memes ridiculing the notion and highlighting the sense of increasing anti-Muslim sentiment. See Hotz (2012).
9. Sidique Khan, from Leeds, was one of the four London 7/7 bombers and their suspected leader.
10. The author must declare an interest and 'insider' knowledge in relation to this point, having worked as an independent consultant during the Pathfinder phase with Birmingham City Council and local youth and women's groups, producing two scoping studies – albeit critically engaged – of the needs and interests of local grassroots organisations, and later sitting on the independent scrutiny panel for the Council's Prevent funding.

References

Abbas, T. (ed) (2005) *Muslim Britain: communities under pressure*, London: Zed Books.

Abbas, T. (2011) *Islamic radicalism and multicultural politics: the British experience*, London: Routledge.

Bagguley, P. and Hussain, Y. (2008) *Riotous citizens: ethnic conflict in multicultural Britain*, Aldershot: Ashgate.

Begg, M. (2014) *Police seized my copy of autobiography of Malcolm X during arrest, to use as evidence of terrorist mindset at trial* @moazzam_begg. [Twitter]. 9 October 2014, https://twitter.com/moazzam_begg, accessed 5 March 2015.

Beider, H. (2011) *Community cohesion: the views of white working-class communities*, York: Joseph Rowntree Foundation.

Bhabha, H. (1997) 'Of mimicry and man: the ambivalence of colonial discourse' in F. Cooper, and A. L. Stoler (eds) *Tensions of empire: colonial cultures in a bourgeois world*, Oakland: University of California Press, pp.152–161.

Cantle, T. (2001) *The Cantle report – community cohesion: a report of the independent review team*, London: Home Office.

Clarke, P. (2014) *Report into allegations concerning Birmingham schools arising from the 'Trojan Horse' letter*, July 2014, https://www.gov.uk/government/uploads/system/uploads/attachment_data/file/340526/HC_576_accessible-pdf, accessed 5 March 2015.

Cobain, I. and Ramesh, R. (2014) *Moazzam Begg was in contact with MI5 about his Syria visits, papers show*, The Guardian, 2 October, http://www.theguardian.com/world/2014/oct/02/moazzam-begg-contact-mi5-agents-papers, accessed 5 March 2015.

DCLG (Department of Communities and Local Government) (2007) *Preventing violent extremism – winning hearts and minds*, London: DCLG.

Faith Matters (2014) *Facebook report: Rotherham, hate and the far-right online*, http://tellmamauk.org/wp-content/uploads/2014/09/Rotherham.pdf, accessed 5 March 2015.

Fanon, F. (2001) *Wretched of the earth* (translated by C. Farrington), London: Penguin.

Fanon, F. (2008) *Black skin, white masks* (translated by C. L. Markmann), London: Pluto Press.

Feldman, M. and Littler, M. (2014) *Tell mama reporting 2013/14 anti-Muslim overview, analysis and 'cumulative extremism'*, Middlesborough: Teesside University, http://tellmamauk.org/wp-content/uploads/2014/07/finalreport.pdf, accessed 5 March 2015.

Gilroy, P. (1982) *The empire strikes back: race and racism in 70s Britain*, Birmingham: Centre for Contemporary Cultural Studies.

Gilroy, P. (1987) *There ain't no black in the union jack: the cultural politics of race and nation*, London: Hutchinson and Co Ltd.

Gilroy, P. (2004) *After empire: multiculture or postcolonial melancholia*, London: Routledge.

Hewitt, S., Spalek, B. and McDonald, L. Z. (2012) *Connected communities: communities defeating or endorsing extreme violence* (AHRC connected communities report), Birmingham: AHRC.

HMG (Her Majesty's Government) (2006) *Countering international terrorism: the United Kingdom's strategy* (presented to Parliament by the Prime Minister and the Secretary of State for the Home Department by Command of Her Majesty), https://www.gov.uk/government/uploads/system/uploads/attachment_data/file/272320/6888.pdf accessed 5 March 2015.

HMG (2008) *The Prevent strategy: a guide for local partners in England – stopping people becoming or supporting terrorists and violent extremists*, London: HMSO.

HMG (2009) *Pursue, prevent, protect, prepare*, London: TSO.

HMG (2011) *Prevent strategy review*, London: HMSO.

Home Affairs Committee (2014) '*Seventeenth report 2014 counter-terrorism chapter 5 the UK's response to the terrorist threat*, 30 April 2014, http://www.publications.

parliament.uk/pa/cm201314/cmselect/cmhaff/231/23107.htm#note133, accessed 5 March 2015.

Hotz, A. (2012) 'Newsweek "Muslim rage" cover invokes a rage of its own', *The Guardian*, 17 September, http://www.theguardian.com/media/us-news-blog/2012/sep/17/muslim-rage-newsweek-magazine-twitter, accessed 5 March 2015.

Kundnani, A. (2009) *Spooked: how not to prevent violent extremism*, London: IRR.

Kundnani, A. (2014) *The Muslims are coming: Islamophobia, extremism, and the domestic war on terror*, London: Verso Books.

McDonald, L. Z. (2002) '*Dress and identities of British Muslim women*', MA dissertation, Department of Social Anthropology, University of St Andrews.

McDonald, L. Z. (2006) 'Islamic feminisms: ideas and experiences of convert women in Britain', PhD Thesis, Centre for Women's Studies, University of York.

McDonald, L. Z. (2011) 'Listening to the experts: Muslim youth work in the UK and its implication for security', *Religion, State and Society* (special issue on *Muslim young people in Britain and Russia: intersections of biography, faith and history*), 39(2/3): 177–189.

McDonald, L. Z. (2012a) 'Engaging young people within a counter-terrorism context' in B. Spalek (ed) *Counter-terrorism: community-based approaches to preventing terror crime*, Basingstoke: Palgrave Macmillan, pp.119–136.

McDonald, L. Z. (2012b) 'Gender within a counter-terrorism context' in B. Spalek (ed) *Counter-terrorism: community-based approaches to preventing terror crime*, Basingstoke: Palgrave Macmillan, pp.100–118.

McDonald, L. Z. (2012c) 'Le Défi de la sécurité: les activistes musulmanes en Grande-Bretagne', *Hommes et Migrations* (special issue on *Les femmes de culture musulmane: participation civique et politique en France et en Grande-Bretagne*), 1209: 44–53.

McDonald, L. Z. (2014) 'Social science, evidence-based data metrics and evaluation: a methodological partnership' in J. Cole and R. Pantucci (eds) *Community tensions: evidence-based approaches to understanding the interplay between hate crimes and reciprocal radicalisation*, London: Royal United Services Institute and Science and Technology Facilities Council.

McDonald, L. Z. and Spalek, B. (2010) 'Anti-social behaviour powers and the policing of security', *Social Policy and Society*, 9(1): 123–133.

McDonald, L. Z., Spalek, B., Silk, D., Limbada, Z. and Da Silva (2012) *Methodology: impacts of counter-terrorism on communities*, London: Institute for Strategic Dialogue.

McGovern, M. and Tobin, A. (2010) *Countering terror or counter-productive? Comparing Irish and British Muslim experiences of counter-insurgency law and policy*, Ormskirk, Lancs: Edge Hill University.

Modood, T. (2005) *Multicultural politics: racism, ethnicity and Muslims in Britain*, Edinburgh: Edinburgh University Press.

Modood, T. (2007) *Multiculturalism: a civic idea*, Cambridge: Polity Press.

Modood, T. (2010) *Still not easy being British: struggles for a multicultural citizenship*, Stoke-on-Trent: Trentham Books.

Phillips, T. (2005) 'Britain "sleepwalking to segregation"', *The Guardian*, 19 September, http://www.theguardian.com/world/2005/sep/19/race.socialexclusion, accessed 5 March 2015.

Quinn, B. (2014) 'Revealed: the MoD's secret cyberwarfare programme', *The Guardian*, 16 March, http://www.theguardian.com/uk-news/2014/mar/16/mod-secret-cyberwarfare-programme, accessed 5 March 2015.

Rozenberg, J. (2013) 'David Miranda detention: Schedule 7 of the terrorism act explained', *The Guardian*, 19 August, http://www.theguardian.com/law/2013/aug/19/david-miranda-detention-schedule-7-terrorism-act, accessed 5 March 2015.

Said, E. (2003) *Orientalism*, London: Penguin Books.

Spalek, B., El Awa, S. and McDonald, L. (2008) *Police-Muslim engagement and partnerships for the purposes of counter-terrorism: an examination*, Birmingham: University of Birmingham/AHRC.

Spalek, B., Lambert, R. and Baker, A. H. (2009) 'Minority Muslim communities and criminal justice: stigmatised UK faith identities Post 9/11 and 7/7' in H. Bui (ed) *Race and the criminal justice system*, London: Sage.

Spalek, B. and McDonald, L. (2009) 'Terror crime prevention: constructing Muslim practices and beliefs as "anti-social" and "extreme" through CONTEST 2', *Social Policy and Society*, 9(1): 123–132.

Spalek, B. and McDonald, L. Z. (2011) *Conflict with and between communities: exploring the role of communities in helping to defeat and / or endorse terrorism and the interface with policing efforts to counter terrorism*, Birmingham: University of Birmingham/AHRC.

Spalek, B., McDonald, L. Z. and El Awa, S. (2011) *Preventing religio-political extremism amongst Muslim youth: a study exploring policy-community partnership*, Birmingham: University of Birmingham/AHRC.

Taussig, M. (1987) *Shaminism, colonialism and the wild man: a study in terror and healing*, Chicago: Chicago University Press.

Weeks, D. (2013) *Radicals and reactionaries: the polarisation of community and government in the name of public safety and security*, PhD thesis, University of St Andrews.

Wikisource (2005) *Tape of Mohammad Sidique Khan*, http://web.archive.org/web/20071013041202/http://en.wikisource.org/wiki/Tape_of_Mohammad_Sidique_Khan, accessed 5 March 2015.

6
The Securitisation of Disadvantaged Communities: The Case of British-Somalis

Don Flynn and Awale Olad

Introduction: the wider context of surveillance

Security studies during the past decade have a strong inclination to emphasise the 2001 terrorist attacks in the United States as a watershed moment for the way in which surveillance policies have subsequently evolved. This can lead to the view that things would have been different had the perpetrators of these actions not succeeded in bringing down the Twin Towers or attacking the Pentagon.

In this chapter, we consider what surveillance looks like from the standpoint of one community, namely Somalis living in Britain. This is a community that knows itself as being under the scrutiny of the authorities for evidence of involvement in terrorist activity. The focus group discussions to which we refer have awareness of this attention as a constant theme, showing how deeply entwined it has become, particularly for young Somalis, in the perception they have of their relationship with the British state.

However, the critical point of our argument is that the record of state surveillance does not follow logic which is exclusively linked with the threat of terrorism. Other characteristics of the Somali community have constituted many of the factors that make it highly visible to the state authorities. Such characteristics include the fact that it is made up of black Africans whose presence in Britain has been greatly expanded by the problematic business of refugee flight; that it is concentrated in the poorest income groups; that its demographic profile is at the young end of the age spectrum; and that it is Muslim.

As theorists in the Foucauldian (Foucault 1995) tradition have noted, the logic of policing and maintaining law and order in modern, complex, diverse societies has required movement away from the punishment of the bodies of malefactors and towards the task of disciplining the masses. In practice, this has meant segmenting the mass of the population into strata according to how people stand in relation to the ownership and control of property. Thus segmented, each stratum can be assessed according to the risk it may represent to the overall system (Lianos 2003). A number of factors come into play at this point, with questions arising about the social values each group is presumed to hold and the role such values play, while reflecting the collective material wealth of each stratum.

Set against these considerations, the British-Somali[1] community has occupied a place in British society which for decades has placed it in the frame for a high level of surveillance by state authorities. During the early phases of this process, the status 'Somali', or indeed 'Muslim', was probably less significant than the fact of being black/African, and the work of monitoring this community's position in society made little distinction between its members and other black and ethnic minority communities. Differentiation began at some point further down the line. Firstly, as some minority ethnic groups achieved higher rates of upward social mobility,[2] it became important to the authorities to distinguish between those who could be seen to be 'successfully integrating' and those who could not be seen to be doing so. Secondly, the fact that some minority ethnic communities were continuing to grow as a result of high rates of immigration also sustained public belief that such communities represented a greater risk than those where rates of newcomer arrivals had dropped to lower levels.[3] Thirdly, the performance of young people from 'risk-presenting' communities, in education and employment, and in their dealings with the police (all areas where social statistics are generated in order to measure integration; see Emua and Jones 2000; Saggar, Somerville, Ford and Sobolewska 2012), provided the authorities with something that felt like an objective measure of integration. A community which scored poorly in relation to these indicators remained a candidate for surveillance.

Our account of the status of the British-Somali community as the subject of state surveillance, at the time of writing this chapter, hinges on a deeper appreciation of the decades-long interest the authorities have taken in this group and the interventions the state has made to attempt to regulate its position in wider society. The role which monitoring now plays in the lives of ethnic Somalis is close to being total, with potentially serious implications for the community's efforts to succeed in British society.

People recorded as being born in Somalia, who figured as residents of England and Wales, were estimated to number 101,370 in the 2011 Census for England and Wales (ONS 2012). This placed Somalis at number 20 in the list of larger immigrant communities in the UK. The absence of a 'British-Somali' ethnic category in the census survey has inclined most informed observers of the community to consider that this was an underestimation, on the grounds that the lack of precision on ethnicity was likely to generate grey areas for Somalis born outside the territory of the troubled state of Somalia: that is, those born in a swathe of countries extending from Ethiopia, Djibouti and Kenya in East Africa, through to Finland, Denmark, the Netherlands and Sweden in Europe.

The evidence from the last two censuses (2001 and 2011) makes it clear that this is a fast-growing community, showing an increase in the 43,519 Somalis who were identified in this ethnic group in the 2001 census survey covering England and Wales (Open Society Foundations 2014: 24). This growth has come from three principal sources: firstly, continuing movement of people as refugees from Somalia and its neighbourhood; secondly, secondary movements of Somalis who have resided in other European Union states with the acquired citizenship of these countries (hence migrating as EU nationals, exercising free movement rights); and thirdly, from the birth of children in ethnic Somali households (Hassan, Musse, Jama and Mohamed 2013).

Yet despite the growing size of the community, Somalis have had a reputation as being relatively 'silent' with regard to what is known about their social and economic situation (Open Society Foundations 2014: 25). Ethnographic studies have begun to appear only in comparatively recent times, prompted in the main by evidence-gathering exercises intended to improve policymaking in such areas as educational and training needs, housing, and health service provision (see, for example, Ali and Jones 2000; Jones 2007; Caspell, Hassan and Abdi 2012). Whilst people of Somali ethnicity are emerging as collaborators and authors of these studies, there is often the sense that the latter are detailing the predicament of a community which is only gradually putting together a consensus on what its needs are.[4]

This raises difficulties for any attempt to understand the impact of security policy on an immigrant community which has been placed close to the centre of official anxieties about the radicalisation of disaffected groups of people. As will be set out in more detail, the

British-Somali community finds itself stumbling across tripwires which signal concern about the prospect of terrorism-related activities on the part of the authorities who watch over them. As Africans, as Muslims with a high proportion being recent refugees, and with many in very disadvantaged socioeconomic sectors, the Somalis appear in frames which suppose that a proportion, albeit still a minority, will incline towards militant jihadism (Baehr 2011: 28).

The issues considered here throw light on the ways in which British-Somalis perceive official interest in their communities through the British government's 'preventing terrorism' agenda, which, to some extent, rebounds on the way they live their lives on a day-to-day basis. These issues are considered from the perspective of authors who are actively involved in civil society movements which aim to aid migrant integration through the medium of democratic agency. This standpoint presumes that social progress will be made as a result of disadvantaged groups being able to make use of the public arena for the robust representation of their needs and interests as a distinct socio-economic-cultural community. To be effective requires that individuals from communities in this situation stand in a relationship to the state which is as close as possible to that of citizenship. The essence of this relationship is that the individual is confident of her/his standing as the bearer of rights in relation to the authorities, and is not merely a subject held in place by state surveillance. What we term the migrants' rights perspective requires that communities mobilise to promote their claims for the consideration of their interests by public authorities, on terms which can be broadly described as social and democratic, though not necessarily with the party political connotation that such a descriptor can imply.

In considering the evidence on these matters, we are influenced by the growing body of work (Morris 2002, Andersson 2014, Bigo, Carrera and Guild 2013) which explores the implications of the proliferation of borders which run between migrant and minority ethnic communities on the one hand and the socio-cultural mainstream of the host country on the other hand. Borders are no longer limited to the physical space that marks the frontier of a state but are also established by a state as mechanisms to control and monitor the movement of people after they have been admitted to its territory, determining for indefinite periods of time their access not just to formal citizenship but also to various social welfare systems and public services, which, when taken as a whole, establish the norms for a decent standard of life within the country. With this in mind, we ask what it means for people in the British-Somali community, who should be increasing their capacity to represent their interests and seek remedies for the social and economic disadvantage they experience, to find that their relationship with the state authorities is structured to a high degree by security policies. In addition, we consider where the state's preventing terrorism agenda stands in the hierarchy of other forms of surveillance of British-Somalis – in particular where these are related to matters arising from their immigration and residence status and other law and order issues.

The growth of community surveillance and 'zero tolerance'

The political discourse which has sustained the drive towards the monitoring and surveillance of communities predates the dramatic rise of the securitisation agenda associated with the aftermath of the 11 September terror attacks in the United States. Elements of this discourse can be found in what came to be known as the 'broken windows' theory of crime, popularised by conservative social commentators in the 1980s (Kelling and Wilson 1982). This theory held that the task of closely monitoring urban environments for early signs of decline was critical to the maintenance of social order. The approach spawned the idea of 'zero tolerance' policing of low-income districts where the decay of neighbourhood infrastructure was considered to be a product of demoralised and alienated local communities. Such a policing approach was triggered by visible signs of deterioration – litter, broken windows, graffiti, abandoned housing – all considered to be signalling the disinterest of neighbourhoods in maintaining standards. Descent into these realms prompted 'respectable' community members to leave, thus leaving behind a population exhibiting pathological features of discontent and irresponsible social behaviour.

The application of the zero tolerance policy in New York City, where it was pioneered in the 1990s, and in London a few years later, had required computer analysis of factors which were considered to be relevant to the onset of decay in neighbourhoods on a street-by-street basis. Among the early indicators of potential trouble was a shift in the demographics of a neighbourhood, with a larger component of the population made up of low-income households with insecure employment statuses, younger aged people, and ethnic minority groups. When surveillance of local communities revealed shifts in these directions, zero tolerance policing was triggered with a range of measures intended to prevent low-level 'anti-social' activity from escalating into more serious types of vandalism and crime.

This approach to policing local communities was taken up with enthusiasm by the Labour government in the years after it came into office in 1997. The Crime and Disorder Act 1998 set down a structure which required local authorities to commit themselves to policing strategies establishing 'youth offending teams' and adopting multi-agency approaches to facilitate the identification and containment of crime through 'community safety partnerships' (Coates and Lawler 2000: 208). The practice of community surveillance became embedded in these structures, providing the agencies now charged with the task of anticipating and preventing disorder from minor to more serious levels, with data gathered at street level. To achieve this, far greater use was to be made of closed circuit television (CCTV) technology, with the period after 2000 seeing a vast expansion of the number of cameras monitoring the movements of members of the public.

Critical sociological perspectives have emerged to account for the expanded role of community surveillance and CCTV technologies, which have been such a marked feature of crime reduction strategies in Britain. Neo-Marxist and Foucauldian accounts stress the role such technologies play in manifesting sovereign state power and imposing discipline across diverse communities (Fussey 2004). Researchers influenced by Marxist perspectives, such as Guy Standing (2011), add emphasis to the function of policing economically marginalised groups in particular. Foucauldian themes, discussed in the works of Kevin Haggerty and Richard Ericson (2000) utilise the idea that the panoptic technologies of surveillance allow order to be maintained, less through dependency on punishing the body and more by way of the regulation of the 'self'.

The point here is that important elements of what is now called 'the securitisation of communities' were in place before what came to be presented as the game-changing terrorist attacks of 11 September in the United States and the 7 July London transport bombings. Surveillance did not begin after these events but was rather extended following a logic which had already swept up groups like the Somalis. Their characteristic demographic features, which highlighted the facts of low income, blackness, adherence to Islam, and problematic migrant status, extended the risk spectrum on which they were located: from the anti-social behaviour, 'illegal immigrant', drug-dealing criminal end, right through to the escalated end of suspect terrorist sympathisers. The themes which have been associated with anti-terrorism securitisation of the community life of British-Somalis had been laid out in the earlier period and were re-legitimised by the supposed added threat of terrorism.

Somalis as subjects of surveillance and monitoring

Studies dealing with the perceptions of people in the Somali community, on how they stand in relation in the gaze of the wider British society in which they live, strongly suggest an awareness of exceptional levels of scrutiny of all aspects of their lives. The Open Society Foundations' (OSF) 'At Home in Europe' project commenced in 2007 and has worked 'to improve the social inclusion of Europe's diverse Muslim communities by examining local government policies and practices in 11 EU cities to determine their effectiveness in achieving meaningful integration' (OSF 2012: 2). The position of Somalis has been an important strand of this work in seven of these cities, and the project's researchers sampled the opinions of members of these community in all the cities, which included Leicester and London in the United Kingdom.[5]

The theme of police surveillance of the community showed up strongly in focus group discussions organised in the OSF's UK studies. Participants in a London round table reported, on one hand, high levels of support for the *principle* of policing, but also strong concern about the way it was carried out in practice. The comments that 'Every civilised country has a police force', and 'You need the police to uphold the law. When you have laws you need people to uphold them', were reported as examples of views typical amongst Somali men in the 18–35 age group (OSF 2014: 107). But alongside this affirmation of the need for law and order was the view that Somalis are the victims of a type of policing which participants in the discussions saw as 'institutionally racist' (Ibid.: 108) The fact of 'blackness' in itself was regarded as being sufficient not only to attract the attention of police officers, but as also being the basis for distinctions made between groups of Somalis, with those of darker skin colour being singled out for special attention (Ibid.).

The logic of zero tolerance policing, requiring as it does the visual monitoring of low-risk issues in order that measures are taken at an early stage to prevent escalation into serious disorder, appears inevitably to bring the fact of 'blackness' into the realm of perceptions of increased risk. The police authorities themselves are well aware of the dangers that might flow from this, and, in the period since the Macpherson Inquiry report into the death of the black teenager, Stephen Lawrence,[6] had taken some measures to counter institutional racism. But practices such as 'stop and search' remained in the armoury of London's police service, and they continued to attract criticism for being disproportionately directed against people from visible ethnic minorities (Equality and Human Rights Commission 2010). The risk continues, in large part because it is not just the individual who is placed under surveillance, but also the neighbourhood in which they live. Section 60 of the Criminal Justice and Public Order Act 1994 permits police officers to suspend the normal requirement that the person being stopped and searched is exhibiting suspicious behaviour, as long as there is credible intelligence about the threat of serious violence in a given area. The criteria for determining what constitutes such a threat are vague, and this led the Independent Police Complaints Commission to rule, in an inquiry in the West Midlands region in 2007, that Section 60 was being used inappropriately (Delsol 2010).

The OSF 'Somalis in London' research, making use of data compiled by the Equality and Human Rights Commission (ECHR) and set out in its 2010 report (ECHR 2010: 38–41), established a strong correlation between the use of stop and search and London boroughs with high proportions of residents from minority ethnic communities. People from black ethnic groups experience stop and search at rates of over 90 per 1,000 in all boroughs, but this rises to 188 per 1,000 in Westminster, and to over 100 per 1,000 in Islington, Hackney, Tower Hamlets and Southwark (OSF 2014: 110–111).

Data from official sources, combined with the evidence of the OSF focus groups, convey the strength of feeling amongst young Somali men, especially about the particularly severe impact on their lives from stop and search. This has the predictable effect of undermining the view that the work of the police service ought to be appreciated as beneficial from the point of view of a community that wishes to live in a society governed by the rule of law. The fact that damage has been done to the relationship which ought to exist between the police and the Somali community has been implicitly acknowledged in initiatives like the establishment of the London Somali Youth Forum (LSYF). This was instigated by the Metropolitan Police's Communities Together Strategic Engagement Team (CTSET). CTSET arose in the aftermath of the terrorist attacks of 7 July 2005 and was intended to be 'responsible for engagement and consultation with the Met's key strategic partners, stakeholders and networks, as well as London's diverse communities, within the context of counter terrorism and security'.[7]

The LSYF website (http://www.lsyf.org.uk/) itself makes no reference to its origins in the post-7 July police strategy. On its home page, it introduces its work in the terms of a voluntary association acting to meet the aspirations of the group it represents:

> London Somali Youth Forum is a youth-led organisation that has been established to meet the needs of young Somali people in their respective boroughs in London.

> Our main objective is to support, empower and inspire young Somalis in London and neighbouring areas through the provision of advice, counselling, mentoring, training and development, community representation, and all other activities that contribute to the above.

The language used in this statement suggests an approach towards the improvement of the lives of young Somalis modelled on a collective uplifting, which, in this form, does not consider the role played by factors external to the community, such as the political, economic and social structures of British society and the role they play in cementing social and economic disadvantage. This would require development of the capacity to question the political environment in which the forum operates, and in particular the relations of power between classes and groups in London. But the origin of the youth forum as an initiative taken by an agency of the state which exercised power over the community – namely the police service – may very well inhibit any evolution in this direction. As the situation stands at present, bodies of this sort are likely to have limited opportunities to develop the independent stance that would allow a more rigorously critical appraisal of the position in which the Somali community stands and the range of actions that would be needed to advance its interests.

But the softer approach of strategic engagement through CTSET-type initiatives has been taken because of recognition that the older edict of obliging community groups to cooperate and reveal all they know to the authorities, which fitted into the operational logic of zero tolerance and stop and search, has encountered its limits. The authorities need to engage with legitimate community leaders if they are to have access to the high-quality intelligence needed to counter terrorism. But this brings up the problem that leaders only obtain this status if they have emerged through the organic processes and life of the community. There are certain things that any community is going to require of its aspiring leaders, and these will include sharing the central values of the larger group and being a part of the consensus of what needs to be done to protect and advance its interests. For the Somali community in Britain, this will include a commitment to the beliefs of Islam and concern about the plight of its people across the diaspora. These are factors which forge leadership within the community but which, from the perspective of state surveillance, will also identify individuals who may be involved in the networks the police consider to be sympathetic to terrorism.

The total policing of communities across a spectrum that extends from 'broken windows' and zero tolerance through to surveillance of potential and/or suspected terrorists, fuses concerns about the social conditions of poor and marginalised groups with those about anti-terrorist agendas which aim to seek out the politicised jihadi-sympathising militant. The drive towards ever more perfect surveillance is therefore bound up with the factors of community life experienced by disadvantaged groups which are deemed to be pathologically ill-adapted to the ways of safe, mainstream society. Alongside the facts of blackness, youth and masculinity acting as triggers for zero tolerance types of policing, there are also issues arising from the community – being of Muslim faith, immigrant background and, in more recent times, adhering to cultural mores which supposedly sanction the genital mutilation of young women – which have raised the visibility of British-Somalis as a community that, for diverse reasons, merits close scrutiny.

British-Somali perceptions of being under surveillance

A focus group discussion in the London borough of Camden, organised in September 2014 by the authors of this chapter, brought together eight people, aged 22–35, of ethnic Somali heritage. Participants included three women and five men occupied in a range of professions: teaching, journalism and law.[8] Two members of the group were prominent in a community organisation which had been established to counter what was seen as the debilitating effects on diasporic communities of clan and tribal systems which prevail amongst Somalis in the home regions of the Horn of Africa. Five had been born in Somalia but had lived their lives since infancy outside that country. One had lived in the United States, and one was a citizen of another EU member state. Henceforth, this focus group will be referred to as the MRN focus group.

The broad outlook of the MRN focus group could fairly be described as sharing a commitment to living in modern, multicultural Britain but also as having a strong sense of the aspects of Somali identity and culture which they intended to retain. Though their socio-economic status might suggest upward mobility and movement away from a community that in general has a lower standing in British society, they were not intending to sever any of the close links they had with their co-ethnics. They felt themselves to be in close contact with the daily concerns and interests of the wider community and could readily draw on anecdotal evidence of the challenges it faced to make their case for policies which would facilitate its acceptance as equal in British society.

The clear consensus amongst the MRN focus group was that the lives of Somali people in British society was subject to regular and routine surveillance, not just by state authorities, but also the media and general public. This was driven by a clearly negative perception of what the community represented to wider British society:

> The question is are we aware that it [surveillance] exists? Since 9/11 and 7/7 a lot of the active people...would be aware of the anti-terror laws. Especially the section 44.[9] It is also connected with the fact that we are Muslims and these are things that are connected with the Muslim community. Somalis who are visible Muslims – especially women wearing the veil and everything, yes, we are aware that the government, the UK government has policies that are supposed to deal with terrorism. (Female, works in education)

The fact of 'being Somali' or 'being Muslim' was the point at which Section 44 powers (which allow a police officer to stop and search an individual or a vehicle) were mentioned by several participants. They believed that the authorities operated a 'tick box' approach to policing, with 'Somali' or 'Muslim' being the foremost items:

> Sometimes they stop me because I just look like a Somali but I haven't ticked none of the other boxes. They have a tick box and they told me they have about 11 boxes. So if you tick half of those boxes – about six or five of them – then you are likely to be stopped. I am for that – absolutely. If somebody ticks five of them they could be the next suicide bomber in central London. And so I must accept that they must be stopped but there are situations where Somalis just tick the first box – that they look like Somalis. (Male, community activist)

Another community activist added,

> All of us tick the one of being Somali. They look like Somalis but it's not fair that I get stopped because I look like a Somali. Sometimes you feel that the government are not doing a fair justice on how they fit the profile of a Somali who just wants to go back [to Somalia] and who has nothing to do [with terrorism]. They are peaceful and law-abiding citizens. They are making a great contribution to society here in the UK. So sometimes the government decision of the security services is not the right approach. It is not a well thought-through process. (Second male community activist)

Participants had detailed knowledge of the government's 'Prevent' strategy, in several instances through their work with organisations which were being considered under the broad remit of the strategy. Prevent was elaborated during the months after the July 2005 bombings of London public transport and is intended as a measure which would tackle what has come to be termed the 'radicalisation' of Muslim youth (Her Majesty's Government, 2011). Participants in the MRN focus group were less inclined to criticise it as having negative consequences, as has been the case with other minority ethnic community activists. A range of criticisms has emerged of the Prevent strategy from a number of state bodies and organisations, including the Commons Select Committee on Local Government and Communities (House of Commons Committee on Local Government and Communities, 2010) and the advocacy organisation CAGE, which has provided an excoriating dissection of Prevent (Mohammed and Siddiqui 2013). A prominent strand of the concerns registered in these reports has been with role that the Prevent strategy plays in monitoring the activities of community organisations. As the CAGE report said, some community projects funded under the terms of Prevent 'were in fact intelligence gathering exercises for the Police' (Mohammed and Siddiqui 2013: 22).

The MRN focus group members with whom the authors (of this chapter) discussed these issues were less anxious about this element of Prevent. This might be due to the fact that they were inclined to the view that radical versions of Islam needed to be countered in the community's own interests because they were often linked to the clan politics of tribal Somali society. In addition, the feeling that the work of the abovementioned London Somali Youth Forum (that had its origins in a Metropolitan Police initiative) could be assessed as positive had blunted at least some aspects of the group's criticism of the Prevent strategy.

The group was very much aware of and highly concerned with aspects of the Prevent strategy which monitored the work of individuals and organisations which had frequent contact with Somalia. Several of the participants were active in projects aimed at supporting the development of people in Somalia, as well as helping to meet the needs of family members back home. They were aware that Prevent meant tracking movements of this sort, and that they themselves had become the subjects of this sort of surveillance:

I was travelling with my friend and he is one of our colleagues who works at [name of organisation] and he comes to him, not me. He looks more Somali than me. But you know the way Somalis look like.

And he holds up my friend for 45 minutes. He [the official] says I've got nothing against you but I have been told that you look like.... The policy is tighter on Somali people. They hire British people to do security checks and of course the government hasn't been consulting or engaging with the Somali community before the legislation. (Second male community activist)

Participants felt that gathering evidence about terrorist threats needed to be sensitive to the fact that leaders from the community were likely to exhibit a number of the characteristics that fitted the profile police used in their tick box alert system. These included travel to Somalia on a frequent basis and the remission of sums of money to the region. From the perspective of community activists, the task of strengthening the level of support from the diaspora was crucial to the task of rebuilding Somalian society and helping it to overcome the factors that were producing jihadism in the home region. In failing to make the distinction between people who were working to achieve these outcomes and ideologically motivated radicals, Prevent was in danger of discouraging a cohort of people who should in fact have been seen as central to overcoming the terrorist threat.

One MRN focus group participant spoke of the sense of anxiety that many in the community felt about the act of remitting money to family members in Somalia:

The ones who work for my NGO are affected by the US legislation on banks and that affected our ability to send back money to our families and loved ones. In places like the Gulf, with the biggest refugee camps in the world, the US legislation holds that you will be liable for money you give and must know who you give the money to. Now we are so fearful about whether we can send a few hundred dollars as a charity to those who have been affected by the violence or the recent famines and droughts in that part of the world. (Male community activist)

In addition to these examples, MRN focus group members spoke of the way in which stop and search practices intersected with the surveillance of people suspected of terrorist-related activity and more mundane forms of delinquent activity typical of the involvement of disaffected youth in crime. Participants described incidents where people stopped for inquiries about their involvement in drug dealing would also be asked about their tribal or clan affiliations. They felt that it was surprising that the police even knew that these things were part of the culture of Somali communities. The matter appeared to have no relevance to petty drug trading, but it could be used to piece together intelligence about allegiances within the community which established the networks and interrelationships which bound people together. They knew of instances where this had led to pressure being put on individuals to act as informers, to report any fragments of information which might be considered of use to the surveillance authorities. Several of the OSF focus group discussions touching on this issue also featured anecdotes about the pressure to become a 'snitch', with young Somalis in particular considering it a point of principle to declare their distance from the authorities and to avoid being seen as a snitch (Open Society Foundation 2014: 116–117).

The entry of the Prevent strategy issue into discussions with the Open Society Foundation focus groups raised the level of indignation amongst some participants about the position of Somalis as a community that was under particularly intense surveillance. Reference was made in this context to the situation in Somalia, where the failure of the national state had opened space for Islamist terrorist organisations to establish authority across a swathe of the country. Awareness of this fact amongst the diaspora had stimulated a number of reactions, from 'anti-tribalism', which had been the longstanding response of the urbanised intelligentsia, through to a view of Islamism as a justified resistance to the ideologies of the developed world which had precipitated the collapse of the state of Somalia. This interpretation of the situation was reinforced when those who were attracted by it moved beyond the mainstream Somali, culturally determined form of Islam and became involved with radicals from other Muslim ethnic communities. The outcome was a commitment to an ideology of global jihad, over which the mainstream of the community had reduced authority.

The negative perception of the impact of Prevent largely formed around the view that it fitted in with western narratives of global jihadism as advanced by Islamists, and appeared to confirm focus group members' notions that Prevent in fact represented the domestic front of an international war against Islam which extended across vast regions of Asia, the Middle East and Africa. The leverage Prevent has provided to sections of the community that are working for the modernisation of traditional and longstanding forms of authority, which include commitment to Islam through to obligations to the extended family, may be acknowledged within the context of youth forums and sports teams supported by Prevent funds, but that funding is generally assessed as meagre, and certainly as constituting too high a price for the advantages it has given to the Islamists.

More pointedly, MRN focus group discussion signalled a strong sense of frustration with the fact that Prevent is an obstacle to the emergence of a British-Somali leadership of the community because it discourages people from coming forward and playing this role. It was seen as infiltrating a space which young community leaders wanted to occupy on their own terms, untainted by the sense of operating on a government-approved licence. Participants in the MRN focus group convened by the authors talked of how their work as professionals, drawing on the social capital that existed in their community, required the maintenance of close contact with people and developments in the region of the Horn and also within the global diaspora. Several of the group members travelled frequently to Somalia, and all were involved in fundraising efforts to support welfare and development needs in the home region. Yet this was precisely the type of activity that drew the most intense scrutiny of the state agencies active on the various fronts of the 'War on Terror'. The attention paid by security agencies to money remitted to Somalia through the *hawala* informal money transfer system generates risks to community activists, because while the informality of the system reduces costs, it increases the importance of trust across all the agents involved in the transaction.[10] Hawala provides an essential channel for the estimated $1.2 billion remitted to Somalia each year by people in the diaspora, accounts for 50 per cent of the country's gross national income, and supports the livelihoods of 40 per cent of its population.[11] Its significance within this scale of financial activity has inevitably attracted the interest and involvement of Islamist groups in the region, and money is filtered through the system to further their aims. Legislation which has its origins in the US Patriot Act allows the intelligence agencies of that country to obtain information stored in data centres which exist on European soil. The British-Somali professionals involved in the MRN focus group were acutely aware that this had the potential to expose them to prosecution, in either a UK or US jurisdiction, if any part of the funds they had been responsible for found their way to one of the Islamist groups operating in Somali. They felt that this exposed them to very severe risk and discouraged the sort of leadership in the affairs of the community that was badly needed.

To summarise, our evidence from focus group discussions of the perception of being a community under surveillance seems to suggest that the feeling of being monitored is intense among British-Somalis. But in common with findings from surveys of other Muslim communities, the issue of Prevent or any other counter-terrorism strategy rarely arises unprompted as a central concern (Griffin Research Consultancy 2013: 8). Somali communities are highly aware that mainstream British society sees their communities as a problem. They feel that their standing as individuals and members of an ethnic group is tainted by narratives highlighting the anti-social behaviour of youth, low employment aspirations, and exceptional housing needs arising from the size of their families, and by their presence in the UK being established through the unpopular processes of migration and asylum-seeking.

However, at the point at which members of the wider Muslim communities are invited to reflect on the types of surveillance that arise from the securitisation strategies of the state, British-Somali community leaders are able to proffer examples of the impact of such strategies on the work they are attempting to do and the problems they present. Strategies like Prevent are challenging for both the perverse effect they have of defining the vision of a jihadi as any young person in the community who aspires to the model of an oppositional radical, and for the fact that they discourage many more British-Somalis who wish to develop initiatives which can be pursued through more mainstream channels. Prevent and similar strategies present a perfect dilemma for the latter group, frustrating not only the hopes group members have of the advancement of their community, but also their personal ambitions as effective leaders. Such strategies assume an important position in the complaints book of Somali activists, with Prevent taking the prize concerning mainstream British society's marginalisation of their community. But this fact notwithstanding, it appears to be a misjudgement to view securitisation as a phenomenon which is uniquely oppressive and dangerous to the community. In many ways, community activists regard it as symbolic of the many things that are wrong with the position of Somalis in British society. The wider frame, in which a range of issues causing discontent exist, has deeper roots, in older and more extensive forms of marginalisation which have marked the experiences of this ethnic group.

Battling surveillance: what do British-Somalis want?

Somalis are one of the longest established African communities in Britain, growing from the settlement of seafarers and merchants in the port cities of Cardiff, Bristol and Liverpool from the late 19th century onwards. Regulations which lasted until 1953 restricted the employment of these early settlers to the shipping industry, but when these ended, members of what was then a small and overwhelmingly male community began to move to cities like Birmingham, Sheffield and Manchester, where there was a demand for labour in industry. Wives and children began to join them from this date, and a second phase of settlement commenced. By the 1960s, students from British Somaliland began to arrive, with a proportion staying on after they had completed their studies (Farah 2000).

Throughout this long process of settlement, the community has retained a strong sense of its Muslim identity and connectedness with a global diaspora through extended family and clan affiliations. Though rarely closed to the extent of avoiding contact with people outside their ethnic group, the triad of 'African', 'Muslim', and 'family' has established a mode of thinking which sees progress and social mobility in community terms, as the uplifting of the entire British-Somali people rather than in terms of the advancement of its most ambitious individual members. Because of this, Somalis have been prone to the criticism that they do not wish to integrate or get on in life, a criticism which is likely to be dispelled after conversation with people from amongst its aspiring professional segments. British-Somalis want a better life, but they seem not to want to leave behind anyone from their community when it comes to getting ahead.

The augmentation of the older Somali migrant groups by the asylum-seeking inflows of the 1980s and 1990s increased the size of the community to the point where now the greater part traces its roots in Britain to these refugee groups. In more recent years, a secondary migration of Somalis from Scandinavian countries and the Netherlands (reportedly driven by their experience of the impatience and intolerance displayed by authorities in the abovementioned countries at their failure to assimilate into mainstream national identities) has augmented the community.[12] Whilst its internal diversity in terms of experiences of travel and life in the developed world has increased during the last three decades, Somalis remain a community bound together by a strong sense of identity forged in Islam, the social life of the Horn of Africa and the Somali language.

From the standpoint of a community which is subject to a particularly rigorous surveillance regime, Somalis see their problematic group status as lying along a continuum of concerns: that is, from the fact of being black/African, immigrant, Muslim, having large families and low incomes, through to having what is seen as a troublesome youth cohort and also connections with a region where the War on Terror is being prosecuted. In evaluating whether any of these factors have greater significance, it is important to take account of the fact that issues of immigration and low income considerably predate the security agenda which has become entrenched after 11 September 2001. British-Somalis were well used to having a problematic relationship with the police, with young males in particular recounting numerous personal experiences of stop and search and of interactions which they felt constituted intimidation.

The field of immigration control has provided an exceptionally rich terrain for inculcation into a regime of intense surveillance. Refugee routes into Britain in the 1980s and 1990s were, as now, heavily policed by immigration enforcement agencies which were charged with powers that allowed raids on homes, arrest and detention for anyone subject to this form of control. By the end of the 1990s, this had taken the form of designated 'green' settlement areas: that is, places where refugees were permitted to live under government dispersal programmes. The forms of financial support to asylum seekers were also changed with the objective of removing individuals from the mainstream monetary economy to firstly, a system of in-kind donation of foodstuffs and other essentials, and secondly, a voucher system which readily identified the person using vouchers as a refugee, at the limited number of shops which were authorised to redeem the special coupons issued by the Home Office. During The New Labour government years, biometric identity cards came into play, which were linked to immigration control databases, and which had the potential to check the movements of individuals at their place of residence and to link up with a range of different welfare and police authorities.

Neither has their journey from being asylum seekers to being part of settled communities ended the surveillance of the British-Somali community on the basis of a more settled immigration status. A requirement imposed on employers by provisions of the Immigration, Asylum and Nationality Act 1996, to check the residence rights of the people who work for them, was reinforced by subsequent legislation in 2006. This produced a system of penalties for employers and limited access to jobs for people from ethnic communities where problematic immigration status was considered to be rife. In more recent times, Somalis, alongside other migrant communities, have reported difficulties in other areas, including registration for National Health services, applications for bank accounts, and dealings with higher education establishments – all arising from apprehensions about residence status.

Somalis live and move through neighbourhoods which bristle with CCTV surveillance and are seen as evidence of a 'Big Brother' state. The

British Security Industry Authority reported in July 2013 that there were 4.9 million of these cameras in operation across the country – around one for every 11 of its people (Barrett 2013). Studies in Birmingham have shown that these are even more concentrated in neighbourhoods which are considered to be predominantly Muslim (Lewis 2010). Somalis walk these neighbourhood streets and attend places of worship well aware of the fact that they exhibit traits and characteristics of a community which is regarded as dangerous and which requires close monitoring. National security is offered as a catch-all justification for the measures described above, but youth in the community suggest another explanation, as expressed in the MRN focus group: 'It is because they don't want us here'.

Yet discussion within the focus groups and on other occasions of meeting and working with young leaders from the British-Somali community shows that most gratefully acknowledge the fact that this community was given a safe haven in Britain, recognising that while the state's governance and police agencies are often insensitive to the needs of a community which has so recently gone through the harshest of times, there are still opportunities to make collective representations to police and public service authorities about the needs of youth and families; and finally, paranoid Islamophobia, if more evident now than before, has still not totally overwhelmed the public mood. A civic-minded leadership is emerging within the community, in the main coming from a group which has made the most of educational opportunities provided in the areas where their families have settled. This group has entered into conversations with wider society on matters which concern the task of raising the social and economic standing of all of the Somali people and not just those individuals with ambition for their personal circumstances.

But this prospect of the collective improvement of the community's circumstances is threatened by the state's surveillance policy. Whether it is monitoring neighbourhoods for signs of broken windows, stopping and searching youth on the streets, or CCTV-ing the gatherings of devout Muslims in the vicinity of mosques, surveillance breaks down the space where communities should be able to gather to consider their own circumstances and needs, and to work out strategies for placing these before the wider society in which they live. The surveillance state operates with guiding principles that confuse the rising community leader with the angry, prospective jihadi. Concern for affairs across the whole of diaspora, community activity that involves the collection of money to send back home, and frequent travel to troubled areas are common to both the community leader and the prospective jihadi. But the all-seeing state myopically fuses the two together and, in the course of doing so, increases the likelihood that some individuals, at least, will react by becoming more like the very thing the public authorities least wish them to be.

Notes

1. 'British-Somali' is used here to refer to people of Somali ethnic heritage who reside in Britain. This group is considerably larger than that comprising Somalis with British citizenship. It includes, for example, those who hold citizenship of Somalia or any of the countries in or adjacent to the Horn of Africa which contain Somali populations, as well as the sizeable number of those who are citizens of other member states of the European Union.
2. Scholars point to differences in the degree of integration of migrant groups, depending on factors such as education levels achieved, occupation and social class position attained, and the quality of networks/social capital established by such groups. See Castles, Korac, Vasta and Vertovec (2002) for a discussion of these issues.
3. Anxiety and scepticism about 'chain migration' and the benefits of immigration feature in some social commentaries. The growth of some migrant communities through fresh waves of newcomers is seen as a particular barrier to integration. For an example of this viewpoint, see Migration Watch UK (2006).
4. The annual Somali Week Festival organised in East London by the Somali Youth and Entertainment organisation, Kayd, is hopefully an indication that momentum is building for the emergence of confident representative voices advocating for the needs of the community. See http://www.kayd.org/?page_id=121, accessed 25 November 2014.
5. The other five cities were Amsterdam, Copenhagen, Helsinki, Malmo and Oslo.
6. The Stephen Lawrence Inquiry Report was published in February 1999 and is regarded as a landmark examination of the attitudes of officers of London's Metropolitan Police towards people in black communities. It led to a large programme of reforms to the police service which were aimed at tackling the problem of institutional racism within the service. See Macpherson (1999).
7. See the Metropolitan Police's 'Total Policing' website at http://content.met.police.uk/Site/communitiestogether, accessed 26 November 2014.
8. This is one of two projects which engages Migrants' Rights Network (MRN) with the Somali community. The second, the London Somali Democratic Engagement Project, works with a younger group of 18–22 year-olds. Discussion in the latter project group is less structured, less about gathering views and more to do with building capacity for advocacy work.
9. Section 44 of the Terrorism Act creates the power to stop and search, without suspicion, any person or any vehicle within a given area specified as 'risky' by the police authorities.

10. For an explanation of how the *hawala* system works, see the account provided by Nashville Public Television at http://ndn.wnpt.org/documentaries/somali/money-transfer/#5, accessed 26 November 2014.
11. Figures cited in the 'Terms of reference of the Working Group Safer Corridor Pilot for UK-Somali remittances', set up by the Department for International Development. See https://www.gov.uk/government/uploads/system/uploads/attachment_data/file/283846/TOR_-_Somalia.pdf, accessed 27 November 2014.
12. For a distribution of Somali-born people, resident in Britain see BBC News (n.d.).

References

Ali, E. and Jones, C. (2000) *Meeting the educational needs of Somali pupils in Camden schools: a report to Camden LEA*, London: Institute of Education, University of London.

Andersson, R. (2014) *Illegality Inc: clandestine migration and the business of bordering Europe*, Oakland: University of California Press.

Baehr, D. (2011) 'The Somali Shabaab militias and their jihadist networks in the West', *KAS International Reports*, Berlin: Konrad Adenaeur Stiftung, http://www.kas.de/wf/doc/kas_23599-544-2-30.pdf?110811121049, accessed 5 March 2015.

Barrett, D. (2013) 'One surveillance camera for every 11 people in Britain, says CCTV survey', *Daily Telegraph*, 10 July, http://www.telegraph.co.uk/technology/10172298/One-surveillance-camera-for-every-11-people-in-Britain-says-CCTV-survey.html, accessed 27 November 2014.

BBC News (n.d.) 'Born abroad: an immigration map of Britain – Somalia', http://news.bbc.co.uk/1/shared/spl/hi/uk/05/born_abroad/countries/html/somalia.stm, accessed 11 March 2015.

Bigo, D., Carrera, S. and Guild, E. (2013) *Foreigners, refugees or minorities? Rethinking people in the context of border controls and visas*, Farnham: Ashgate.

Caspell, J., Hassan, S. and Abdi, A. (2012) *Meeting the needs of Somali residents*, London: Tower Hamlets Homes (Business Development Team).

Castles, S., Korac, M., Vasta, E. and Vertovec, S. (2002) *Integration: mapping the field*, Volume I (Home Office report 28/03), London: The Stationery Office.

Coates, D. and Lawler, P. (2000) *New Labour in power*, Manchester: Manchester University Press.

Delsol, R. (2010) 'Section 60 stop and search powers' in S. Denison (ed) *Ethnic Profiling: The Use of 'Race' in UK Law Enforcement*, London: Runnymede, http://www.runnymedetrust.org/events-conferences/econferences/ethnic-profiling-in-uk-law-enforcement/the-report/young-people-and-section-60/section-60-stop-and-search-powers.html, accessed 25 November 2014.

Emua, A. and Jones, C. (2000) *Meeting the educational needs of Somali pupils in Camden schools: a report to Camden LEA*, London: Institute of Education, University of London.

Equality and Human Rights Commission (2010) *Stop and think: a critical review of the use of stop and search powers in England and Wales*, London: EHRC.

Farah, N. (2000), *Yesterday, tomorrow: voices from the Somali diaspora*, London: Continuum.

Foucault, M. (1995) *Discipline and punish: the birth of the prison*, New York: Vintage Books.

Fussey, P. (2004) 'New Labour and new surveillance: theoretical and political ramifications of CCTV Implementation in the UK', *Surveillance & Society* (special issue on CCTV), 2(2/3): 251–269, http://www.surveillance-and-society.org/articles2(2)/newlabour.pdf, accessed 27 November 2014.

Griffin Research and Consultancy (2013) *Communities' views on the government's Prevent strategy within Hackney* (report for London Borough of Hackney), Hitchin: Griffin Research and Consultancy.

Haggerty, J. D. and Ericson, R. V. (2000) 'The surveillance assemblage', *British Journal of Sociology*, 51(4): 605–622.

Hassan, F., Musse, M., Jama, J. and Mohamed, F. (2013) *Mapping of the Somali diaspora in England and Wales*, Geneva: International Organisation for Migration, http://unitedkingdom.iom.int/sites/default/files/doc/publications/Mapping-of-the-Somali-diaspora-in-England-and-Wales.pdf, accessed 26 November 2014.

HM Government (2011) *Prevent strategy* (presented to Parliament by the Secretary of State for the Home Department by Command of Her Majesty), London: The Stationery Office, https://www.gov.uk/government/uploads/system/uploads/attachment_data/file/97976/prevent-strategy-review.pdf, accessed 25 November 2015.

House of Commons Communities and Local Government Committee (2010) *Preventing violent extremism: sixth report of session 2009–2010*, London: The Stationery Office.

Jones, A. (2007) *The unexpected community: the needs and aspirations of Birmingham's Somali community*, Birmingham: Human City Institute.

Kelling, G. L. and Wilson, J. Q. (1982) *Broken windows: the police and neighborhood safety*, Washington DC: The Atlantic, 1 March, http://www.theatlantic.com/magazine/archive/1982/03/broken-windows/304465/, accessed 23 November 2014.

Lewis, P. (2010) 'Surveillance cameras spring up in Muslim areas – the targets? Terrorists', *The Guardian*, 4 June, http://www.theguardian.com/uk/2010/jun/04/birmingham-surveillance-cameras-muslim-community, accessed 25 November 2014.

Lianos, M. (2003) 'Social control after Foucault', *Surveillance & Society*, 1(3): 412–430, http://www.surveillance-and-society.org/articles1%283%29/AfterFoucault.pdf, accessed 5 March 2015.

Macpherson, W. (1999) *The Stephen Lawrence inquiry: the report of an inquiry by Sir William Macpherson of Cluny*, London: TSO, https://www.gov.uk/government/uploads/system/uploads/attachment_data/file/277111/4262.pdf,, accessed 25 November 2014.

Migration Watch UK (2006) *The Effect of immigration on the integration of communities in Britain* (Briefing Paper 10.22), http://www.migrationwatchuk.com/Briefingpaper/document/113, accessed 5 March 2015.

Mohammed, J. and Siddiqui, A. (2013) *The Prevent strategy: a cradle to grave police-state*, London: CAGE.

Morris, L. (2002) *Managing migration: civic stratification and migrants' rights*, Abingdon, Oxford: Psychology Press.

ONS (2012) 'Country of birth (detailed) local authorities in England and Wales' (Table QS203EW, Column AR), *2011 Census*, https://www.nomisweb.co.uk/census/2011/qs203ew, accessed 4 March 2015.

Open Society Foundations (2012) *At home in Europe: promoting inclusion*, London and Budapest: Open Society Foundations, http://www.opensocietyfoundations. org/sites/default/files/promoting-inclusion-leaflet-20130726_0.pdf,   accessed 20 November 2014.

Open Society Foundations (2014) *Somalis in London*, New York and London: Open Society Foundations.

Saggar, S., Somerville, W., Ford, R. and Sobolewska, M. (2012) *The impacts of migration on cohesion and integration* (Final report to the Migration Advisory Committee), London: MAC, https://www.gov.uk/government/uploads/system/ uploads/attachment_data/file/258355/social-cohesion-integration.pdf, accessed 4 March 2015.

Standing, G. (2011) *The precariat: the new dangerous class*, London: Bloomsbury Academic, http://dx.doi.org/10.5040/9781849664554, accessed 5 March 2015.

Part III

Populist Responses to Securitisation and Migration in a Crisis Europe

7

The Rise of Italian Populism and 'Fascism of the Third Millennium' in the Age of Migration and Security

Emanuele Toscano

Introduction

From a sociological point of view, the themes of security, risk and fear are inherent in late-modern society and linked to the processes of globalisation, de-traditionalisation and individualisation that are its key features (Giddens 1990; Beck 1992). These themes have combined with the rapidly declining systems of protection which, over the last 50 years, have been a defining trait of economically advanced countries – a trait that, if anything, has become even more glaring against the backdrop of the ongoing economic crisis since 2008. The social risks that appeared to have been overcome by the protection systems that were developed in the postwar years (Galantino and Ricotta 2014), through social and welfare policies, are once again emerging, this time exacerbated by fears (Furedi 2002) and the perceived insecurity arising from globalisation and its consequences at the economic, political, social and cultural levels.

In this light, the relationship between security and migration flows has always been a key issue in Italian public debate. It is a topic which, starting from the 1990s, has increasingly been dealt with in scientific terms, becoming the subject of much research in the area of social sciences (Barbagli 2008; Galantino and Ricotta 2014). The aim of this chapter is to analyse how perceptions and demands for security have changed in Italy with regard to the complex phenomenon of migration and how the matrix of racist discourse has taken up a different configuration over the past 10 years, starting, above all, with the dimensions of culture and identity.

Immigration and security in Italy

Migrants in Italy

The trend of net emigration from Italy, which had developed since the country's unification in the mid-19th century, started to reverse in the 1970s. Before long, Italy had gradually started to attract an ever-greater number of 'foreigners', recording migration flows which were in line with those experienced by other European nations. The constant growth of undocumented migrants led to the enforcement of specific legislation, including regularisations,[1] which over the years attempted to govern migration flows. It is therefore no surprise that the first piece of immigration legislation, governing asylum seekers and migration flows, only came into effect in 1990: the so-called *Legge Martelli* (39/1990), during the incumbency of the Christian-democratic government headed by Giulio Andreotti.

With the collapse of the socialist regimes in Eastern Europe, and the constant rise of the foreign-born population in Italy, the issue of immigration became increasingly prominent on the political agenda and in public debate. Consequently, both centre-left and centre-right governments passed two organic laws, the *Turco-Napolitano*[2] in 1998 and the *Bossi-Fini* in 2002. Currently in force, the latter was, for a time – starting in 2009 – integrated with a series of additional measures, designed by then-Lega Nord (Northern League)[3] internal affairs minister Roberto Maroni and known as the 'security package',[4] which introduced the crime of *immigrazione clandestina*, subsequently abolished in 2013.

According to the national statistics bureau (ISTAT), Italy's foreign-born population grew exponentially from 1971 to 2011, at a significantly higher rate than the overall population. The numbers of migrants in Italy jumped from 2.2 'foreigners' out of 1,000 inhabitants in 1971, to 23.4 out of 1,000 in 2001. Ten years later, that ratio had gone up even further, rising to 65 migrants out of every 1,000 inhabitants (Caritas Migrantes 2012: 85). This demographic trend has been confirmed by data emerging from the censuses that take place every decade: over the past 40 years, the number of migrants[5] in Italy has grown from 58,000 in 1971 to over 4.3 million in 2013: that is, 7.4 per cent of the total population. This rise can be ascribed partly to the net emigration rate and partly to the birth of babies on Italian soil having foreign-born parents. Latest data, in fact, show that 15 per cent of all newborns (Istat 2013: 4) have migrant parents, an unequivocal sign of a migrant population that is increasingly well settled in the country.

In terms of geography, the distribution of migrants in Italy continues, as in the past, to be somewhat varied. If until 1991, half of the migrant population lived in the north, today some two-thirds live and work there. Only 14 per cent live in the southern regions of the country where the integration process is more difficult and where, as we will observe later, the exploitation of migrants is more consistent.

Out of the foreign-born resident population, the largest migrant group consists of those born in Romania and makes up 21 per cent of the total. This is followed by Albanians (11 per cent), Moroccans (10 per cent), Chinese (5 per cent), and Ukrainians (4 per cent) (Caritas Migrantes 2014: 439). As for religion, the latest figures showed that over 53 per cent of migrants were Christians – mostly of the Orthodox denomination – while 33 per cent were Muslims. Although well represented, the large religions of the East (Hinduism, Buddhism, Sikhism, and Shintoism) are in a minority. These figures show that it is substantially wrong to reduce the multi-religious phenomenon that has developed in the wake of immigration exclusively to Islam (Ibid.).

Immigration and security

Notwithstanding toughening measures aimed at deterring migrant flows and the profound economic and social crises that have continued unabated since 2008, Italy has continued to record a net immigration rate, also as a consequence of the large number of migrants from Africa following the turmoil triggered by the so-called Arab Spring and worsening ethnic and religious conflict in the sub-Saharan regions of the continent.

While immigration has continued to increase, starting from the end of the last decade, Italy has recorded a countertendency in the rate of reported cases and arrests for violent drug- and prostitution-related crimes and theft involving 'foreigners' – a rate that had continued to rise for two decades (Barbagli and Colombo 2011). ISTAT figures (2012) have highlighted that a significant number of migrants (17 per cent) were charged with offences connected to their being in the country irregularly. Also, not all migrant groups were involved in criminal activities: Romanians, Moroccans and Albanians form part of the groups which alone account for more than 50 per cent of total reported criminal offences.[6] As Barbagli and Colombo showed (2011), to understand the reasons why individuals from these three migrant groups stand accused for the majority of these crimes, it is necessary to take into account two structural elements of Italy's migrant population: increased structuring and selection. Immigration in Italy has in fact undergone a significant change, and the diversity of nationalities making up the migrant population has diminished considerably. The bulk of Italy's foreign-born population today is made up of fewer migrant nationalities than in the past. In addition, the diversity of nationalities, which had been a feature of immigration in Italy, has progressively waned as national communities have settled and grown in size. The largest migrant groups (Romanians, Moroccans, Albanians) thus coincide for the most part with the three national communities in which most crime is committed and recorded.

Recent research (European Observatory on Security 2014) aimed at recording social perceptions and representations of security in Italy and Europe showed that Italians were ambivalent with respect to migration, highlighting an attitude both of openness and concern at the same time. Half of those interviewed in the observatory's survey said that migrants helped open the country to new cultural input, while 44 per cent considered immigrants as an economic resource. And finally, 80 per cent viewed the concession of citizenship to migrants' children born in Italy in a favourable light (Ibid.: 9); at the same time, though, those respondents showed concern over the phenomenon of migration, undoubtedly also as a consequence of the economic downturn and job crunch. About one-third of respondents saw the phenomenon as 'a danger for public order and for the security of individuals', while a similar number believed immigrants were 'a threat to jobs' (Ibid.). Significantly, when compared to data from the same survey conducted in 2012, these figures increased five and seven times respectively (Ibid.). However, that same survey also showed that the immigration-criminality connection was not the uppermost security concern for Italians, as it had been in 2007–2008. What citizens fear most today is the economic crisis and the country's political instability.[7] Up to 2008, the perception of insecurity linked to the presence of immigrants, and of crime arising because of them, was due to the media emphasis on a number of violent crimes involving immigrants,[8] and to the ensuing introduction of restrictive measures (such as the 'security package'; see note 4) by successive centre-right governments led by Silvio Berlusconi. These security policies levered the crisis of traditional crime prevention social models by paving the way to preemptive action (Garland 2001), focusing, that is, on developing models and practices aimed at protecting citizens against insecurity, rather than taking action to offset the causes of the crime (Galantino and Ricotta 2014).

The various faces of racism after 9/11

Having examined the migrant presence in Italy more closely and how this and insecurity arising from criminality appear to be linked, we now turn our attention to how the dramatic events of 9 September 2001 have influenced security policies and have driven the spread of racism in Italy over recent years. As expected, the terrorist attacks which hit New York generated a wave of reactions from the international political world and also from a vast swathe of the scientific community. The latter analysed the causes and consequences of the tragic event from political, social and legislative standpoints. While generating strong clamour and emotion, the attacks were only partly accountable, in Italy, for the spread of racist attitudes and behaviour towards migrants.

Various forms of racism developed in Italy after 2001 that can be roughly grouped under three different configurations: (a) 'institutional racism', driven above all by political parties such as the Lega Nord, which more than any other party rode the wave of anti-Islamic sentiment that had flared up after 9/11, by including religious discourse within the broader critique of the migratory phenomenon that has impacted Italy; (b) criminal racism involving violent and criminal acts against migrants which has led to a rise of innocent victims; (c) populist racism fanned by extreme right movements (though not only by them) which, alongside the declining forms of biological racism, have sustained discourses aimed at repositioning the link between cultural differences and social instability and insecurity in the area of immigration.

We will now consider these different forms through which racist discourse has developed in Italy over the past decade, focusing on cases that can be individually ascribed to these different types of racism.

Institutional racism

The definition of institutional racism, as deployed here, encapsulates the multifarious expressions of racist discourse taken up in media and political arenas with regard to the representation of migrants (especially those from Muslim-majority countries). It also pertains to the antagonistic positions held by parties such as the Northern League towards migrant and Muslim populations.[9]

Several studies on media representation in Italy of the 9/11 events (Allievi 2003; Amico and Villano 2007; Battistelli, Pasini and Palareti 2008; Massari 2006) showed that there has been a systematic confusion between Islam as an international political threat and the presence in Italy of Arab migrants, through the erroneous equation that all Arabs are Muslims. In particular, Massari (2006) shows how Italian media focused, in the initial phase, immediately after the attacks (12–16 September 2001), on the events which had occurred and on the emotional dimension, as support and solidarity was expressed to the American people. No reference was made of the Muslim presence in Italy at this point, nor were Muslims linked to the attacks. Media attention then broadened, in the successive phase (during the month after the attacks), to include in-depth analyses of Islam and its cultural aspects, trivialising the representation of the latter and highlighting the potential threats posed by a large Muslim presence in Italy. Massari (2006: 98) shows that Lega Nord campaigns at this time started to put the accent on alleged links between Muslims resident in Italy and the potential terrorist threat they represented.[10] In the third phase – one month after the attacks – media coverage as well as political discourse tended to blur, as Islam and Muslims in Italy were persistently depicted as a potential threat.

Through his research, Massari then singles out a third period, covering the final part of 2001 where there was a lowering of tones, as the threat linked to the Islamic presence in Italy gradually ebbed. Further research (Battistelli, Pasini and Palareti 2008) analysing both the Italian and US press, carried out in the years after 2001, confirmed what Massari had found regarding the use of the terms 'Arab' and 'Muslim' – terms which were associated with the idea of religious fundamentalism and therefore with a potential terrorist threat. A closer look at the Italian press, in fact, reveals that there was almost inevitably a correlation between the word 'Arab', international terrorism, and the Muslim presence in Italy, thereby contributing to the stoking of a discriminatory attitude towards migrants in general. But with respect to the US press, whereas the opposition between 'us' and 'them' mostly applied to foreign policy themes, 'in the Italian press' – the researchers say – 'the opposition occurred in the daily lives of everyone, pitting Italians against their own migrant neighbours' (Battistelli, Pasini and Palareti 2008: 458). This was the position the Lega Nord sustained in political rallies and initiatives (along with allusion to the themes inherent in the 'clash of civilisations' paradigm; see Huntington 1993), thus contributing to a flaring up of internal conflict. At the same time, the Lega Nord trivialised representations of immigrant communities by generalising the cultural and religious differences which existed between migrants themselves (Allievi 2003). The Lega Nord party consequently activated what Gal and Irvine (1995) call the 'cancellation process' whereby a social group is misrepresented as being homogeneous; all internal differences are consistently ignored. The Lega Nord's narrative is best exemplified by the numerous declarations made by one of its MEPs, Mario Borghezio, who said, at a rally against the construction of a mosque in Milan, a few months after the 9/11 attacks, 'It is inadmissible that centres such as these stay open, quite obviously frequented by pro-terrorist abettors. We must shut them down to send a signal that is loud and clear: fundamentalists in Italy have no right of speech'.[11]

The firm opposition against immigration – especially involving people from Muslim-majority countries – has continued to be a mainstay of the Lega Nord policy in the post-9/11 period, as evidenced by the blatantly racist behaviour of the party's prominent exponents. For example, Giancarlo Gentilini, a former mayor of the northeastern city of Treviso, became famous for his anti-immigrant policies and hate speeches against migrants who live there,[12] while in another episode, Lega Nord members of the Trento provincial council put forward a motion for the institution of separate wagons for migrants in commuter trains. And finally, in another instance of institutional racism, MP Roberto Calderoli, speaking in 2006 about freedom of expression, appeared on TV wearing a T-shirt bearing an image of the prophet Mohammad,[13] prompting a spate of strong reactions in the Arab world, namely in Libya where a street protest in Benghazi against the Italian government called the armed forces into action and resulted in the deaths of 11 protesters.

Criminal racism

While institutional racism occurs predominantly in northern Italy – where the Lega Nord party is strongest and where the majority of Muslim immigrants live – racism elsewhere, including the south, has not been limited to political and institutional discourses. In some cases, especially in the southern regions of the country, racism has been expressed in physical acts of violence against the local immigrant population, often orchestrated by the Mafia and other local criminal organisations (Andrisani, Bontempelli, Callaioli, Chiodo, Faso, Miraglia, Naletto, Olivieri, Pona, Pugliese, Rivera and Traina 2011).

On 18 September 2008, a hit squad of the Camorra, a local crime syndicate originating in Campania, fired shots on a penny arcade at Castel Volturno, in the province of Naples, killing six African immigrants from the sub-Saharan region (Togo, Liberia and Ghana). The act of violence was part of a turf war waged on a Nigerian crime syndicate which controlled local drug trafficking and prostitution on behalf of local Camorra clans. The episode, which stood out for its gruesome brutality, highlighted the racist dimension of Camorra clans, which base their action on strong racist prejudice against migrants. The killings triggered a strong reaction on the part of local migrant communities, which staged violent protests against the criminal syndicates and also the government and local institutions who were accused of having abandoned the local territory in the hands of the *camorristi*.

Castel Volturno was not the only case in which migrants resorted to violent protest to highlight the precarious conditions in which they were often forced to live. Most immigrants in the south work in agriculture, which is a job sector that structurally requires a large number of migrant labourers (Macioti and Pugliese 1991). These workers are often exploited, live in unsuitable conditions, and have no employment or social rights whatsoever. In 2010, following the shooting of two Africans, the migrant community employed in the orange-picking sector in the Gioia Tauro plain staged a violent revolt in the city of Rosarno against the local citizens and crime syndicate, namely the *Ndrangheta*, which in that region controls not only agriculture but also drugs and arms trafficking. The revolt, which lasted several days, shed light on the inhuman conditions in which migrants were forced to live, the exploitation they underwent, and their difficult relations with local inhabitants (Filhol 2013).

Yet these forms of criminal racism cannot be ascribed exclusively to criminal organisations or to the exploitation of immigrants in the agricultural sector, nor can this form of racial prejudice be said to occur only in the south. Among the many examples of aggression and violence against migrants, one involved an attack carried out against a Roma camp by the residents of a neighbourhood in the outskirts of Turin. Hosting numerous Roma families, that illegal camp was torched after a teenager claimed to have been raped by two Roma youths. As it turned out, the girl's claim proved to be entirely false.

A final example that can be used to understand the criminal forms that racism can take concerns the killing in Florence of two Senegalese street hawkers, shot to death by an extreme right militant who then took his own life.

Populist racism

Finally, there is populist racism, a form that has developed in the last few years and is quite distinct from the other typologies of racism we have outlined. Populist racism, in fact, upholds a position whereby cultural relativism has progressively pushed aside the biological matrix which continues to underpin the previous two types of racism. Theories that national and ethnic communities are the expression of a specificity of human nature, and are therefore irreducible and different from all others, first developed and gained prominence in the 1970s (Barker 1981; Miles and Brown 1989; Taguieff 2001; Wieviorka 1995). A universal racism based on the dominance of one race over the others, and on the concept of race as a biological category, was gradually replaced by a vision of racism based not on domination, but on the exclusion of and distancing between cultures (and therefore between races) with a view to safeguarding the uniqueness of each and to offsetting the risk of a universalist acceptance (Germinario 2002).

These 'differentialist' positions, often considered less dangerous than racism grounded in a biological matrix, have gained some success in Italy and are openly sustained by numerous political formations ranging from the extreme right, namely CasaPound – which we will analyse more closely below – to the Movimento 5 Stelle, Beppe Grillo's '5-Star movement', which, in the last legislative elections, snatched 25 per cent of the votes.

As within the 5-Star movement – which claims to be 'neither rightist nor leftist' – there cohabit political cultures which are often at odds with each other,[14] and it is impossible to define a unitary position on the issue of immigration. For this reason, reference is made here to the positions held by the movement's founders, Beppe Grillo and Gianroberto Casaleggio, and other keynote exponents. Grillo has, on various occasions, vented his aversion to the idea of granting automatic citizenship to the children of immigrants who are born in Italy (the so-called *ius soli*), defining the issue as being 'senseless,' casting his anger against the 'do-gooders of the left...who will place the burden of their deliriums squarely on the shoulders of Italians'.[15] 'Help them at home' is also the mantra adopted by 5-Star exponents every time a boat carrying migrants from sub-Saharan Africa and the Maghreb sinks on its way to Lampedusa.[16] These declarations reiterate the need to oppose 'illegal' immigration by eliminating the root causes of migration to Italy and Europe, 'because immigrants must stay at home, because Africa is their home and because countries like Italy have limited ability to absorb them'.[17] According to 5-Star MP Luigi di Maio, the costs of immigration are borne entirely by Italians whose tax revenues are seen to pay for the costs of maintaining asylum seekers: 'This is sheer folly given the conditions this country is in'.[18] While these positions are not openly racist in terms of race purity and homogeneity, these statements highlight the identity and cultural aspect of immigration, seen as a cost to be borne by the community as a whole and not as an opportunity. It is an approach that neglects and simplifies the actions society should be taking with regard to social conflict, to the issues of stratification, and to ascending and descending mobility generated by the immigration phenomenon (Wieviorka 1995).

Within the framework of this typology of racism, it can be argued that separate treatment should be given to the role of the extreme right, namely the CasaPound movement.

CasaPound: 'fascists of the third millennium'

Established in Rome in 2003, following the occupation of a building in the city centre, CasaPound,[19] an extreme-right movement, soon put down roots and spread nationwide. That occupation, as with the others which followed across the country, came with a precise demand, spelled out in the banners displayed immediately following the occupation of the buildings: 'house rent is usury', 'say no to the high cost of living'. The aim of the occupation was to give a home to 20 Italian families and to state the crucial importance of house ownership while rejecting the local government's housing policies. The name chosen for the movement and its symbol – a stylised turtle – encapsulate all that the movement stands for: that is, the right to a home (turtles are animals which carry their homes with them at all times) and the fight against usury, represented by Rome's intolerably high housing rents, with prices being driven by large real estate companies. Ezra Pound, the American poet, also held this position regarding the right to property and the fight against usury.[20] As a consequence of CasaPound's drive to modernise discourse, iconography,[21] as well as expressive and stylistic codes, both media and political analysts have been led to consider CasaPound as the expression of third-millennium fascism to highlight the movement's break with Italy's neo-fascism and extreme right.

Although CasaPound's initial political action focused on social housing, before long the movement had broadened its field of interest to include issues arising from globalisation and migration.

CasaPound and immigration

CasaPound's position regarding the issue of immigration is highly articulate and complex compared to the traditional all-out rejection of immigration that has been a constant feature of extreme right movements elsewhere. CasaPound has distanced itself not only from the clash of civilisation theories (Huntington 1993) – which, as we have seen earlier, pit white, Christian, Anglo-western populations against the Arab and Islamic worlds – but also from those theories which sustain a form of identity based on an anti-immigration stance in the name of an alleged 'unsoiled whiteness' to be defended and preserved. CasaPound rejects these positions because they are considered to be the exclusive outcome of a reactionary, defensive and trivialising vision – a vision dictated by anger that does not generate the conflict that will drive a radical change in the status quo. The following can be read in a document in which the movement outlines its position on immigration:[22] for CasaPound, 'there is no such thing as a policy without an overall vision of the *polis*, without outlining an organisational structure of the state, without engaging a cultural and social struggle, without launching a counter-offensive even at a meta-political level, without spiritual commitment'.[23] For CasaPound, 'the ultimate enemy of our people and of our tradition is never another people or another tradition but is that which is hostile to all peoples and traditions' (15). In this light, the struggle against globalisation is all encompassing and seen as the enemy, inasmuch as it is a homogenising phenomenon from a cultural point of view, a harbinger of the attempt to impose the political hegemony of financial lobbies. This struggle against globalisation finds expression in the rejection of what CasaPound calls the 'multiracial society' which it rejects from political, cultural and social points of view:

- From the political point of view, the intensification of the phenomenon of migration embodies the failure on the part of national states to protect their own citizens.
- From the cultural point of view, multiracial society is believed to be the outcome of a process driven by globalisation, which is destroying and standardising all cultural differences.
- From the social point of view, the migration phenomenon must be opposed because it leads to declining rights and protections for all individuals.

CasaPound considers the presence of irregular migrant workers in the labour market to be a form of unfair competition levered by unscrupulous entrepreneurs. In particular, immigrants are considered to be the new slaves of global society, instrumental within the entrepreneurial system, illegal trade and the interests of organised crime. The positions upheld by CasaPound can be traced back to a criticism of the multicultural mode, which, as Wieviorka (2001) explains, had led the social sciences to articulate a broad and complex debate.[24] Migration is viewed as an obligatory option that is imposed on individuals, the consequence of the impoverishment of nations whose economic resources have been expropriated by multinationals. For this reason, argues CasaPound, ways should be found to govern migration flows by cooperating with non-European countries with a view to stimulating their development and to toughening restrictions so as to deter migrant inflow in Italy. These positions do not come with claims of racial superiority over migrants, marking a clear separation with the neo-fascism of the postwar years. In this light, citizenship is one of the key elements of CasaPound's action, aimed at linking a stronger citizenship with a stronger national state and a stronger Europe within a vision of citizenship which binds together rights and duties at a national and macro-regional, rather than universal, level. The state/father and citizens/children metaphor emerged often in the interviews within the framework of the research conducted by the author,[25] as militants showed their preference for the federalist option in Italy. In fact, as a militant maintained during an interview,

> The same concept that is expressed at a political level between the state and citizens can be expressed through the metaphor of the relationship between father and children. What a father wants is to make sure that his children are well, that they have a good education, find a decent job, and have a house – if you know what I mean.... And that's exactly what a state must want for its children. If a family is alright, no head of the family would have any issues about helping the neighbour (F., 24 years, Rome)

CasaPound has strongly rejected all attempts made to label it a racist movement. On various occasions, it has reiterated its ideological distance from the racist theorisations which have always been a feature of the Italian extreme right. In fact, one of the slogans of CasaPound is 'Zero per cent racism, 100 per cent identity'.

CasaPound's positions on immigration and, more generally, on the relationship between different cultures and communities, can be traced back to a current of thought that had already gained some prominence during the 1980s in France. Upheld by the *Nouvelle Droite*, and namely by its chief theoriser, Alain de Benoist, the basic tenets of this cultural matrix are (Germinario 2002):

1. a critique of neoliberalism and the minimisation of the impact of market economics;
2. offsetting the Westernisation and Americanisation of the world which has led, according to the *Nouvelle Droite*, to the homogenisation of communities, eliminating all cultural and national specificities;
3. rejection of egalitarianism, which is viewed as the consequence of the combination of individualism and mass society, stressing, at the same time, the beneficial effects of difference.

Conclusions

Over the past decade, as we have observed, Italy has witnessed growing immigration, a phenomenon that has also featured the attendant implementation, especially by successive centre-right governments, of a series of measures aimed at restricting migrant inflow and strengthening urban security (Ganalintino and Ricotta 2014). While the dramatic attacks of 11 September 2001 on the Twin Towers in New York only partly contributed to toughening security measures, they went a long way towards shifting the political and media focus on immigration and the presence in Italy of a large Muslim community. In line with a trend common to all European countries (Ignazi 2006), the issue of race as a biological and universal category has been increasingly sidelined by new – but just as dangerous – forms of institutional racism. Mainly driven by the Lega Nord party, and featuring a strong aversion to and suspicion of Muslim presence in Italy, this form of racism has combined with the rise of populist racism, grounded in the rhetoric of the exaltation of cultural differences and irreducibility. These latter positions have struck a strong chord with the new movements of the radical right, such as CasaPound, a movement which has been capable of renewing the language and characteristic positions of Italian neo-fascism with regard to immigration.

Notes

1. By this we mean the various forms of amnesty which have been granted at various points since the 1980s to irregular migrants already in Italy. These measures, taken in 1986, 1990, 1995, 1998, 2002, 2007, 2009, 2012 and 2013, triggered a fully fledged form of collective, vertical social mobility for millions of people who had either entered the country via irregular means or who had remained in Italy after the expiry of their residence permits – so-called overstayers. According to Barbagli (2006), amnesties for irregular migrants are a feature of countries where immigration is a relatively new phenomenon: for example, Italy, Greece and Portugal.
2. Law 40/1998, known as the Turco Napolitano law, introduced temporary detention centres – the Centri di Permanenza Temporanea (CPT) – for irregular migrants. The CPT were subsequently renamed CIE – Centri di Identificazione ed Espulsione (identification and deportation centres), following the enforcement of the Bossi Fini law (2002) and the successive Security Package of 2009. These structures introduced the concept of administrative detention in Italy, a legal provision depriving persons deemed to have violated an administrative rule (such as that of not possessing a residence permit) of individual liberties.
3. The Northern League, founded in the late 1980s by Umberto Bossi, is a political party characterised by a strong autonomist drive for the independence of Italy's northern regions against what is seen as a corrupt and centralised state. With the election in 2013 of Matteo Salvini as the party's new national secretary, the Northern League has focused on contrasting issues such as immigration and same-sex marriage.

4. The security package empowered local police forces to counteract irregular migration. It provided for the conviction of landlords renting homes to irregular migrants and established the criminalisation of irregular migration.
5. In contrast with the UK, the concept of ethnic minorities is not used in Italy to describe long-established communities of migrant origin.
6. Such criminal offences, based on surveys of the whole population (that is, both Italians and migrants) include homicide and attempted homicide, theft with violence and deception, car theft, burglary, theft in public places (Barbagli and Colombo 2011). That these criminal acts are committed impacts strongly on public opinion and shapes perceptions of crime and its perpetrators significantly.
7. As the European Observatory on security (2014) has highlighted, immigration and its links with criminality are perceived above all as a source of insecurity in countries like the UK and Germany, where economic concerns are less widespread.
8. Among these crimes, the one which had the strongest impact on public opinion was no doubt the murder of 47-year-old Giovanna Reggiani, who was brutally raped and killed as she was returning home on 30 October 2007, by a 24-year-old Romanian citizen who was living in a Roma camp near the Tor di Quinto railway station in Rome.
9. The term and concept 'institutional racism' is originally attributed to Stokely Carmichael, a black African-American civil rights activist. It has since been defined variously. For a recent definition as accepted by a European state – the UK – see Macpherson (1999).
10. During this phase, Lega Nord distributed flyers to party supporters gathered at a rally held by party leader Umberto Bossi in Venice on 17 September 2001, with the slogan 'clandestini = terroristi islamici' ('Illegal immigrants = Islamic terrorists') hoping to ride the strong emotional wave of public opinion that the 9/11 terrorist attacks had produced.
11. See *L'Unità*, 20 October 2001, http://cerca.unita.it/ARCHIVE/xml/25000/22458. xml?key=islam&first=401&orderby=0, accessed 20 August 2014.
12. In 1997, during his first mayoral mandate, Gentilini removed the benches near the main railway station because migrants frequented the area. Known for his many slurs against immigrants, the former mayor was condemned in May 2014 for having instigated race hate in the course of a public rally in 2008, during which he invited citizens 'to wipe the streets clean of all these ethnic groups that are ruining our country...enough of these Muslims, they must go back home...I don't want to see councillors who are black, yellow, brown, grey'. See 'Festa di popoli – Gentilini', http://youtu.be/_ WCZNQJkV3E, accessed 14 September 2014.
13. The t-shirt Calderoli was wearing bore a reproduction of a vignette published the previous day by the French newspaper *France Soir*, of the prophet Mohammed who, according to Islamic beliefs, should not be depicted in any way.
14. The 5-Star Movement (M5S) was started by the comedian Beppe Grillo and the web strategist Gianroberto Casaleggio in 2009. Starting as a civic movement, it managed to obtain 25.5 per cent of the vote in the last general election of 2013, becoming the second most moved party. Party members underline how the M5S is not a party but a movement that cannot be placed on the classical left-right scale. The M5S stand for five main issues: (1) sustainable transport,

(2) sustainable development, (3) environmentalism, (4) e-connectivity and (5) public water. For an analysis of the positions and strategies of the 5-Star Movement, reference can be made to the work by Biorcio and Natale (2012), among others, and to number 1/2013 (year XIV) of the review *Comunicazione Politica*, which is entirely dedicated to an analysis of the 5-Star Movement as a political phenomenon.

15. See http://www.beppegrillo.it/2012/01/la_cittadinanza.html and http://www.beppegrillo.it/2013/05/ius_soli.html, accessed 14 September 2014.
16. On the night of 3 October 2013, a ship sank off Lampedusa following a fire on board, killing 360 migrants who were making their way to Italy.
17. See http://www.alessandrodibattista.it/vegetarianismo-poverta-e-immigra zione/, accessed 14 September 2014.
18. See http://youtu.be/dswJz2_dhU4, accessed 14 September 2014.
19. The analysis of the CasaPound movement is based on wide-ranging research conducted by this author with Daniele di Nunzio. See Di Nunzio and Toscano (2011) and in English, Di Nunzio and Toscano (2014).
20. Ezra Pound (1885–1972), an American poet and thinker, was a staunch supporter of Benito Mussolini and the fascism of the *Repubblica Sociale*. His positions have been taken up by the Italian radical right; his writings and poems against usury (in particular *Cantos XLV*) are viewed as a critique of modern wars, capitalism, and American political, economic and cultural hegemony.
21. For example, the movement has abandoned the Celtic cross – the long-time iconic symbol of Italian neo-fascism – and has replaced it with the stylised turtle, CasaPound's trademark symbol.
22. See http://www.casapounditalia.org/2013/09/sul-fronte-dellessere-le-pro-poste-di.html, accessed 14 September 2014.
23. CasaPound Italia (2013) 'Sul fronte dell'Essere. Immigration, identity, citizenship: data, solutions and misunderstanding according to CasaPound vision', http://www.casapounditalia.org/2013/09/sul-fronte-dellessere-le-proposte-di.html, accessed 14 September 2014.
24. The literature on multiculturalism is immense and has involved not only sociologists, but also scholars in other human and social science disciplines in its theoretical debate. Reference is made in particular to the works of Kymlicka (1995), Taylor (1992) and Wieviorka (2001) and to Volume 16(1) of the review *Theory, Culture and Society*, which hosted an important international debate on these and attendant issues.
25. The ethnographic research was conducted over a period of 18 months, from April 2009 to November 2010, with 25 in-depth interviews with CasaPound leaders, members and activists recorded in Rome.

References

Allievi, S. (2003) *Islam italiano. Viaggio nella seconda religione del paese*, Turin: Einaudi.

Amico, C. and Villano P. (2007) 'L'ombra delle Torri. Una ricerca sulla rappresentazione mediatica dell'arabo dopo l'11 settembre 2001', *Psicologia Contemporanea*, 199: 54–61.

Andrisani, P., Bontempelli, S., Callaioli A., Chiodo S., Faso G., Miraglia, F., Naletto, G., Olivieri, M. S., Pona, A., Pugliese, E., Rivera, A. and Traina, I. (2011) *Chronicles of ordinary racism. Second white paper on racism in Italy,* Roma: Lunaria.

Barbagli, M. (2008) *Immigrazione e sicurezza in Italia,* Bologna: Il Mulino.

Barbagli, M. and Colombo A. (eds) (2011) *Rapporto sulla criminalità e sulla sicurezza in Italia 2010,* Rome: Fondazione ICSA.

Barker, M. (1981) *The new racism,* London: Junction Books.

Battistelli, P., Pasini, S. and Palareti, L. (2008) 'La Costruzione del nemico dopo l'11 settembre. L'effetto dell'identità dell'aggressore sulla rappresentazione del terrorismo', *Psicologia Sociale,* (1): 139–156.

Beck, U. (1992) *Risk society: towards a new modernity,* London: Sage.

Biorcio, R. and Natale, P. (2012) *Politica a 5 Stelle. Idee, storia e strategie del movimento di Grillo,* Milano: Feltrinelli.

Caritas Migrantes (2012) *Dossier Statistico Immigrazione. 22° Rapporto,* Rome: IDOS.

Caritas Migrantes (2014) *Dossier Statistico Immigrazione. Dalle discriminazioni ai diritti,* Rome: IDOS.

Di Nunzio, D. and Toscano, E. (2011) *Dentro e fuori CasaPound. Capire il fascismo del Terzo Millennio,* Roma: Armando Editore.

Di Nunzio, D. and Toscano, E. (2014) 'Taking everything back. CasaPound, a far right movement in Italy' in A. L. Farro and H. Lustiger Thaler (eds) *Reimagining social movements. From collective to individuals,* London: Ashgate, pp.251–262.

European Observatory on Security (Osservatorio Europeo sulla Sicurezza) (2014) *La Grande incertezza* (VII rapporto sulla sicurezza e l'insicurezza sociale in Italia e in Europa), Bologna, Rome, Vicenza: Fondazione Unipolis/Demos and Pi/ Osservatorio di Pavia.

Filhol, R. (2013) 'Les travailleurs agricoles migrants en Italie du Sud. Entre incompréhension, instrumentalisation et solidarités locales', *Hommes and Migrations,* 1301: 139–147.

Furedi, F. (2002) *Culture of fear: risk taking and the morality of low expectation,* London: Continuum.

Gal, S. and Irvine, J. (1995) 'The boundaries of languages and disciplines: How ideologies construct differences', *Social Research,* 62: 976–1001.

Galantino, M. G. and Ricotta G. (2014) *Domanda di sicurezza e politiche locali. Il caso del Lazio,* Milan: Franco Angeli.

Garland, D. (2001) *The culture of control: crime and social order in contemporary society,* London: Oxford University Press.

Germinario, F. (2002) *La destra degli dei. Alain de Benoist e la cultura politica della Nouvelle Droite,* Turin: Bollati Bolinghieri.

Giddens, A. (1990) *The consequences of modernity,* Cambridge: Polity Press.

Huntington, S. (1993) 'A clash of civilization?' *Foreign Affairs,* 72(3): 22–49.

Ignazi, P. (2006) *Extreme right parties in Western Europe,* Oxford: Oxford University Press.

ISTAT (2012) *Rapporto annuale 2012* (Annual Report 2012). *La situazione del paese,* Rome: ISTAT.

ISTAT (2013) 'La Popolazione straniera residente in Italia – bilancio demografico anno 2012', www.istat.it, accessed 14 September 2014.

Kymlicka, W. (1995) *Multicultural citizenship: a liberal theory of minority rights,* Oxford: Oxford University Press.

Macioti, M. I. and Pugliese, E. (1991) *Gli immigrati in Italia,* Rome-Bari: Laterza.

Macpherson, W. (1999) *The Stephen Lawrence inquiry: the report of an inquiry by Sir William Macpherson of Cluny,* London: TSO, https://www.gov.uk/government/uploads/system/uploads/attachment_data/file/277111/4262.pdf, accessed 9 March 2015.

Massari, M. (2006) *Islamofobia. La paura e l'Islam,* Rome-Bari: Laterza

Miles, R. and Brown, M. (1989) *Racism,* London: Routledge.

Taguieff, P. A. (2001) *The force of prejudice. On racism and its doubles,* Minneapolis: University of Minnesota Press.

Taylor, C. (1992) *Multiculturalism and the politics of recognition,* Princeton: Princeton University Press.

Wieviorka, M. (1995) *The arena of racism,* London: Sage.

Wieviorka, M. (2001) *La Différence,* Paris: Fayard.

8
Identitarian Populism: Securitisation of Migration and the Far Right in Times of Economic Crisis in Greece and the UK

Gabriella Lazaridis and Anna-Maria Konsta

Introduction[1]

Western states have sought to integrate securitisation measures within migration regimes as asylum seekers and other migrant categories come to be seen as agents of social instability or as potential terrorists seeking to exploit immigration systems. Security concerns have topped western political agendas since the attacks of 9/11, and given that these attacks were carried out by non-state agents, the Cold War argument that security should also be about combating non-military threats was resurrected by governments in the west. Included among the non-military threats to state security is migration, the idea being that liberal migration regimes advance cross-border risks – for example, that of terrorism – while more restrictive regimes minimise such threats and improve national and societal security. In the Greek case, harsh austerity measures imposed upon Greek citizens resulted in even harsher anti-immigration measures imposed upon immigrants. Securitisation of migration in Greece, especially after the outbreak of the current economic crisis in the country, was followed by the emergence of a populist far right party as a considerable political force.

In the current European political climate, with political institutions in the process of configuring themselves in accordance with the new realities of the post-financial crisis environment, the potential for populist groups to attract large numbers of followers is of renewed importance. In light of this, this chapter looks at *majority identitarian populist* parties in the UK and Greece: two countries with contrasting historical and politico-economic trajectories, both affected by the current economic crisis but to different degrees and dealing with the crisis in different ways. Focusing on the core narratives of two *identitarian populist* parties, the BNP in the UK and Golden Dawn in Greece, we show how they take advantage of the securitisation of migration and how, via populist actions, exclusionary practices are promoted through the construction of Otherness. These actions are commonly heralded as answers to the contemporary hardships encountered by citizens in their daily lives, such as changes in the economy, work and social organisation, and range from profound hostility to immigration and multiculturalism in the UK, to covert and overt violence against the Other in Greece.

Populisms and identitarian populism

In the last 20 years, the populist trend in Europe has been investigated by academics, while the term 'populism' itself has crossed the boundaries of academic debates into the political arena, and into everyday language. In-depth analyses of populism (for example, Betz 1994) feature scholarship focusing on radical right parties (Kitschelt 2007), the new populist right (Laycock 2005; Mudde 2004), far right parties (Taggart 2004), the right-wing populism (Helms, 1997; Laclau 2005), radical right populism (Rydgren 2003), or simply the populist parties (Fella and Ruzza 2009). The distinction extends the taxonomy to include neo-liberal populism and national-populism (Betz 1994). Populism has been dismissed as being nothing more than a rhetorical style common to politicians, as described in Canovan's (1981) concept of 'politician's populism'. Some have described populism as a 'thin ideology', able to borrow ideas from a range of political perspectives (Stanley 2008: 95), or as lacking an ideological base. This has led to calls (Roxborough 1984) for eliminating the concept, given the difficulties in providing a clear-cut definition, because of its wide geographical and chronological extension and its multifaceted nature. Sartori (1970) speaks of 'conceptual stretching' – namely, distorting the concept when it does not fit the case under examination and adjusting it to denote too large an array of political tendencies. A consequence of these differences is that some scholars prefer to talk about 'populisms'. Reflecting this uncertainty, the label populism has been applied to a massive array of parties, groups and narratives, from Russian Narodnicks to Italian comedians such as Bepe Grillo.

There are three key elements in populism. Firstly, populists claim to speak on behalf of a mass that can be defined as members of a national community that share a culture, a language, interests or the belief in the values of belonging to a group or culture. As such, the construction of the 'people' is rendered a genuine, homogeneous and democratic sovereign (Canovan 1999), in other words, an ideal totality (Laclau 2005). Secondly, populists cast the people in opposition to an elite. Political elites and intellectuals are accused by populists of being undemocratic, incapable, unproductive and privileged, distant or alienated from the people or lacking in the plebescitarian quality of common sense (Mény and Surel 2002). Finally, and as a result of the conception of the mass, populists identify some form of threatening Other. Groups that are Othered are depicted as depriving the 'sovereign' people of their rights, values and prosperity, thus explaining why the elites and the mass are seemingly disconnected (Albertazzi and McDonnell 2008). Zaslove (2008: 323) discusses how adept populist groups are at identifying dangerous Others who lie 'outside the heartland' and the lack of ideological boundaries with populist parties on both the left and right. Zaslove (Ibid.) argues that parties of the right are more likely to point to 'immigrants', 'environmentalists', the 'unemployed' and 'feminists' as scapegoats. This list could include homosexuals, the disabled, asylum seekers and other minority groups.

These three components illustrate the basic elements of populism but are still fluid enough to allow for the massive array of *populisms* seemingly on offer in the political marketplace. These essential building blocks can almost endlessly be ripped up and reconfigured to form new narratives with a range of groups filling the various roles of the mass, elite and Other. This paper focuses on a particular interpretation of populism that we have termed *majority identitarian populism*. The *majority identitarian populist* narrative centres on the concept of identity as a tool for determining who belongs to the mass. This can be based on any number of characteristics such as religion, ethnicity or values. Majority *identitarian populists* claim to speak for what they see as the (current) majority group.[2] The Other is usually a group considered not to belong to the mass, as defined by the organisation. The Other in *identitarian populist* narratives differs in some key respects which can include ethnicity, but could also be based on citizenship status, language skills, religion or a mixture of different or unspecified criteria. Elites are often presented as either unable to prevent the threat presented by the Other, and therefore as incompetent, or actively conspiring against the mass. Frequently, this role is filled by political leaders seen as complicit in mass immigration or European integration or both (depending on the nature of the Other).

In some cases, they may even be presented as engaged in conspiracy, colluding with the Other against the interests of the mass. The final stipulation of *majority identitarian populism* is the need for the populist narrative to be central to the party. What Canovan (1981) terms 'populist calls' alone is not sufficient. To be considered a majority *identitarian populist* party, the organisation must not be operating in a wider social context. This definition, in practice, takes in many of the parties that have been described as radical or far right, but it excludes mainstream political parties that may make populist calls.

Methods

A series of semi-structured interviews were carried out between May and September 2013 in both the UK and Greece with members of *identitarian populist* movements and parties. Interviewees included youth members, intermediate activists, and in some cases, senior figures and were analysed through a grounded theory approach.

The process of obtaining interviews in the Greek context was revealing about the nature of the organisations being contacted. In most cases, initial contact was made through personal contacts of the researchers, as official path routes proved to be ineffective. This approach demonstrates that Greek politics are still heavily dominated by a network of interpersonal and, in a way, clientelistic relationships. Golden Dawn's members were keen to provide information, especially about their ideological background, in an effort to disconnect it from pro-Nazism allegations. In some cases, interviewees were reluctant to engage with us, especially older members, whereas younger individuals with university education, and in some instances studies in the UK, were more open to participate in a UK university-originated research.

In the UK, in most cases initial contact was made through email inviting subjects to an interview. The email was deliberately very open about the funding and scope of the project, and included a link to a project description hosted on the university website. In cases where no email address was available, contact was made over social networking sites. For example, contact was made with members of the Young BNP through their Facebook page. In some cases, interviewees were reluctant to engage with members of the academic community. One mid-level organiser from the BNP refused to be interviewed on the grounds of the National Union of Students' (NUS) 'no platform policy', which prevents members of the BNP from speaking on NUS-affiliated campuses. Other possible subjects were extremely reluctant to talk and exhibited strong concern for their personal privacy and a desire to maintain anonymity, even from the researchers.

What makes qualitative research in this area so difficult is that academics are often perceived as being part of the elite and therefore incapable of being honest brokers who objectively and dispassionately communicate the words of research subjects without twisting them to their own ends.

Case studies

Greece

A shift in Greek politics occurred after the global economic crisis of 2008 and the collapse of the Greek economy in 2010. This was followed by a number of rescue packages from the European Union (EU) and the International Monetary Fund (IMF) (Matsaganis 2011; Georgiadou, Kafe and Nezi 2012) and by unprecedented harsh austerity measures which affected society as a whole and increased poverty[3] (Marinakou 2013) to such an extent that some commentators go as far as to claim that Greece is now facing a humanitarian crisis (Politaki 2013). Following the austerity measures, the social contract (Rousseau 1762), according to which self-interested, rational, but equal human beings agree with one another to live together under common laws and create an enforce-ment mechanism managed by a civil authority or government (in the past, the sovereign) has started to break down in three ways: first, the Eurozone mechanisms under the German umbrella preserve the neo-liberal ideology of the free market, and whose response to the crisis is to apply more of the same and quicker: privatisations and removing workers' rights, among other things, all of which had formed the basis of the contract. Second, the workers and their union representatives see the contract as one-sided, and failing to include them. Third, the Euro-crisis destroys not just jobs, but the very underpinnings of society. People who took actions that were prudent at the time are increasingly at the mercy of forces beyond their control, managed by unknown economic centres, strong central European governments, and European elites. At the same time, the Greek state during the management of the crisis has become increasingly a repressive force, and the austerity measures threaten its own existence and legitimacy. There is an increasing mistrust – not only towards government, but also towards the political system as a whole. Moreover, the Greek immigration framework has created inequalities even among immigrants, and has created 'plastic' subjectivities easily mouldable by public authorities; in this sense, a plastic or protean citizenship emerged for immigrants in Greece (Konsta and Lazaridis 2010; O'Brien 2013). Immigration featured very prominently in most political party programs and public discourses as a fundamental security concern.

The financial and economic crisis in Greece resulted in a shift of the Greek immigration policy, and harsh austerity measures imposed upon Greek citizens resulted in even harder anti-immigration measures. Securitisation of migration has largely affected a great portion of youth in Greece. Second generation immigrants, but also children who enter the country as asylum seekers from countries such as Syria, end up in detention centres with adults, and are often separated from their families. Public debates on the adoption of a new anti-racist legislation have reached a deadlock, and the country seems to be divided in a hate/anti-hate discourse mainly focused on illegal immigration. Harsh austerity measures imposed upon Greek citizens are not the only reason for this deep division in society. Non-effective public policies over the past 20 years related to immigration in the country that led to securitisation of migration have played an important role, as has the application of the securitisation lenses to migration by the media, which has amplified the perceived threats to Greek identity, values and security that this phenomenon poses and enabled the Greek people to interpret, categorise and evaluate migration accordingly.

A new generation of stateless people is emerging in Greece. These are second-generation immigrants, in some cases, with no citizenship rights in any country in the world, since being born, raised and educated in Greece has left them with no cultural ties with the homeland of their parents. In February 2013, the council of the state, the highest administrative court, in Greece upheld to annul Law 3838/2010, which fast-tracked the naturalisation process for second-generation immigrants. Essentially, the court declared unconstitutional the provision that gave the right to vote to municipal and prefectural elections to immigrants holding a temporary residence permit, and the provision that allowed second-generation immigrants to acquire Greek citizenship only because they are born in Greece or after having studied for six consecutive years in a Greek school. The Greek authorities would need to reconsider every naturalisation already granted under the 2010 law's conditions.

The Greek state's policies on securitisation of migration have been dominated so far by realist ideas, which consider the state as the only object of security (Karyotis 2011: 15), and have largely neglected the people-centred or human security approach. According to Hannah Arendt (1976), in order to make human rights possible, the right to have rights must be ensured. From this derives the notion that human security approach is based on humanitarian principles. The underlying principle is making the individual and communities secure. To achieve this, citizenship cannot be viewed as a contractual relationship between state and individual, but as an association based on solidarity and mutual responsibility among all members in society, including immigrants and their children.

In this socioeconomic context, a number of newly formed or smaller *identitarian populist* political groups of the far right emerged on the Greek political scene; some (the Independent Greeks and the Golden Dawn) gained political representation in the Greek Parliament after the May and June 2012 national elections.

The results of the 2012 national elections[4] may have been largely determined by the degree of public anger at the EU-IMF rescue package for Greece and the desire to deliver a shock protest vote against the two main established parties: the conservative New Democracy and the socialist PASOK. Nevertheless, immigration also featured prominently in most party programmes and public discourses as a fundamental security concern. Golden Dawn was the most spectacular beneficiary of the securitisation of the immigration debate, rising from 0.29 per cent in 2009 to almost 7 per cent in 2012 and winning respectively 21 and 18 parliamentary seats in the May and June 2012 elections. The electoral system in Greece is 'reinforced proportionality', according to which a party must secure at least 3 per cent of the vote to be represented in parliament, and the party that wins the plurality of votes cast is awarded an extra 50 seats. Before the 2012 national elections, Golden Dawn never managed to be represented in the Greek Parliament due to this threshold.

The social process behind the magic rise of the Golden Dawn is based on the general unreliability of the political system and the democratic institutions, and the systematic breakdown of important institutions by the political elites. According to the European social survey, Greek citizens in 2002 were asked how highly they would rank their trust in parliament and politicians on a scale of 0 to 10 (10 the highest score); 61 per cent and 80 per cent, respectively, gave responses from zero to five. In 2010, 92 per cent and 96 per cent, respectively, ranked their trust from zero to five, which is among the lowest trust in political institutions within Europe, and the country has diverged further from the EU average on the trust dimensions ever since.[5] In this context, the young have lost trust in politicians and political institutions. And this belief may fuel violence as their response. Following the killing of 15-year-old Alexis Grigoropoulos by a police officer on 6 December 2008, school and university students rose up in an unprecedented outpouring of rage. Spontaneous demonstrations, mostly organised by email and SMS, shook towns and cities across the country.

A further factor explaining the rise of the Golden Dawn has been the lack of another powerful conservative political pole to compensate for a shift to the extreme right (Marvakis, Anastassiadou, Petritsi and Anagnostopoulou 2013: 5). New Democracy and LAOS, which used to be the major representatives of the Right in Greece, were accused by many of their supporters of collaborating with the EU and IMF against the interests of Greek people. The phenomenon of the Golden Dawn interests academics of the far right in Greece, and new literature is being published discussing its rise in the Greek political system (Xenakis 2012; Doxiadis and Matsaganis 2012; Georgiadou and Rori 2012; Zouboulakis 2013; Ellinas 2013; Koronaiou and Sakellariou 2013).

Golden Dawn campaigned in both 2012 national elections based on concerns for unemployment, austerity and the economy, as well as virulent anti-immigration rhetoric. In May 2012, action squads organised by Golden Dawn, terrorised for days immigrants detained in special facilities in the outskirts of Patras, which is the third largest city in Greece. The level of public tolerance towards, or even support for, such actions is difficult to gauge. However, recent opinion polls[6] show that support for Golden Dawn jumped from 6.9 per cent to 11.5 per cent after the 2012 parliamentary elections, a percentage which ranked Golden Dawn as the third political party in electoral support behind New Democracy and Syriza (the coalition of the radical left).

Golden Dawn has been developing a social programme, including the delivery of free or minimal cost food among the most unfavoured strata of ethnic Greeks. Under the slogan 'Return Greek people's money to the people', they have organised open food donations in central squares all over Greece. In one of the public food donations in Athens, Golden Dawn MP Ilias Panagiotaros refused to give food to an old immigrant lady and urged her to go and ask for food from the left coalition party Syriza, which, according to his opinion, is the protector of immigrants (Koronaiou and Sakellariou 2013: 336). Another area of activism in which Golden Dawn allegedly engages is offering protection for victims of crime, a service that has been appreciated by citizens and utilised by the police, who refer Athenians to Golden Dawn for help, especially when immigrant crime is involved. The party, however, demands allegiance in return for their service. The myth of the little 'boy scouts' of the Golden Dawn has widely been reproduced by the media.

One of the actions Golden Dawn took after the 2012 elections was to create a blood bank. Announcements and slogans such as 'donate blood – save a Greek soul' were widely circulated, and it was clearly stated in the text accompanying this announcement that the blood is 'only for Greeks'.

Golden Dawn can be characterised as a majority *identitarian populist* party that places the identity of the majority, defined as ethnic Greeks, at its centre. As a Golden Dawn activist told us, 'Greek is only the person born by two Greek parents'. And another one said, 'I am against inter-racial marriage because it goes against the purity of our race'. Another health initiative has been the formation in December 2012 of 'Medicines Avec Frontiers', in opposition to the international organisation 'Medicines Sans Frontiers'. In their inaugural announcement, they stated that the service is only for Greeks and called on Greek doctors to participate. They also state that 'almost 3 million illegal immigrants are treated by the Greek hospitals for free and this is the basic reason why the health system is in this mess' (Koronaiou and Sakellariou 2013: 334).

As far as unemployment is concerned, Golden Dawn's anti-immigrant rhetoric is summarised in their repeatedly used slogan, 'every foreign worker is a Greek unemployed'. Incidents like the recent one in a straw-berry production farm in southern Greece where Bangladeshi strawberry pickers were shot, but luckily only slightly injured, by their supervisors for demanding to get paid for six months of unpaid work,[7] have been supported by Golden Dawn's anti-immigrant rhetoric. Although in this particular case, Golden Dawn has publicly refused its involvement and condemned the shootings, it made an official announcement that these issues arise because jobs were stolen from Greeks and given to illegal immigrants, and the only solution to the problem is the imme-diate expulsion of all illegal immigrants.[8] Members of Golden Dawn have reportedly been involved in numerous incidents of hate speech and crime based on victims' national, ethnic, religious, and sexual iden-tities and are profoundly opposed to immigration; when asked about Golden Dawn's immigration policy a prominent Golden Dawn activist told us, 'first...we shut down our borders...second...all those who are currently inside the country with no documents, no papers, will be sent back'. When he was asked where they would go, he replied, 'Let them go wherever!'

A document posted on the Golden Dawn site – 'political positions' – stated that all illegal immigrants would be arrested and sent to special detention centres pending repatriation, where 'the conditions would not resemble a 5-star hotel'.[9] In addition, all of the Golden Dawn interviewees were against the creation of a mosque in Athens, and they expressed concerns regarding the increase of Muslim immigrants in the country. Furthermore, one Golden Dawn member characterised the Roma population in Greece as 'Bulgarian/Turkish-gypsies who have nothing to do with the Roma in Europe, and should be kicked out of the country, since they are here just to work as professional beggars'.

All Golden Dawn interviewees expressed concerns about Zionism, and many openly denied the Holocaust, arguing that the figure of the death toll of the Jewish population, at the hands of the Nazis during WWII, had been largely fabricated. The party's spokesman, in a public speech in the Greek parliament in June 2013, admitted openly that Golden Dawn members denied the holocaust.[10]

Today's youth in Greece is possibly the first generation since the Second World War that will be worse off than their parents. Youth unemployment is exceptionally high with European figures reporting a youth unemployment rate greater than 50 per cent; according to data released by the Greek Statistical Authority, in May 2013, unemployment rates in the age groups between 15–24 and 25–34 years were 64.9 per cent and 37.7 per cent, and the overall unemployment rate for all age groups amounted to 27.6 per cent.[11] According to the president of the Afghan community in Athens, Golden Dawn recruits people from a very young age, and they participate as minors in action squads, which attack immigrants in specific neighbourhoods in Athens such as Agios Panteleimonas and Plateia Atikis. Younger activists are thought more likely to receive lenient treatment from the police.

Moreover, Golden Dawn has formed a nonprofit organisation, which they have named OAED (in Greek), after the acronym of the official state organisation for the unemployed, which literally means 'Manpower Employment Organisation', but in the case of the Golden Dawn organisation, the acronym means 'Group for Unemployed Hard-Hit Greeks' (Koronaiou and Sakellariou 2013: 335). The purpose of this organisation, which operates illegally, according to the Greek Ministry of Labour, is to find jobs only for Greeks;[12] it does this in collaboration with local Golden Dawn offices.

Golden Dawn also has a growing presence among students in state high schools around the country and targets pupils at primary schools. Its official website recently hosted pictures of neatly dressed six- to ten-year-olds, accompanied by parents, at a 'national awakening' session held at a Golden Dawn branch office outside Athens. The session included a discussion on 'the Olympian gods, the ancient Greek pantheon and the Christian faith'.[13] It is quite active through the Internet, where it mainly promotes issues related to the party's social programme. There are also websites supportive of Golden Dawn, which are devoted to nationalist ideals.[14] Finally, Golden Dawn operates a number of blogs. A heavily visited blog is the party's New York-based blog, 'Xaameriki' (http://xaameriki.wordpress.com/). Young people are mobilised via such sites. Younger activists are thought more likely to receive lenient treatment from the police. In the Greek context, youths participate in *identitarian populist* parties such as the Golden Dawn in order to feel a sense of belonging, security and protection against a collapsing world. Golden Dawn, in particular, with its military-like organisation, provides a sort of structure and stability in a disintegrating and deconstructed society. When asked about youth participation, a Golden Dawn interviewee responded,

> Certainly there is an increase...certainly it is growing every day...in major cities of Greece...Athens...Thessaloniki...the percentage of the youth participation in Golden Dawn is far ahead of the other parties...far ahead...it means that...desperate young person...seeing that there is no hope...turns to nationalism...thinking that this closed system...might spare him the problems of...uh...monopolies and globalisation.

Another reason why the young are attracted to the Golden Dawn may be the party's social action programme, which may create a sense of meaning in their lives, making them feeling useful in a society with high youth unemployment (around 60 per cent in 2015). All our interviewees felt quite strongly about their party's social action programme, and they were keen to promote it as the 'only alternative to the failure of the Greek welfare state'. A Golden Dawn member said in relation to this,

> With the various social actions, and the gatherings we organise, like the ones where children are learning about Greek history and ideology...so this is how our ideology is cultivated. Beyond that, someone who has lost his job...has been mugged 17 times by foreigners...they have raped...uh...his wife...uh...or his mother...uh...and is a victim of too many unlawful acts committed by all these scums...it is possible to come to us...slowly they see and they are fully nurtured by our ideology...all those votes and even

more so were not from members of the Golden Dawn party. ... they are from sympathisers who are potential political soldiers of the People's Association ... through our various social actions which, as you see, are continuing and ... uh ... unstoppable.

UK

Despite the financial crisis, the UK offers a relatively stable and prosperous backdrop for populist politics and the mobilisation of young people. Following the 2010 UK general election, the UK is led by a coalition of the centre-right Conservative and centre Liberal Democrat parties. Such a coalition is unusual in the UK, due to the use of single member plurality voting. In opposition sits the Labour party, which is struggling to recover from an unpopular premiership by Gordon Brown. Current polling information suggests that the Labour Party is currently in the ascendancy, sitting around 8 per cent, above the Conservatives, with the Liberal Democrats at 11 per cent.[15]

Following the financial crisis, the dominant theme in UK politics is the government's austerity drive, characterised by large scale cuts across many government departments, as part of what David Cameron described in 2009, following significant contractions in GDP, as the 'Age of Austerity'.[16] Grimshaw and Rubery (2012) have described the impact of coalition approach towards the welfare state as being negative for young people in the UK: tripling the level of university fees, revoking the Educational Maintenance Allowance (EMA),[17] and extending the age at which young people were considered to still be dependents and therefore unable to qualify for independent housing benefits (raised from 25 to 35).

Young people (under 25) have suffered disproportionately compared to older workers during the financial crisis, as displayed by the youth unemployment rate (Bell and Blanchflower 2011: 264). In 2012, of those able to work, 21 per cent of those under the age of 25 were unemployed, compared to 5.7 per cent of those aged between 25 and 74.[18] For comparison, the figure for under 25s in 2000 was 12.2 per cent. The UK youth unemployment figure compares favourably with the European average, 23 per cent unemployment amongst under 25s. The unemployment rate covers only those available and actively seeking work, so the true impact of the recession may be larger. The idea of a lost generation has also been encapsulated in the figures for those 'not in education, employment or training' the so-called NEETS. The office for National Statistics currently estimates that 1.09 million people between the ages of 16 and 24 fall into this category (ONS 2013).

It becomes clear then that whilst young people in the UK are far from the worst off in Europe, they are facing challenges. Despite this, there is little sign that young people are organised politically, and most research suggests that they do not engage in formal collective action through electoral politics. Recent figures, collected by the Hansard Society (2013: 21) show similarly low levels of political participation by 18–24 year olds, with only 12 per cent of those questioned reporting that they were likely to vote, down from 22 per cent the previous year. This is against an overall figure of 41 per cent of citizens reporting that they were certain to vote in the event of a general election (Ibid.: 18). However, there is evidence that less formal and more individualistic participation in the UK is relatively common, especially amongst young people, such as petitions and boycotts. This trend is consistent with wider social change, as society goes through a process of individualisation that has made it difficult, for younger people especially, to connect with formal, organised political parties (Pattie, Seyd and Whiteley 2004: 87; Henn, Weinstein and Wring 2002).

Outside of the formal political parties in the UK, all of whom have youth wings, there are a range of political organisations, many of them conforming to the *identitarian populist* framework established above, that may attempt to mobilise supporters; these include the British National Party (BNP), a nationalist political party that has long been perceived as the face of far-right politics in the UK. The BNP won two seats in the 2009 European elections with close to a million votes, a ninefold increase on their previous total, making them the most successful extreme right party in the UK (Ford and Goodwin 2010: 4). The 2009 European parliamentary election, however, marked the electoral high-point for the BNP, and was the result of concerted effort by the party since 1999 to present itself as an electable force in UK politics. In both the 2010 general election and the regular council elections since, the BNP has suffered a reversal of fortunes. It retains its two MEPs (although one MEP resigned from the party in 2012); it is still without representation at the national level and has only two remaining local councillors. The electoral ups and downs of the BNP have been accompanied by a constantly evolving ideological position. From 1999 onwards, and under the leadership of Nick Griffin, the BNP has sought to undergo a process of modernisation designed to break the connection to fascism exhibited by crude racism and anti-Semitism and replace it with a softer and more socially acceptable programme (Eatwell 2004; Atton 2006; Mammone 2009; Rhodes 2009; Goodwin 2010). Halikiopoulou and Vasilopoulou (2010) argue that post-1999, the BNP's manifestos reveal a shift in their understanding of the nation and nationalism. Whilst race forms a significant basis for the BNP's nationalism, this is increasingly alongside narratives that emphasise civic values such as rule of law, citizenship and political rights (Ibid.: 588).

From the viewpoint of the *identitarian populist* template, the BNP's discourse clearly matches the three elements described: protection of the mass, identification of a threatening Other, and anti-elitism. Beginning with how the BNP understands and represents itself, its members, and the majority of the British public (that is, the mass), the 2010 BNP election manifesto was clear: ethnicity remains a component of the BNP's understanding of British identity and the party had a focus on protecting the rights of the 'indigenous' British (BNP 2010: 12). The ambiguities of this approach can be seen in the following extract from the manifesto:

> The BNP recognises the right of legally settled and law-abiding minorities to remain in the UK and enjoy the full protection of the law, on the understanding that the indigenous population of Britain has the right to remain the majority population of our nation. (Ibid.: 16)

In this context, indigenous is synonymous with 'white'; however, this is far from the kind of exclusionary language associated with ethnic nationalism. The evolving position on who constitutes the mass within the UK is partly confirmed through interviews with activists. One middle-aged, female BNP activist maintained the focus on natural divisions between peoples, saying, 'We're all put in our countries for a reason'. Further questions however revealed a more complex understanding of identity. The same activist, whilst maintaining the importance of ethnic distinctions in constructing citizenship, invoked the concept of civic citizenship based on the shifting narratives described in the analysis of Halikiopoulou and Vasilopoulou (2010). Quite what civic citizenship amounts to, and the status of civic citizens in relation to the 'indigenous' British, is not made clear: 'Well, they can't be British English, can they? How can a black man or a Pakistani – he's a Pakistani – how can he be English? He can't – he should never deny his heritage, anyway, but they can be civic citizens'.

In a separate interview, a middle-aged, male BNP activist, when asked if British identity included a cultural as well as a racial component, responded, 'The way we live our lives, the English live their lives. Yeah, I think it's unique'. He went on to suggest that if minorities were prepared to assimilate (westernise), only then they could be considered to be citizens: 'Well, they fit in, wherever they want to fit in. If they want be westernised, that's fine. But there's not a lot to say about that'.

Representing the mass in this way, even if it's not entirely based on an ethnic interpretation of British identity, inevitably results in the establishment of an in-group and an out-group: those who are not part of the mass the BNP claims to represent. The BNP 2010 manifesto presents a wider range of targets for this type of Othering behaviour, namely immigrants, EU, Muslims and those convicted of a crime. Speaking with activists, however, they chose to dwell on two central concerns: immigration and European integration.[19] Opposition to both these trends seems to stem from the nationalist stance of the BNP, with both immigration and closer European integration felt to be a threat to national identity. In discussing immigration, interviewees did not specifically attack immigrants themselves, and instead often presented themselves as sympathetic to but rejecting immigration, primarily on resource grounds. The following example from a young BNP (YBNP) activist strongly emphasised what they see as the economic case for halting immigration:

> You can't sustain an unprecedented amount of people coming and staying, for the most part, because we're an island, we're very small and it is an issue and it needs to be resolved. Because we're overpopulated as it is.

When pressed for detail, specific forms of immigration were considered more acceptable than others. For example, when asked about overseas students coming to the UK, one YBNP activist stressed that he did not consider this to be part of wider immigration patterns: 'That's on a different level altogether, isn't it? If people come here for education, it's separate'.

Whilst it was clear that immigration was perceived to be a central political problem for the BNP, as the quote below from another YBNP activist illustrates, the focus of criticism is on political leaders as opposed to immigrants:

> But I think where the main problem lies is, not the people that come here, but the issue would be that we allow this to happen. For them to come here and it doesn't help them in any way, it's much more than what we would help them in another way. I think there's all kinds of solutions to that sort of immigration.

The anti-elitist element in BNP literature is one of the strongest components in the BNP's manifesto. In a section entitled 'Counter jihad', the

manifesto argues that mainstream political parties have been responsible for encouraging mass immigration, which they argue will lead to
'most of Europe colonised by Islam within a few decades' (BNP 2010: 5).
Here one must bear in mind that the 7 July 2005 London bombings had
given new impetus to questions of socioeconomic, as well as cultural,
exclusion and alienation in Muslim communities. Prime Minister Tony
Blair made this connection explicit in a major speech just one month
after the bombings, when he claimed that 'coming to Britain is not a
right. And even when people have come here, staying here carries with
it a duty. That duty is to share and support the values that sustain the
British way of life'.

Other activists we interviewed expressed a profound disconnection
from mainstream politics, accusing political figures of being arrogant,
shallow, and in one case, traitorous: 'Teddy [Edward Heath] took us into
the EU illegally – he was a traitor and a bastard because he did commit
treason against this country without a shadow of a doubt'.

Having established their brand of politics, we now go on to explore
how the BNP has sought to engage with young people. Evidence to
date suggests that BNP activists are predominantly drawn from older
cohorts, rather than from the young, a trend that Goodwin puts down
to the coming of age of many older groups during the Powellism of
the 1960s and 70s in the UK, and therefore as identifying to a greater
extent with the 'exclusionary' BNP (2010: 42). In contrast, online the
BNP is active on Facebook, and analysis of the groups Facebook page
has shown a majority of those who have joined the BNP Facebook
group are under 25: 62 per cent of the sample of 82,700 (Bartlett,
Birdwell and Littler 2011: 34). The BNP also maintains a specific youth
wing that is active on Facebook – Young BNP – which currently maintains an active Facebook page (with 955 'likes'). BNP campaign material stresses the importance of the YBNP as part of the wider BNP party
structure, arguing,

> The success of our youth wing, the YBNP, is one of the most impor-
> tant objectives of the Party. After all, it is for the rights and freedoms
> of our own children and grandchildren that we are fighting, and we
> have to recruit new, young activists or the party would gradually die
> off! (BNP Activists Handbook, n.d.: 40)

However, given the low levels of youth involvement in politics in the UK,
and the seemingly shrinking levels of support for the BNP (see above),
increasing membership of YBNP seems likely to be challenging. This

was recognised by the YBNP members interviewed, who put the size of the YBNP in their region at 100–200. There was also a clear recognition that formal YBNP membership was often secondary for looser and more informal relationships with the party. Increasingly, it was reported, the YBNP had supporters rather than members; however, this was seen to be common to all political parties: 'Supporting, active yeah, but you're problem is, there are a lot more supporters than there are active people. It's always a big problem with all politics, I would say'. They also felt that many young people who could be attracted to the BNP were put off by the stigma attached to the party:

> Yeah, even then there's a lot more activists than you get made aware of, simply because of other external factors, such as the stigma that comes with the BNP and they don't wish to be seen in pictures and such.

None of the interviewees were able to give details about any recruitment drives targeted at young people specifically, and given the apparent size of the YBNP, and in spite of claims made in the activist handbook (BNP n.d.) it seems that YBNP remains a small-scale group. Both the YBNP members interviewed fit the profile, suggested by Goodwin (2010), of self-starters. On encountering a BNP street stall at the time of the last general election (2010) both claim to have done further research into political parties and compared their policy positions, including researching material online:

> We joined the Youth BNP when we met them at a stall. They had a stall held in [place name], which was the British National Party in general. And they're there often, and they give out leaflets and such, and we took, I took one of the leaflets, and I was interested by what I read, and I looked into it further and decided it was right for me.

Surprisingly, however, members of the YBNP saw themselves as being exceptional amongst their peers for their interest in politics and were critical of those not politically engaged:

> I think people should realise its significance, especially youth, of politics. If you're not paying attention to a governing body that controls every aspect of your life until you die, then you're just socially inept. And I find it stupid that people go, 'I don't pay attention to politics.'

Well you whinge about this, you whinge about that, or you like that. But you don't think to yourself, 'Hold on, I actually have power to make a change in this governing body'.

Conclusions

Data collected from activists in both the Golden Dawn and the BNP has revealed a surprising amount of diversity in the parties' understanding of who they represent, and in their attitudes and praxis towards the other and their appeal to young people.

Both groups fit the template of *majority identitarian populism* as identified in the theoretical section. Despite this, there was considerable variation with how they constructed their specific brands of populism. For the Golden Dawn, the mass was constituted firmly by 'ethnic' Greeks born of two Greek parents. Manifesto material from the BNP reveals a similar ethnic component, although with imprecise emphasis on both parents' origins being British, promising to defend the 'indigenous' British. However, face-to-face interviews with BNP and YBNP members, unlike those of the Golden Dawn, reveals a mindset potentially less extreme than the reputation of the party suggests. Unlike the Golden Dawn, electoral necessity has seemingly led to the BNP attempting to ameliorate some of its most exclusionary tendencies, as shown by the willingness to extend civic citizenship to those born outside of the UK. Undoubtedly, this should not be considered citizenship on equal terms with the 'indigenous' population.

In constructing the Other, Golden Dawn interviewees were overt in the criticism of migrants and ethnic minorities, such as the Roma. Moreover, securitisation of migration state policies in Greece has fuelled Golden Dawn's anti-immigrant rhetoric. In contrast, the BNP interviewees exhibited little direct hostility towards immigrants and British minorities. Every BNP interviewee was careful to stress their inclusive credentials and to counter accusations of racism, and unlike Golden Dawn, none of the interviewees was directly critical of immigrants themselves. In part, this is likely down to acute sensitivity and awareness of previous portrayals of the party in the media and academia. In other words, everyone was likely on their best behaviour. The fiercest criticism from the BNP interviewees was reserved not for the Other, but for the elite. Mainstream political parties, characteristically referred to as the 'old gang' in BNP literature, are described as being arrogant and out of touch with the majority of the public (BNP 2010: 18). On the other hand, the Golden Dawn, having won a substantial number of sears in the Greek parliament, gauged their criticism towards the EU and IMF, and comparatively slightly less to the state apparatus.

In relation to the recruitment of young people, both the Golden Dawn and the BNP demonstrated an awareness of the importance of young people to the future of their parties. Whilst the Golden Dawn was clearly optimistic about its ability to recruit new and youthful members, the BNP was decidedly less so. This may be partly explained by the vastly different social situations. Whereas the UK has come through the economic crisis comparatively well, the financial pressures and rapidly degenerating social circumstances of the Greek case may well be acting as a recruiting sergeant for Golden Dawn. There is also some evidence that Greek society may be predisposed towards nationalist and exclusionary narratives. For example, a survey conducted by the National Centre for Social Research at the end of the 1990s illuminates in a better way how the young people understood then the meaning of 'nation': largely as a homogeneous organic and cultural group (Stratoudaki 2005). More than 80 per cent of the adolescent students *inter alia* agree with the preservation of Greek traditions and habits against conditions of globalisation and open borders, and a common biological, racial origin of the Greeks. The same survey found that one in four students placed in the first place the traditional nationalist values of 'pride for the homeland "and" religious faith'. According to Halikiopoulou and Vasilopoulou (2010), the economic crisis may be exacerbating deeper tendencies towards extremism present in Greek society, perpetuated by a highly centralised education system.[20]

Both the Golden Dawn and the BNP are legitimate political parties with a clear focus on contesting elections. For this reason, it is difficult to brand either party extremist in the sense that they are outside the boundaries of liberal democratic systems. However, both parties clearly adopt discourses that serve to establish out- and in-groups, and seek to exclude those that do not fit within the specific mass the party claims to represent. Nevertheless, interviews with activists reveal a marked difference in the extent of Othering behaviour in the two organisations. Whilst Golden Dawn activists focused their criticism on migrants themselves, the BNP activists reserved their strongest attacks for political elites. The different foci may go some way to explaining the seemingly different levels associated with each organisation. Whilst there are a number of accounts linking Golden Dawn to organised political violence directed at migrants, there is seemingly less evidence linking the BNP explicitly to it.[21]

Notes

1. This publication has been produced with the financial support of (a) the Fundamental Rights and Citizenship Programme of the European Union (Justice and Home Affairs), as part of a project on 'Hate speech and populist othering in Europe through the racism, age, and gender looking glass' (Grant Number Just/2012/FRAC/AG/2861) and (b) the EU's Daphne initiative for a project on 'E-engagement against violence' (Grant Number JUST/2011/DAP/ AG/3195). The contents of this publication are the sole responsibility of the authors and can in no way be taken to reflect the views of the European Commission. We would like to thank the RAGE and E-EAV teams for their support.
2. This stipulation was included to differentiate between minority populist groups, which could conceivably include separatist groups and some religious extremists.
3. See, in this respect, data from Eurostat: http://epp.eurostat.ec.europa.eu/ statistics_explained/index.php/People_at_risk_of_poverty_or_social_exclusion, accessed?
4. Voting is compulsory legally, but with the constitutional reform of 2001, there is no more penal prosecution. See: http://www.hellenicparliament.gr/ Vouli-ton-Ellinon/To-Politevma/Ekloges/.
5. See: http://www.opendemocracy.net/yannis-theocharis/reinstating-trust-in-greek-psyche.
6. See: http://news247.gr/eidiseis/dimoskopiseis.
7. See: http://www.neurope.eu/article/suspects-manolada-farm-shootings-arrested.
8. See: http://www.economist.com/blogs/charlemagne/2013/03/greek-politics. http://news247.gr/eidiseis/politiki/xrysh_aygh_gia_manwlada_amesh_ apelash_olwn_twn_lathrometanastwn_oristiko_telos_sthn_paranomh_ ergasia_twn_allodapwn.2217104.html
9. See http://www.xryshaygh.com/assets/files/politikes-theseis.pdf, p. 18.
10. See: http://news247.gr/eidiseis/politiki/kasidiarhs_arnhthhke_to_olokautwma_ mesa_sth_voylh.2284457.html.
11. See http://www.sigmalive.com/inbusiness/news/greek/59564.
12. See http://www.neolaia.gr/2012/09/28/xrysh-aygh-grafeio-ergasias-ellines/#. UXnRhUpiOTw.
13. See http://www.economist.com/blogs/charlemagne/2013/03/greek-politics.
14. See http://ethnikismos.net/.
15. See UK Polling Report for a frequently updated aggregate levels of support for the three main parties: http://ukpollingreport.co.uk/.
16. Full text of the 'Age of Austerity' speech can be found here: http://www. conservatives.com/News/Speeches/2009/04/The_age_of_austerity_speech_ to_the_2009_Spring_Forum.aspx.
17. The EMA was a small payment made to those between the ages of 16–18 and in education.
18. European unemployment data is available from Eurostat: http://epp.eurostat.ec.europa.eu/portal/page/portal/eurostat/home.
19. Interviewees also expressed opinions on a variety of other social issues, including homosexuality; these will be reported in another paper.

20. See: http://blogs.lse.ac.uk/europpblog/2013/01/29/greece-golden-dawn-education/.
21. There is some limited evidence that the BNP has a particular culture of violence expressed in internal party narratives. It is not possible to expand on this research, however, to claim that the BNP itself participates in or endorses violent acts. See: a 'Hope Not Hate' report written by Goodwin and Evans, available here: http://www.channel4.com/media/c4-news/images/voting-to-violence%20(7).pdf.

References

Albertazzi, D. and McDonnell, D. (eds) (2008) *Twenty-first century populism: the spectre of Western European democracy*, Basingstoke: Palgrave Macmillan.

Arendt, H. (1976) *The origins of totalitarianism*, San Diego: Harcourt.

Atton, C. (2006) 'Far-right media on the Internet: culture, discourse and power', *New Media & Society*, 8(4): 573–587.

Bartlett, J., Birdwell, J. and Littler, M. (2011) *The new face of digital populism*, London: Demos.

Bell, D. N. F. and Blanchflower, D. G. (2011) 'Young people and the Great Recession', *Oxford Review of Economic Policy*, 27(2): 241–267.

Betz, H-G. (1994) *Radical right-wing populism in Western Europe*, New York: St Martin's Press.

BNP (British National Party) (2010) *Democracy, freedom culture and identity*, British National Party General Elections Manifesto 2010.

BNP (n.d.) 'Activists and organisers handbook', http://www.bnp.org.uk/PDF/activists.pdf, accessed 15 August 2015.

Canovan, M. (1981) *Populism*, London: Junction Books.

Canovan, M. (1999) 'Trust the people! Populism and the two faces of democracy', *Political Studies*, 47: 2–16.

Doxiadis, A. and Matsaganis, M. (2012) *National populism and xenophobia in Greece*, London: Counterpoint.

Eatwell, R. (2004) 'The extreme right in Britain: the long road to modernization' in R. Eatwell and C. Mudde (eds) *Western democracies and the new extreme right challenge*, London: Routledge, pp.62–81.

Ellinas, A. (2013) 'The rise of the Golden Dawn: the new face of the far right in Greece', *South European Society and Politics*, 18(4): 543–565.

Fella, S. and Ruzza, C. (2009) *Reinventing the Italian right: territorial politics, populism and 'post-fascism'*, London: Routledge.

Ford, R. and Goodwin, M. J. (2010) 'Angry white men: individual and contextual predictors of support for the British National Party', *Political Studies*, 58(1): 1–25.

Georgiadou, V., Kafe, A. and Nezi, R. (2012) 'The radical right parties under the economic crisis: the Greek case', 62nd Political Studies Association Annual Conference, Belfast, 3–5 April.

Georgiadou, V. and Rori, L. (2012) 'Stable party strength in an unstable political landscape? The case of the Golden Dawn' in R. Gerodimos (ed) *Greek elections: June 2012* (Greek Politics Specialist Group, Political Studies Association), http://www.gpsg.org.uk/wp-content/uploads/2012/06/GPSG-Election-June-2012-Pamphlet.pdf, accessed 15 August 2013.

Goodwin, M. J. (2010) 'Activism in contemporary extreme right parties: the case of the British National Party (BNP)', *Journal of Elections, Public Opinion, and Parties*, 20(1): 31–54.

Halikiopoulou, D. and Vasilopoulou, S. (2010) 'Towards a 'civic' narrative: British national identity and the transformation of the British National Party', *The Political Quarterly*, 81(4): 583–592.

Hansard Society (2013) *Audit of political engagement 10. The 2013 Report*, London: Hasard Society.

Helms, L. (1997) 'Right-wing populist parties in Austria and Switzerland: a comparative analysis of electoral support and conditions of success', *West European Politics*, 20(2): 37–52.

Henn, M., Weinstein, M. and Wring, D. (2002) 'A generation apart? Youth and political participation in Britain', *The British Journal of Politics and International Relations*, 4(2): 167–192.

Karyotis, G. (2011) 'The fallacy of securitizing migration: elite rationality and unintended consequences' in G. Lazaridis (ed) *Security, insecurity and migration in Europe*, Aldershot: Ashgate.

Kitschelt, H. (2007) 'Growth and persistence of the radical right in post-industrial democracies: advances and challenges in comparative research', *West European Politics*, 30(5): 1176–1206.

Konsta, A. and Lazaridis, G. (2010) 'Civic stratification, "plastic" citizenship and "plastic subjectivities" in Greek immigration policy', *Journal of International Migration and Integration*, 11(4): 365–382.

Koronaiou, A. and Sakellariou, A. (2013) 'Reflections on "Golden Dawn", community organizing and nationalist solidarity: helping (only) Greeks', *Community Development Journal*, 48(2): 332–338.

Laclau, E. (2005) *On populist reason*, London, New York: Verso.

Laycock, D. (2005) 'Visions of popular sovereignty: mapping the contested terrain of contemporary western populisms', *Critical Review of International Social and Political Philosophy*, 8(2): 125–144.

Mammone, A. (2009) The eternal return? Faux populism and contemporarization of neo-fascism across Britain, France and Italy, *Journal of Contemporary European Studies*, 17(2): 171–192.

Marinakou, M. (2013) *Report EAPN Greece: poverty in Greece – facts and figures*, http://www.eapn.eu/images/stories/docs/EAPN-MEMBERS-publications/2012-poverty-facts-and-figures-GREECE-Maria-Marinakou.pdf, accessed 30 April 2013 and 15 August 2015.

Marvakis, A., Anastassiadou, M., Petritsi, I. and Anagnostopoulou, T. (2013) 'Youth paves the way by in which way? Youth and far-right in Greece', Friedrich Ebert Stiftung, July (in Greek).

Matsaganis, M. (2011) 'The welfare state and the crisis: the case of Greece', *Journal of European Social Policy*, 21(5): 501–513.

Mény, Y. and Surel, Y. (2002) 'The constitutive ambiguity of populism' in Y. Mény, and Y. Surel (eds) *Democracies and the populist challenge*, Basingstoke: Palgrave Macmillan, pp.1–24.

Mudde, C. (2004) 'The populist zeitgeist', *Government and Opposition*, 39(3): 541–563.

O'Brien, P. (2013) 'Clashes within Western civilization: debating citizenship for European Muslims', *Migration Studies*, 1(2): 131–155.

ONS (2013) 'Statistical bulletin: young people not in education, employment or training (NEET), May 2013, http://www.ons.gov.uk/ons/rel/lms/young-people-not-in-education--employment-or-training--neets-/may-2013/statistical-bulletin.html, accessed 16 August 2013.

Pattie, C., Seyd, P. and Whiteley, P. (2004) *Citizenship in Britain: values, participation and democracy*, Cambridge: Cambridge University Press.

Politaki, A. (2013) 'Greece is facing a humanitarian crisis', *The Guardian*, 11 February, http://www.guardian.co.uk/commentisfree/2013/feb/11/greece-humanitarian-crisis-eu, accessed 30 April 2013.

Rhodes, J. (2009) 'The banal national party: the routine nature of legitimacy', *Patterns of Prejudice*, 43(2): 142–160.

Rousseau, J-J. (1762) *The social contract*, http://ebooks.adelaide.edu.au/r/rousseau/jean_jacques/r864s/, 29 April 2013.

Roxborough, I. (1984) 'Unity and diversity in Latin American history', *Journal of Latin American Studies*, 16(2): 1–26.

Rydgren, J. (2003) 'Meso-level reasons for racism and xenophobia: some converging and diverging effects of radical right populism in France and Sweden', *European Journal of Social Theory*, 6(1): 45–68.

Sartori, G. (1970) 'Concept misformation in comparative politics', *American Political Science Review*, 64(4): 1033–1053.

Stanley, B. (2008) 'The thin ideology of populism', *Journal of Political Ideologies*, 13(1): 95–110.

Stratoudaki, H. (2005) 'Nation and democracy: views on the national identity of adolescents', *Epitheorisi Koinwnikwn Erevnwn*, 116: 23–50.

Taggart, P. (2004) 'Populism and representative politics in contemporary Europe', *Journal of Political Ideologies*, 9(3): 269–288.

Xenakis, S. (2012) 'A new dawn? Change and continuity in political violence in Greece', *Terrorism and Political Violence*, 24(3): 437–464.

Zaslove, A. (2008) 'Here to stay? Populism as a new party type', *European Review*, 16(3): 319–336.

Zouboulakis, S. (2013) *Golden Dawn and the church*, Athens: Polis (in Greek).

9
Securitisation of Migration and Far Right Populist Othering in Scandinavian Countries

Gabriella Lazaridis and Vasiliki Tsagkroni

Introduction

Almost three decades after Klaus von Beyme argued that 'there is virtually no comparative literature on the topic' (1988: 14) far-right parties have started drawing considerable attention from scholars. From the mid-1980s onwards, Europe has faced a new phenomenon of radicalisation, which from its first occurrence was difficult to define. Since the first appearance of contemporary far-right parties, various labels, such as 'extreme right' (Carter 2005; Ignazi 1996; Hainsworth 2000), 'right-wing populism' (Decker 2004), 'ethno-nationalism' (Rydgren 2005), 'anti-immigrant' (Fennema 1997), 'radical right' (Minkenberg 1998; Kitschelt and McGann 1995) and 'far right' (Marcus 2000) have been used to describe and classify this new political family.

This family encourages welfare and redistributive social policies, but defends ethnic nationalism, which provides the basis for selective social care policies. It promotes demands for direct democratic enrichment of political expression and a wider, plebiscitary form of political participation, while preferring authoritarian and hierarchical structures (see Georgiadou 2008). In other words, welfare chauvinism, radical anti-immigration policies, referendum policies and national priority (Hainsworth 2000), along with the decline of established sociocultural and sociopolitical systems and the minimising of the role of the state (Betz 1994) are characteristic of the rise of far-right parties since the 1980s.

Guided by leaders with a flair for expression in front of the media, these parties are considered 'the most prominent representatives of a new political entrepreneurialism' (Ignazi 1997; Mudde 2002; Betz 1998; Eatwell 2000). As Mudde (2002) observes, although most of these parties are branded as pariahs, they have managed to launch themselves as what we would call significant 'topographies' in the political field and have posed a substantial challenge to established political agencies across several western European countries (see also Betz 1994).

What is it that makes these parties so popular? Since their first appearance, their rise has been associated with embracing a strong negative attitude towards migrants and with the portrayal of migrants and ethnic minorities as dangerous Others. The threat of immigration and multi-culturalism appear to be prioritised in the political agenda of the far-right family: migrants are perceived as a security threat and linked with a wide range of sociopolitical, welfare and economic issues. The opposition of the extreme right towards immigration and multiculturalism can be traced back to ethnocentric perceptions of the nation, and the expression of racism underlines its welfare chauvinistic discourse (see Hainsworth 2000). Through anti-immigration policies and xenophobia, the Others become the scapegoats for any problems a country faces: economic crises, violence and crime, and rising unemployment rates. The purpose of this chapter is to look at the rise and popularity of the far right in Scandinavia. We examine the ways in which they use the securitisation of migration and the alleged threat that migrants pose to 'our' state, economic and ontological security and identity, as a means of justifying and legitimising their anti-immigration, racist and xeno-phobic rhetoric and praxis.

The choice of Scandinavia is not accidental. In one geographical area, where social democracy has been established for over half a century, and the political system is characterised by stability, the occurrence and success of far-right parties is of particular interest. These parties, such as the Danish People's Party (Dansk Folkeparti, DF) (1995 to present) or the Norwegian Progress Party (Fremskridtspartiet, FrP) (1973 to present), the Sweden Democrats (Sverigedemokraterna, SD) (1988 to present) and the Finns Party (Perussuomalaiset, PS) (1995 to present), are essentially a subset of far-right parties, and much discussion has taken place in the past about whether or not they should be included in the wider family of the European far right (see Mudde 2002; Hainsworth 2008).

Despite their differences – for example the SD in Sweden has its roots in the neo-Nazi scene, whereas in Norway and Denmark, both FrPs began as anti-tax parties; and in Finland, the PS was originally identi-fied by its opposition to the EU – the emerging theme of immigration is common in all four countries, and each nation's culture and identity is perceived as being under threat. Bearing this in mind, according to Mudde (2002), the common view of most researchers, with regard to the parties in Scandinavia, is that they are extreme mostly because of their policies on immigration and their support for welfare chauvinism. This chapter starts with the definitional groundwork of securitisation of migration, followed by its association with the far-right parties. The focus is then transferred to the specific cases of the Nordic countries. After an overview of the political opportunities in the area, the chapter attempts to identify and analyse the discourse of hate in relation to migration and populist Othering in these far-right parties.

Popularity and success of the far right

As stated above, during the past 40 years, far-right parties have emerged in several western European countries and experienced an increase in their electoral share: not only at a national level, but also at regional and international levels. Golder (2003) argues that the emerging electoral support for far-right parties has often been seen as a compelling influence on government coalitions and policy assessments. Anastasakis (2000: 5–6) proposes a model of four approaches to 'the rise, resilience and nature' of the far-right parties: (a) historical, as a legacy of the fascist era, (b) structural, in terms of a socioeconomic context, (c) political, in terms of political actors, and (d) ideologico-cultural, as in xenophobic rhetoric.

The fascist element can be traced back to changes which occurred in the postwar era (Anastasakis 2000; Hainsworth 2000; Moufahim 2007). Moreover, after the economic crisis of the 1970s, which created social and economic difficulties, followed by the decreasing level of productivity, higher rates in unemployment and a broader gap between rich and poor (Hainsworth 2000), the far-right parties successfully addressed such distress by focusing on issues related to socioeconomic changes, unemployment and immigration, which eventually raised their level of support among voters. The third feature involves the dimension of protest voting: in which votes can be translated as a protest against the political system but nevertheless have ideological roots (Betz 1994). Mistrust of established political parties has created a climate of discomfort within a section of voters who have chosen 'to turn their back on politics or to use the ballot as a means of protest' (Anastasakis 2000: 14). Thus, voters choose to project their dissatisfaction upon the established political parties by voting for a party which is considered a pariah of the system (Coffi 2004). This role of the outsider – often attributed to far-right parties – is not only due to their position of targeting the established political system, but also due to the criticism they receive from conventional political parties. As Fennema and Van der Brug (2006) argue, by denouncing the established political system, the parties of the far right become more appealing to the electorate who want to punish the mainstream parties by casting a protest vote. Finally, the last dimension concerns the xenophobic attitudes of the far-right parties. According to Betz (1994), the latter have exploited the opportunity created by the failure of established political parties to address critical issues which are considered highly significant by a part of the electorate, such as immigration.

The success of far-right parties in Western democracies is not only based on a favourable political environment but also on leadership, organisational structure and political culture. These parties' charismatic leadership, capable of setting the political and programmatic direction, and a closed hierarchical and centralised organisational structure, 'with-decisions being made at the top by a relatively circumscribed circle of party activists and transmitted to the bottom' (Betz 1998: 4), has allowed them to react rapidly to evolving issues (such as immigration), and to take advantage of 'changing political opportunities' (see Hainsworth 2000).

Securitisation of migration and the far right

Hainsworth (1992: 7) defines immigration as 'the extreme right's issue par excellence'. Immigration ideologies which incorporate strong sentiments of xenophobia are among the most characteristic themes of the far right, with a distinguishing popular appeal within the electorate. Xenophobia – literally, fear (phobia) of the foreigner (xenos) – is the sentiment in which far-right parties ground their welfare-chauvinist policies and anti-immigration measures (see Davies and Lynch 2002 in Moufahim 2007). Several scholars have adopted the label 'anti-immigration parties' (see Fennema 1997) rather than any other definition. This sees far-right parties as focusing on a 'single issue' (Hainsworth 2008), that of immigration, with the mobility and presence of migrants framed as a security issue.

The link between migration and security is socially constructed through public discourse and/or the social practices of various actors who have the legitimacy and vested interests to perform such a linkage and enter into framing struggles with each other in order to safeguard these very same interests and legitimacy (Scheufele 1999; Lavenex 2001).

Frames operate like lenses which magnify a subset of potentially relevant considerations, while blurring others (Nelson, Clawson and Oxley 1997; Druckman 2001). The application of these lenses to migration, in our case by far-right political parties and movements, amplifies the perceived threats that this phenomenon poses and promotes 'a particular problem definition, causal interpretation, moral evaluation, and/or treatment recommendation' (Entman 1993: 52), enabling and empowering the audience to interpret, categorise and evaluate migration accordingly (Benford and Snow 2000). In this way, public debate about the impact of migration on host societies and their social practices can potentially be entrapped in the logic of security.

This type of framing constitutes an attempt to push a social issue from normal politics into the realm of security, by presenting it as a threat to the fundamental values of an order (Buzan, Wæver and Wilde 1998). When an empowering audience accepts this frame as the predominant one for defining and dealing with an issue, then this issue becomes 'securitised', legitimising in this way the adoption of urgent policy responses to block its development, which otherwise might not have been possible (Ibid.). Securitisation, then, takes place when political leaders utilise the rhetoric of threat in order to legitimise the deployment of emergency measures with the consent of a specific audience, pushing in this way an area of normal politics into the security realm (McDonald 2008: 567). In simple terms, a social issue is securitised not due to its objective importance as a security threat, but because it is presented as such (Karyotis 2007: 3).

A plethora of empirical studies produced since the mid-1990s on a wide range of issues and national contexts have identified security practices (see Bigo 2002), legal frameworks (see Basaran 2008), and visual images (see Moller 2007) as central to the social construction of the 'migration-security nexus'.

Fear and unease constitute the basis of (in)securitisation. Anxiety about 'potentialities' and 'likelihoods' creates the urge to tame the uncertain at all costs and by any means, which relegates the Other to 'the category of cultural and even racial infrahumanity'[1] (Aradau and Van Munster 2009: 693). This opens the door to the most exploitative and cruel treatment that human beings are capable of inflicting on one another.

Framing the migration issue as a security threat has been strengthened in the wake of 11 September 2001, which consolidated migration as a threat to national welfare systems and identities, European values and the cultural homogeneity of EU member states. What unites far-right parties is their particular commitment to some sort of ethnic exclusionism – hostility to foreigners, immigrants, Third World asylum-seekers, and similar out-groups – as well as aggressive nationalism or localism.

As already mentioned, the parties of the far right project xenophobic sentiments, underline the threat of mass immigration and the potential creation of a multicultural society, and propose strict immigration control and asylum policies. In France, since the early 1970s, the National Front (Front National, FN) has adopted an anti-immigration rhetoric and called for 'assisted repatriation' (see Hainsworth 2008). Comparable examples are found in the Belgian Vlaams Blok, the Italian Northern League (Lega Nord, LN), the Swiss People's Party (Swiss Schweizerische Volksparteiand, SVP) and in the Austrian Freedom Party (Freiheitliche Partei Österreichs, FPÖ), among others. Norris (2004: 132) argues that immigration is the signature issue of the far right, and the fear of the Other that drives policies on immigration, asylum seekers and multiculturalism. Rejecting any form of multiculturalism is essential within the far-right ideology and is often the reason that these parties have been accused of racism. The nation and national identity, along with ethnic and religious homogeneity, are seen as needing protection from perceived threats: for example, asylum seekers, Muslims, immigrants, and homosexuals. In addition, far-right parties 'postulate a homogenous society where national identity is passed on through blood and heredity' (Hainsworth 2000 in Moufahim 2007: 31). Difference is seen as a threat to the stability of society.

For far-right parties, immigration is strongly related to the concept of nation. The nationalistic myth is characterised by the effort to construct an idea of nation and national belonging by using ethnic, cultural and political criteria of exclusion, and to condense the idea of the nation into an image of collective homogeneity (see Minkenberg 2004). Defending ethno-nationalism, the parties of the far right argue for a homogeneous environment in which the nation is consistent with the state (Eatwell 2000). Thus, they disregard or belittle any foreign elements that can be differentiated from it. The nation is perceived as a unit which shares identical cultural and ethnic origins, and individuals who do not share these features should not be considered as part of it (Hainsworth 2008). In addition, the homogeneity of the nation reflects issues like welfare chauvinism. The socioeconomic policy of welfare chauvinism introduces a notion of 'our own people first', an exclusionist approach adopted by the entirety of far-right parties. Based on this principle, state funds and jobs should be reserved for natives, rather than immigrants, and, along with that, the state should protect the national economy against 'foreign competition' (Mudde 2002: 175). For Kitschelt and McGann (1995), what has contributed to the structure of far-right parties' economic rhetoric has been the general anxiety over growing global competition.

Until the 1960s, the Nordic countries had homogeneous societies that lacked political or intellectual traditions related to xenophobia and racism. The sudden appearance of 'guest workers' from the late 1960s onwards did not reveal immigration to be a major issue because unemployment rates during this period were almost negligible, and migrant workers had no problem taking on the difficult jobs which the indigenous populations refused to do (see Bjørklund and Andersen 1999). As will become apparent further on in this chapter, this changed in the 1990s.

Political opportunities in a seemingly steadfast political system

The emergence and consolidation of new parties in the Nordic democracies makes it more interesting, as these countries had maintained a very stable party system from the 1920s. A basic condition for the emergence of new parties since the 1970s, which managed to attract a large proportion of voters from existing vested parties in Scandinavia, was the convergence of policies and programmes of social democracy. A part of the electorate abandoned their traditional choices in terms of partisan support, and started experimenting with the newly launched far-right parties.

In Scandinavia, the increase in social welfare depended less on the net electoral power of social democratic parties and more on the relationship between a broadly united moderate left (see Kitschelt and McGann 1995). The established political parties from social democratic and conservative backgrounds had an incentive to differentiate themselves in the area of electoral competition in order to attract young voters. Such electoral strategies, however, complicated the formation of coalitions among non-socialist parties. As a result, even in cases where a coalition government was successful, it was almost impossible to change public policy beyond the social democratic establishment.

Before 1973, the year in which Progress Parties dynamically appeared in both Denmark and Norway, the two countries were experiencing radical changes in their political landscape. In Denmark in 1968, after almost two decades of domination by the Social Democrats, a newly formed coalition government emerged between the Conservative People's Party (Det Konservative Folkeparti, DKF), the Radical Left Party (Det Radikale Venstre) and the Danish Social Liberal Party (Venstre, Danmarks Liberale Parti). The new government found it very difficult to escape from dominant social democratic policies; this caused great resentment and frustration in the electorate, and a renewed social democratic coalition government replaced it in 1971. It is around that period that an unprecedented climate of alienation, with a great degree of distrust for the political parties, was created. In addition, other changes that appeared at that time formed an even more fertile climate for the appearance of new parties. Alienation became stronger due to multilayered simultaneous changes in social liabilities and structures, discomfort with raising tax benefits, and discontent due to the unreliability of the political system. Political debate and related class alliances resulted in unprecedented electoral instability and, in conjunction with the fragmentation of the party system, favoured the emergence of the Danish FrP, which adopted a rationale against tax and the political establishment, and which succeeded in penetrating into the political system and attracting a large part of the voters.

At this same time (the late 1960s and early 1970s), the political landscape of Norway did not differ much from the Danish one. In 1965, after long domination by the Social Democratic Party, the Labour Party (Arbeiderpartiet, A/Ap) ascended to power in a coalition government involving the Conservative Party (Høyre), the Centre Party (Senterpartiet, Sp), the Christian Democratic Party (Kristelig Folkeparti, KrF), and the Liberal Party of Norway (Venstre). Although the new government had moved back to the political centre, it was not able to detach itself from policies that had previously been linked to the social democratic governments. In both Norway and Denmark, on the eve of the rise of the new far-right parties, the mainstream parties seemed unable to provide a substantial alternative.

Additionally, in 1972, and after a strong campaign from the social democratic parties in Denmark and Norway, referenda took place on the accession of the countries to the European Economic Community, ultimately resulting in 63.4 per cent in favour of integration in Denmark, and 53.5 per cent against integration in Norway. The referendums brought about broad mobilisation and polarisation among voters and the party elites, especially in the case of Norway. As previously mentioned, the prevailing distrust of political parties and the deterioration of relations between voters and parties created the ideal conditions for the formation of new parties. The fact that the late 1960s and early 1970s were the most expansive periods of the welfare state, characterised by an unprecedented increase in taxation, also contributed to this.

However, these conditions did not prevail in Sweden, where the Social Democrats remained in government until 1976, a period where the welfare state presented its most expansive policy, and in contrast to the previous cases of Norway and Denmark, political mistrust was at relatively low levels (see Widfeldt 2015). Nevertheless, the coalition of non-socialist parties, in the case of Sweden, had similarly not been separated from the Social Democratic policies of the past and was characterised by separatist movements and volatility. New parties started to develop in Sweden only after the 1980s. From 1986 until the elections of 1991, the government formed by Social Democrats (Sveriges socialdemokratiska arbetareparti, SAP) faced problems, not only political but also economic. Two decades after Denmark and Norway, Sweden was experiencing a structural change that affected traditional relations between the working class and the SAP. This view is reinforced by the fact that three new parties almost simultaneously made their appearance: the Christian Democrats (Kristdemokraterna, KrD) in 1991, the Green Party (Miljöpartiet de Gröna, MdG) in 1988, and finally New Democracy (Ny Demokrati, ND), also in 1991.

Finland, on the other hand, was the only Nordic country that strongly resisted the influence of the rising new far-right movement until the foundation of the Finns Party (Perussuomalaiset, PS) in 1995. Unlike other European countries, in Finland no significant efforts from parties belonging to the far-right family were made, and the roots of this phenomenon can be located in two key factors related to the development of far-right ideology: the political system and immigration. Initially, the social structure of the country started to change, along with the mentality of specific social groups that had traditionally been dedicated to the established parties but now started to declare themselves open to political alternatives. As Pekonen, Hynynen, and Kalliala (2001) extensively describe, the economic growth in the country was associated with organic decentralisation, and helped create a new middle class, which did not appear to be loyal to a specific political party. In this environment, the social groups lost their cohesion, significant effect of turning their backs on parties that they had previously supported. More specifically, in the urban centres, there was a growing dissatisfaction with the whole political scene; the traditional political identity was lost, the party involvement was significantly reduced, and the short-period electoral behaviour caused parties to lose their strong political support (see Pekonen, Hynynen and Kalliala 2001). Finally, the partisan coalitions did not leave much room for growth of far-right ideology and organisations associated with this kind of ideology.

The Scandinavian representatives of the far right

From the late 1980s onwards, a spate of far-right parties is observed across Europe, which did not leave the Scandinavian countries unaffected. As discussed above, despite the success of parties that are associated with the far-right ideology, mainly in Denmark and Norway, the case of Scandinavia differs from that of Europe. The parties appearing on the Scandinavian political scene seem closer to a moderate conservatism (see Widfeldt 2015) and would hardly qualify as traditional representatives of the far-right family, in comparison to the French FN or the Greek Golden Dawn (Chyrsi Aygi, GD), for example. Nevertheless, within the political system of these countries, they appeared as main exponents

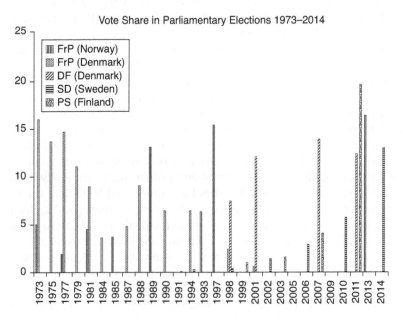

Figure 9.1   Electoral share of far-right parties in national parliamentary elections in Scandinavia (1973–2014)

of extremist rhetoric, which includes them in the European far-right family (see Mudde 2002).

The appearance of the Progress Parties (Fremskridtspartie) in the late 1970s in Denmark and Norway started as a protest movement against high taxes, subsidies and state intervention. In the years that followed, the parties recorded failed policies, changes in leadership and organisational structure: in other words, a general learning process which gradually led to right-leaning authoritarianism having a positive impact on the electorate (see Kitschelt and McGann 1995). The success of these parties raised fundamental questions about whether they could keep their voters in the years that followed. From Sweden, where success seemed short-lived (in the case of ND); to Finland, where the breakthrough occurred only in 2011 through PS; to Denmark and Norway, where the far-right DF and FrP parties are gaining recognition, an increasingly diversified picture is emerging, especially in the light of Nordic countries' similar political systems, structures, and cultural identities.

In 1972, Mogens Glistrup, in Denmark, launched a newly formed party called Fremskridtspartiet (FrP, 'Progress Party'). The party rapidly increased in popularity as a party of protest by adopting liberal political and economic rhetoric. Its basic proposal was to reduce taxes and cut government costs. In the national elections of 1973, a year after its creation, the Danish FrP was able to win 28 out of the 179 seats in parliament – that is, 15.9 per cent of the votes – and became the second party in power in the country. In the 1975 elections, it managed to maintain the number of votes, winning 13.6 per cent, and capturing 24 seats in parliament, and in the 1977 elections, it won 14.6 per cent and 26 seats. In the mid-1980s, there was minimal support for the party, and in 1994, the party only gained 6.4 per cent of the vote. In 1995, leading members of the group dropped out, an action that fundamentally weakened the party, which received very low rates in the elections that followed until 2005, when the party no longer took part in elections (see Andersen and Bjørklund 2008).

A year later, in 1973, in Norway, the Fremskrittspartiet (FrP, 'Progress Party') was founded by Anders Lange, more as a protest movement against high taxes, subsidies and state intervention. The inspiration for the foundation of the party came from the unexpected success of the Fremskridtspartie, FrP in Denmark (see Bjørklund and Andersen 1999; Kitschelt and McGann 1995; Hainsworth 2000; Georgiadou 2008; Betz 1994; Ignazi 2003). The name originally was Anders Lange's Party for a

Strong Reduction in Taxes, Duties and Public Intervention. In the elections that year, the party received 5 per cent of the vote and four seats in the national parliament. The political message of the party changed over time, thus changing the social profile of the voters. In the beginning, the party mainly focused on the tax issue, describing tax levels, subsidies and regulations as unacceptable. Gradually, it began to defend positions in favour of the free market, arguing for government interventionism and against the social democratic 'nanny state', and from the mid-1980s until today, the prominent issue has been immigration. In 1977, the party was renamed the Progress Party (FrP).

The success of 1973 was not repeated in the 1977 election, where the Norwegian FrP failed to elect a member in the national parliament. The party in 1989 made a strong breakthrough and returned as the third largest party with 13 per cent of the popular vote. In 1997, the FrP was the third party again, with 15.3 per cent. Before the elections of 2001, its popularity reached a very high level, but the involvement of senior members of the party in sex scandals and the undemocratic interior treatment of the president's domestic opponents – who eventually resigned and formed a new party called Democrats (*Demokratene*) – left the party again in third place, with a 14.6 per cent share. The coalition government was formed after the elections under the Bondevik, composed of Christian Democrats (Kristelig Folkeparti, KrF), the Conservative Party (Høyre) and the Liberals (Venstre), but it depended on the support of the FrP. To ensure this support, the coalition government announced that their policy would include tax cuts, accelerated privatisation, and the licensing of construction of a natural gas power plant (FrP 2015). The announcement of support from Carl I. Hagen, chairman of the Norwegian FrP, was accompanied by a list of further requirements as a condition of cooperation.

As a result of these pressures, members of the party presided over the government's standing parliamentary committees on finance and social issues: for example, social welfare. Moreover, the withdrawal of the party's more extreme elements allowed Norway's traditional parties to sit down with the FrP at the negotiating table (see Bjørklund and Andersen 1999). In the elections of 2005, the party almost doubled its strength by winning 22.1 per cent of the vote and 38 seats in the national parliament, thus occupying the second-strongest electoral force in the country, a position that was held in the elections of 2009 when the party gained 22.9 per cent of the vote. In the elections of 2013, with Siv Jensen as the president of the party (the successor to Carl Hagen since 2006), although the FrP lost some of its electoral support, it gained 13.6 per cent and managed to form its first coalition government with the Conservative Party.

In the mid-1990s, personal conflicts within the parliamentary group of the FrP in Denmark accompanied a concentration of power around the president, Pia Kjaersgaard. In 1995, Kjaersgaard, along with Kristian Thulesen Dahl, Poul Nødgaard and Ole Donner, left the FrP and formed a new party, the Danish People's Party (Dansk Folkeparti, DF) (Ignazi 2003). At first, the new party did not deviate ideologically from its predecessor (see Bjørklund 1999), but it soon abandoned the last remnants of neoliberalism, carried as a legacy from the FrP, and focused on other issues, such as immigration and nationalist appeals.

The DF, making its first election appearance in 1998, managed to win 13 seats in parliament, with 7.4 per cent of the vote. In the elections of 2001, the party was able to increase its share to 12 per cent, winning 22 seats in the national parliament, thus ranking third in the voting power position in the country. The DF supported the coalition government of the Conservative People's Party (Konservative Folkeparti, KrF) and the Liberals (Venstre) under Prime Minister Anders Fogh Rasmussen in return for hard requirements, such as more stringent policies on the issue of immigration (Pedersen and Ringsmose 2004: 5). In the elections of 2005, it further increased its vote share to 13.2 per cent, with 24 seats in parliament. In the following years, the DF's popularity rose sharply in the opinion polls, after the controversy created by the Danish newspaper *Jyllands-Posten*'s publication of Muhammad cartoons. In the 2007 elections, the DF managed to maintain its share of 13.8 per cent of the vote and increased its seats in parliament to 25, a number minimised to 22 in the last elections of 2011, in which it gained 12.3 per cent of the popular vote. In 2012, the leadership of the party passed to Kristian Thulesen Dahl, after Pia Kjærsgaard's retirement.

The dynamic movement in Sweden was made when the New Democracy (Ny Demokrati, ND) party managed to win 6.7 per cent of the vote in national parliamentary elections in 1991. The party was founded on 4 February 1991 by Bert Karlsson and Ian Wachtmeister (see Rydgren 2001), and its campaign caught the attention of the media, with a particular style that was reminiscent of no other traditional political campaigns (see Taggart 1996). Its programme focused on four key elements: vested political parties and politicians do not represent the 'people', the need to reduce tax rates and privatise public services, and the need to reduce the number of immigrants. ND, even before its formal establishment as a party, seemed particularly popular in the polls, an estimation that was proved right in the electoral results, where the party won 25 parliamentary seats with 6.7 per cent of the popular vote. In the years that followed, the governing parties would seek the cooperation of ND in parliamentary committees, but would seek even greater cooperation with the party leadership. Internal conflicts, omissions and lack of party discipline would make such cooperation more difficult and would play a catalytic role in the development of the party (see Andersen and Bjørklund 2008). In the Survey of 1992, the party gained 10 per cent. With the resignation of the party leader, Wachtmeister, in February 1994, public support seemed to crumble (see Widfeldt 2001). What began as a strong political alliance between Karlsson and Wachtmeister resulted in conflict and litigation, which made co-operation impossible. After the resignation, neither Wachtmeister nor Karlsson wanted to remain in charge, a fact that left the party without any leadership.

The sudden success of the ND in Sweden didn't last long compared to the FrP and the DF. Personal conflicts between the founders, the heterogeneity of the parliamentary group, amateurism in everyday politics, dislike of any form of party organisation, and the shift of conservative parties to the right drastically reduced its chances of success (Ignazi 2003: 159). In the 1994 parliamentary elections, the party would receive just 1.2 per cent of the vote, and in 1998, only 0.2 per cent.

Today, the leading far-right party is the Sweden Democrats (Sverigedemokraterna, SD), which has managed to gain marginal votes nationally and a few elected representatives in local elections. Founded as a successor to the Sweden Party (Sverigepartiet) in 1988 from the merger of the FrP and the racist, far-right group Keep Sweden Swedish (Bevara Sverige Svenskt), the party, like other far-right parties in Europe, tried to self-identify as a representative of 'true democracy' (see Widfeldt 2000). Nevertheless, the party was not able to shrug off its origins, which were often underlined by journalists in an effort to remind the public that the SD had been associated with Nazi or racist organisations (Widfeldt 2000). For years, the party's initial electoral impact would be reduced. In 1995, Mikael Jansoon became the party's leader. Under the leadership of Jansson, the SD started distancing itself from its extremist elements, which caused the most radical supporters to leave and establish a party called the National Democrats (Nationaldemokraterna) (see Rydgren 2005), a split that proved to be a key development in the party's 'electability' (Widfeldt 2015: 184). Despite eliminating references to extremism, the burden of the party's origins remained, and the SD could not establish itself in the national political scene. In 2005, in another internal split, Jimmie Akesson replaced Jansson. The new leadership created a modernised environment, a reform that proved beneficial for the party's electoral success. In the 2010 elections, the party finally managed to enter parliament with 5.7 per cent of the vote, doubling its support in the latest elections of 2014, by gaining 12.9 per cent and winning 49 seats in parliament. From a party that self-identified with 'nationalism' (SD 1999, 2005) to its most recent redefinition – 'social conservatism' (SD 2011) – the party's emphasis is on nation and nationalism and its rhetoric is strongly linked with the issues of immigration and opposing multiculturalism (see Widfeldt 2015).

In 1995, after the collapse of the Finnish Rural Party (Suomen Maaseudun Puolue) a newly formed party emerged, led by Simo Sioni. The party was named True Finns (Perussuomalaiset), later known as the Finns Party. The new party focused its political rhetoric on nationalism, and under the leadership of Timo Soini, it won three seats in the 2003 election (Kestila 2006: 174). In the March 2007 election, it managed to increase its share to 4.1 per cent and occupy five seats in the national parliament. In the parliamentary elections of 2011, the party had a breakthrough and gained over 19.5 per cent of the popular vote, establishing itself in the national political scene. The party's social agenda supports the Nordic tradition of policies based on social-democratic origins, but it is the ethno-nationalist populism, focusing on Euroscepticism and welfare policies that makes PS one of the main representatives of the far right in the area.

The rhetoric of extremes: immigrants as the new face of threat

The issue of immigration began to appear on the political agenda of parties in Scandinavia in the mid-1980s, when there was a qualitative change in migration – unskilled workers were replaced by refugees seeking asylum (Ignazi 2003). From 1990 onwards, a rapidly growing immigrant population and public interest in juvenile delinquency, unemployment and dependence on social benefits, brought immigration to the fore as an issue that affects citizens' voting decisions. Moreover, parties began to engage with the issue of immigration in their rhetoric and specifically emphasised their opposition to the prospect of a multicultural society as a result of the increasing number of immigrants in their country (see Van Spanje and Van der Brug 2005).

Although the immigration issue was key, the anti-immigrant political rhetoric on the part of the ND and SD was by far the toughest in
the history of the Swedish parliament. ND, for instance, believes that
political refugees have to take loans and not benefits, that immigrants
should be expelled from the country if connected to criminal cases, that
children of immigrants should not have the right to be educated in their
mother tongue, and that the determination of refugee status should
have stricter criteria (Widfeldt, 2001). Proposals for changes in policy
towards refugees and migrants on the part of ND had direct support from
incumbent parties, leading to the party being lambasted and accused of
racism. But since 1989, the policy affecting refugees became tougher
(see Dahlström 2004). The official position of both the non-socialist
government of 1991–1994 and the socialist government after 1994 was
that the country had received a large number of political refugees and
could not continue to accept them at such a rate (Widfeldt 2001: 16). In
1996, parliament approved a government proposal that included rejection of some conditions for asylum and abandoned the concept of de
facto refugees. This attitude was criticised by the opposition as a hardening of the Swedish asylum policy, and the government was accused
of introducing policies similar to those proposed by the ND a few
years before.

In Norway, from 1990 onwards, the rapidly growing population of
immigrants and public interest in juvenile delinquency, unemployment
and dependence on social benefits made immigration a debating issue.
The FrP led the debate, igniting intense political controversy by highlighting aspects and causes. In its manifesto of 1977, the party requested
limiting migration in order to secure jobs. In 1985, the party reacted
to subsidised housing and grants for learning the mother tongue,
projecting them as discrimination against Norwegians (Bjorklund and
Andersen 1999: 7). Having said that, the party argued that it favoured
free migration, provided immigrants could maintain themselves without
state support. At the same time, it stressed that only Norwegian citizens
have the right to reside in Norway. In its electoral manifesto of 1985,
the party self-identified as 'liberal', based on the Norwegian constitution, Norwegian and Western tradition and cultural heritage, and its
roots in Christian values (FrP 1985). The party declared its view of a
society with limited state power in order to protect the rights of the
individual.

During the 1987 campaign, the number of people seeking asylum
in Norway tripled compared to 1986, which brought up issues associated with immigration – for instance, the potential exploitation of

the welfare state – and this in turn resulted in support for an anti-immigrant party. It is in 1987 that Carl Hagen quoted a letter which he claimed held information implying a conspiracy among Muslim immigrants who planned to take over Norway, indicating a serious security issue for the country (see Hagelund 2003). For Hagelund (2003), the argument and the emphasis on the immigration issue transformed after 1987, leading to a combination of the party's welfare argument from the early 1980s (claiming that immigrants were receiving preferential treatment), and fears concerning the preservation of the country's cultural heritage. In 1993, it supported the view that a society without ethnic minorities is the ideal justifying its beliefs on the grounds that in multicultural societies conflicts arise very easily. In this election campaign, Hagen once more addressed the electorate with securitisation of migration rhetoric, where immigrants are attributed responsibility for importing a culture of violence and a 'gang mentality' (Widfeldt 2015: 97). That same year, FrP proposed the integration of existing migrants and severe restrictions on the entry of new migrants, mainly from non-western countries, while at the same time declaring that everyone had to fight against all forms of discrimination and racism.

Although the legislation on asylum became more stringent in Norway, there were still huge differences between the traditional parties and the populist far right represented by the Norwegian FrP. The other parties accused members of the FrP of racism and xenophobia, while the FrP responded that it was against policies for refugees and distinguished itself from other xenophobic parties in Europe, such as the French FN. Hagen notes that he was the only person responsible for expressing the views of the party on immigration. During the 1997 campaign, the identification of Hagen with his political opponents – for example, Jean-Marie Le Pen of the French FN – provoked an angry reaction: 'Le Pen is a disgusting racist. His ideological positions are far from the ones represented by the FrP' (Bjørklund 2011: 286). Characteristic, however, is the statement by Hagen: 'Not all Muslims are terrorists, but all terrorists are Muslims' (Aftenposten 2005a). Under Norwegian law, three years of legal residence in the country is enough to give the right to vote in local elections, and seven years is enough to grant citizenship; the FrP strongly opposed both. A proposal by Hagen in 1999, to establish a form of language test as a prerequisite for granting citizenship, was sharply criticised and characterised as extreme.

Nevertheless, in her work on the FrP immigration policies, Hagelund (2003) highlights a reference from the party's manifesto of 1997, in which immigration and conflict have been used in their main argument. In the same document, FrP identifies immigration as a key factor that escalates the danger of conflict in the country and should be considered an ongoing threat (55).

Although the split of the party in 2001 removed the most extreme elements (perceived to be strongly racist), the party never stopped expressing its views in various ways which went beyond commonly accepted limits. A typical example is Hagen's speech at Levende Ord's religious festival in July 2004 in which he argued, *inter alia*, that an attempt should be made to convert all Muslims living in the country to Christianity. The next day, other party officials were even more extreme: They asked 'to criminalise the ideology and practice of Islam and to outlaw such Nazism', comparing the Quran to Hitler's *Mein Kampf*. They even stated, 'The Prophet Muhammad urged them to kill all infidels' and 'Religion (Islam) as practiced is a threat to our social system and way of life' (Pettersson 2004).

The chairman of the Conservative Party, Erna Solberg, claimed after Hagen's announcements at the festival, 'The speech proves that this is the reason that the party FrP does not participate in any government', and 'the behaviour of Hagen hampers cooperation' (Pettersson 2004). Despite the public outcry, Hagen returned to the subject a few months later, in November 2004. In the parliamentary debate on the 'White Paper on Security', he proposed the monitoring of groups that invite Islamist politicians and establishing approval procedures for imams in Norway. 'Hagen mixes immigration policy in the debate on the safety and how to protect the Norwegian society from terrorism. But our readiness to confront the terrorists does not mean that we should stigmatise and watch all Muslims in Norway. This is just disgusting' (Aftenposten 2004).

Moreover, in 2000, the police chief asked – on the pretext of overrepresentation of refugees in forensic statistics – to detain those applicants who did not have travel documents, a practice abolished in Norway in 1996 after the suicide of a man while he was in custody. During the 2005 campaign, the party printed a brochure focusing on 'criminal' immigrants, stating that 'the perpetrator is of foreign origin' (Aftenposten 2005b). Harsh criticism from other parties, and particularly from Prime Minister Kjell Magne Bondevik, was expressed; Bondevik claimed that the FrP was 'playing games exploiting the fear of immigrants' (Ibid.). The pamphlet argued that many immigrants are law-abiding citizens who do a fantastic job for Norway, but unfortunately there are too many who are not. The statistics clearly show that crime is rising among immigrants. The Prime Minister continues, saying 'The FrP claims that it has nothing against the law-abiding immigrants who are in Norway on legal establishment and rejects discrimination based on colour, race and national or religious affiliation' (Aftenposten 2005a).

In Denmark, the immigration issue also dominated policies after the mid-1980s and would quickly be incorporated into the agendas of the political parties, with a significant part of the population believing that immigration was one of the country's most important problems. The immigration issue was a significant compromise in a reordering of social cleavages in the party system (Andersen and Bjørklund 2008: 387) and was highlighted as a trademark for both Danish FrP and DF. In 1983, the country adopted a revised law, strengthening the position of refugees and migrants. In the years that followed, and with the number of asylum seekers increasing, a more conservative attitude on the part of the government towards immigrants was adopted, and in 1986, the law was tightened with the support of the government of Conservative Party Progress and the Social Democrats.

Religion is examined through the prism of culture and diversity in western societies, with Denmark by definition being considered Christian, and Islam representing a completely different culture, one incompatible with Christian–Western values. Glistrup (Founder of the Progress Party in Denmark) states that his party's purpose is to free the country from Muslims and proposes their expulsion from the country. In a speech, he compared Muslims in Denmark to a drop of arsenic in a glass of clean water (Wren 2001: 155). Another way to comprehend the attitude of the Progress party towards the Muslims is to look at occasional statements from members of the press, which in most cases are extreme and provocative. In these statements, Muslims are considered collectively to be exploiters of the welfare system at best, and at worst, terrorists and threats to the security of the country. Bo Warming, a party member, stated, for instance, 'The only difference between Muslims and rats is that the rats do not receive social benefits', while Vagn Andersen, another member believes, 'The state gave jobs to immigrants. Many of them work in the food industry, which can poison our food and endanger the agricultural exports. Another way of terrorism is to poison water supplies' (CERD 2003). A party press release states, 'the cultural enrichment of the country brought to the Danes only negative outcomes and rapes by Muslims who do not respect our citizens and for this reason must be treated like intruders in the country. Politicians should deport them' (FrP 2001). In reaction to these statements and others at the party conference in 2001, the Muslim MP, Kamal Quereshi, fled the UN Committee on the Elimination of Racial Discrimination in 2003 (see Kamal Quereshi v. Denmark Communication No. 27/2002 U.N. Doc. CERD/C/63/D/27/2002 2003).

The DF, on the other hand, in its manifesto, states that the goal of the party is to ensure the freedom of Danes in their own country and the development of society in accordance with the Danish culture, which is defined by the sum of Danish history, experience, language and customs. The foundation of the country is the cultural heritage of the Danes, which must be maintained and strengthened. The Christian faith is an integral part of life in Denmark. Throughout the text, there is a widespread view that Denmark has a religious, cultural and ethnic homogeneity. The party declares its opposition to any attempt to convert Denmark to a multicultural society, arguing that Denmark is not and has never been a country of immigrants (DF 2001).

In 2006, polls showed soaring popularity due to the controversy created by the publication of cartoons of Mohammed. 53 per cent of Danes supported the newspaper, despite a public apology from its director and the Danish Prime Minister (*Jyllands-Posten* 2006). The party executive's belief is that the violent reactions of Muslims in this instance revealed the serious problem facing Europe of the presence of an Islamic minority that does not respect fundamental rights such as freedom of the press. One problem that they themselves have identified and highlighted in the party congress after 11 September 2001, is that the speakers referred to Muslims as 'our enemy'. The solution proposed by the MP and a member of the Council of Europe, Morten Messerschmidt, is to drastically reduce the number of immigrants from Muslim countries: if no action is taken within a few years, the Muslims will make up the majority of the population in Europe, and this will spell the end of European culture (FrontPage Magazine 2006).

In November 2005, MP Louise Frevert unveiled on her personal site a series of statements against Muslims, most of which are already in a book published in 2004. In short, a political statement, under the heading 'Articles that nobody dares to publish', she states, 'they believe that we must adapt to Islam, and have convinced so the priests and leaders....they believe that it is their right to rape and beat Danish citizens....we spend time and money to integrate Muslims but the result does not change. The cancer spreads unchecked while we talk' (International Network Against Cyber Hate, Inach annual report 2005).

The Committee against racism and intolerance of the Council of Europe, in its report on Denmark, published in May 2006, considered that the situation in the country had worsened compared with previous years and noted a pervasive xenophobia and intolerance, especially against Muslims. The support of the DF to the government allowed the party to promote laws and measures that adversely affected the position of minorities. Particular reference was made to police reluctance to prosecute party members or supporters for inciting racial hatred, allowing its members to make statements to the media that were openly racist and offensive to minorities, while the party did nothing to curb them (Council of Europe, European Commission against Racism and Intolerance, third report on Denmark 2006).

In the party's election campaign of November 2007, the DF blamed Muslim immigrants for not respecting Danish traditions, claiming that their only concern is the exploitation of the generosity of the welfare of the country. A related poster of the party, which featured a group of women wearing the projected headscarf, was entitled, 'Follow the traditions and customs of the country or else leave'. The party in its programme included a series of law proposals targeting immigrants, arguing, 'There is every reason to tighten the screws, because the Danish prices are under pressure', and 'the main concern of the Danes should be the preservation of their identity'. Migration and its securitisation seem to play a decisive role in the electoral process of political parties in Scandinavia, since their popularity increased when they included the question of securitisation of migration in their program (Ivarsflaten 2003: 18). It is not surprising that many scholars (Fennema, Bjørklund, Andersen) have these parties listed as 'anti-immigration parties'.

In the manifesto of 2009, immigrants, and more specifically 'non-ethnic Danes', were used in the framework of – among others – housing, education and crime (DF 2009). The DF emphasised their negative influence on Danish society (in Widfeldt 2015: 142–143). The party illustrated securitisation of migration in strongly worded rhetoric, in which immigrants could 'kill us', and their 'ideology of evil' should be 'forced out of the Western Civilisation' (Ibid.: 144).

As mentioned above, the Swedish SD tends to focus on the nation itself. Assimilation to the host country is a top priority: 'the more different to Sweden the culture and identity of an immigrant, and the bigger the group of immigrants, the more difficult the assimilation process' (SD 2011). For this party, immigration is not only a problem, but also a threat to the country's national and cultural identity and its welfare and safety. Having said that, the anti-immigration rhetoric of SD has been carefully supported by policies that have also been sanitised. Focusing on the anxiety of preserving Swedish culture, the party centres on the notion of 'open Swedishness', indicating that immigrants can be accepted and are welcomed in the country, as long as they abdicate their identity and adapt to the Swedish principles.

In its official manifesto of 2005, the party underlines that it 'condemns multiculturalism as well as racism and teachings where the ethnic origin is the only, or most important aspect when deciding if a person is, should be, or could be a part of our nation' (SD 2005). For Widfeldt, the opposition to multiculturalism places the party within the 'ethno-pluralist 'equal but separate' doctrine (2015: 197). By keeping its roots to the xenophobic 'Keep Sweden Swedish' movement, the party emphasises the importance of protecting the dominance of the country's own culture from any possible threats.

Similar to the cases of Norway and Denmark, SD in Sweden mobilises the securitisation of migration in its rhetoric and links the subject of immigration to problems and challenges in the its society, such as unemployment or crime. In one of his speeches, Akesson directly linked unemployment to asylum seekers, claiming that if the number of asylum seekers in the country rose, the number of jobs available would decline. Being the country with the most asylum applications per person in the world, Sweden, according to Akesson, should support fewer asylum acceptances, require immigrants to take language tests, and decrease immigrants' welfare benefits. Additionally, in one of his interviews in 2011 on BBC, Akesson underlined, 'Immigrants are in general little bit more criminal than Swedes born in Sweden, and that's a fact' (BBC 2011).

The strongly anti-immigration values of the party are often supported publicly by other members, who do not hesitate to portray publically the threat they believe the country faces from large numbers of immigrants. Niclas Nilsson, group leader on the Kristianstad council, estimates that the number of immigrants in the country is proof of the poor immigration policy in western Europe and stressed that Swedish people 'don't feel at home any more'. In one of his interviews, he underlined, 'The problem we have is basically with the Muslims. They have difficulty assimilating, so much of their culture is based on Islam' (Crouch 2014). He continued, highlighting the threat to the nation's 'Swedishness' posed by the growing numbers of Muslim immigrants in the country. Furthermore, Akesson in his speech in Sölvesborg, in July 2014, characterised Islamism as the Nazism and Communism of today and claimed, 'It has to be met with disgust and much stronger resistance than has so far been the case'. He continued, stating SD's commitment to give the Swedish Security Service (Säpo) extended powers to compress the number of Islamist immigrants in the country (SD 2014). The success of SD's 'Swedes First' rhetoric, for Hainsworth (2008), can be translated as an attempt to moderate and mobilise the party's extremist image by imitating the example of the FrP and DF.

In Finland, discrimination and racism towards Others started emerging after the 1980s (Isaksson and Jokisalo 1998). As mentioned above, the main focus of the PS was Euroscepticism and immigration policies, retaining a populist profile traced in parties participating in the far-right family. The rhetoric of the party has nationalist and xenophobic elements, underlining that the state of Finland was established to safeguard the interests of the Finnish people (PS 2011). The immigration issue was extensively emphasised in the official manifesto of the party. Restrictions concerning the entrance and residence of immigrants in the country, calls for protection of the national sovereignty and stringent immigration policies were emphasised. The same manifesto states, 'Basic Finnish immigration policy should be based on the fact that the Finns should always be able to decide for themselves the conditions under which a foreigner can come to our country and reside in our country' (PS 2011). Social-democratic welfare, combined with nationalism and xenophobia, were valuable for attracting support for the party, a well-known recipe for success in the far-right party family.

The party's rhetoric often includes elements of extreme nationalism. A characteristic example is MP Juho Eerola's statement in 2010: 'I'm attracted to fascism and especially the economic policies carried out by Benito Mussolini – We could learn a lot from that model'. Similarly, James Hirvisaari, another party member, while referring to multiculturalism, compared it to evil and underlined, 'the terrorist attacks are due to the supporters of multiculturalism. The real culprits are not the Muslims (what can they do about their madness) or those criticising immigration (although they are often blamed) but multiculturalists who are hankering after the richness and glory of Islam here in the deep north' (Korhonen 2012: 215). PS has managed to address the sense of security in the country, along with nation, national identity and Finnish culture, and to draw the attention of the electorate, creating an emotional connection with the voters by adopting the culture of fear discourse regarding the potential threat of immigration.

Conclusions

The increase in the number of immigrants to a country is considered to be a catalyst and often can be translated as a key factor for the support of far-right parties. Along with nationalism, anti-immigration policy is a political identity attribute. The rhetoric against asylum seekers and migrants is one of the most important issues that has contributed to the emergence of far-right movements in recent decades. In Finland, asylum seekers and immigration are a relatively new phenomenon in comparison to the rest of the Nordic countries.

In Sweden, on the other hand, the influx of mainly non-European immigrants rose steadily between 1970 and the 1990s, which gave it a multicultural identity similar to other western European countries (Rydgren 2001: 13). Xenophobia, which began to be strongly expressed at the time, offered the far-right parties an extremely effective rhetorical tool. While xenophobia is not a mentor-voting criterion *per se*, most of the voters for far-right parties appear to have xenophobic attitudes.

In Sweden, the majority of voters feel positive about the idea of reducing the proportion of immigrants received by the country since the late 1980s. However, until 1991, the issue of migration did not belong to the prioritised agenda, neither that of the parties nor that of voters. After 1994, the immigration issue seemed to disappear again as an important determinant of voting. The economic crisis appears to have had the effect of increasing the emphasis on the importance of traditional issues such as the economy or public welfare, while neglecting issues such as immigration (Rydgren 2001: 14–15). During the late 1990s, the immigration issue came back to the forefront, and nowadays it is placed high on the list of political parties and individuals.

As Widfeldt (2015) notices in his work, *Extreme Right Parties in Scandinavia*, immigration can be measured as a key factor for the increasing support of the far-right parties in the area. The anti-immigrant policy, from the 1980s onwards, along with the liberal market, welfare chauvinism, law and order, and populist speech will be the key traits that characterise the FrP and the DF.

The behaviour of the right-wing parties and their attitudes have changed radically over the years. Typical is the case of parties in Denmark, where it became very clear that the ambition for power and holding responsible positions was decisive as regards organisational changes within the party. In a multiparty system such as the Nordic countries have, far-right parties present a reliable option, something that, without party discipline and centralised control, would not be possible.

The emergence of FrP in Norway and the DF in Denmark has shown that far-right parties have now won their place in the political landscape of these countries, and most are unlikely to disappear. Although these parties, as presented above, deviate from the existing image of far-right parties in general, they seem to be powered by the same source as other parties in Europe: the issue of migration and its securitisation. The tradition of Scandinavian social democracy seems not to leave unaffected the evolution of the parties contemplated, although among the far-right family, they clearly present a more moderate profile compared with other parties belonging to the same family in Europe.

Many explanations have been given for what may have contributed to the – until recently unsuccessful – appearance of far-right parties in Finland and Sweden. These range from electoral systems, to political personalities and internal problems. Regardless, the explanations are once again in contrast to the conditions prevailing in the countries examined, as there is a long tradition of coalition government, immigration levels are high in all countries, and the economic situation and taxation does not differ radically. The fact that no far-right party in Finland and Sweden had significant success for years, and the rapid emergence of SD and PS, prove that these countries were not safe from a potential materialisation of a strong far-right movement.

Despite their differences and background, what the Scandinavian parties present is a rhetoric, with strong populist elements, where immigrants are hazards and states should be alerted as the countries are under threat. Contributing to the rising senses of xenophobia and Islamophobia, securitisation of migration is more than a theory in the case of the far-right parties under examination. The fear of Islam in recent years is a key element of their policy. Their very strong need to preserve their cultural identity leads far-right parties to take an uncompromising position against immigrants, especially against Muslims living in their country who are carving their mark where freedom of the individual and freedom of speech are considered indisputable, thus breaking the values that were considered essential in their culture and history. In other words, neither the parties discussed in this chapter, nor the openly racist and violent right-wing activists, operate in a societal vacuum. The success or failure of these parties depends on which discourses are dominant, as this environment provides better or poorer breeding grounds for hate-speech and violent acts, which are a serious threat to fundamental democratic values and jeopardise the right to security for many minority inhabitants.

Note

1. Cultural/racial inferiority.

References

Aftenposten (2004) 'Carl Hagen: is Christianity a bridge?', http://www.aftenposten.no/english/local/article860793.ece, accessed 15 January 2014.
Aftenposten (2005a) 'Carl Hagen: all terrorists are Muslims', http://www.aftenposten.no/english/local/article1103526.ece, accessed 11 March 2015.

Aftenposten (2005b) 'Progress party brochure sparks racism charges', http://www.aftenposten.no/english/local/article1097512.ece, accessed 15 January 2015.

Allen, C. and Nielsen, J. S. (2002) *Summary report on Islamophobia in the EU after 11 September 2001*, Vienna: European Monitoring Centre on Racism and Xenophobia (EUMC).

Anastasakis, O. (2000) 'Extreme right in Europe: a comparative study of recent trends' (Discussion paper 3), the Hellenic Observatory and the European Institute, London: London School of Economics and Political Science.

Andersen, J. G. and Bjørklund, T. (2008) 'Scandinavia and the Far Right' in P. Davies and P. Jackson (eds) *The far right in Europe. An encyclopedia*, Oxford: Greenwood World Publishing, pp.147–163.

Aradau, C. and Van Munster, R. (2009) 'Poststructuralism, continental philosophy, and the remaking of security studies' in V. Mauer and M. Dunn Cavelty (eds) *The Routledge handbook of security studies*, London: Routledge, pp.73–83.

Basaran, T. (2008) 'Security, law, borders: spaces of exclusion', *International Political Sociology*, 2: 339–354.

BBC HARDtalk (2011) 'Jimmie Akesson: Swedish immigration is "extreme"', http://news.bbc.co.uk/1/hi/programmes/hardtalk/9372832.stm, accessed 11 March 2015.

Benford, R. D. and Snow, D. A. (2000) 'Framing processes and social movements: an overview and assessment', *Annual Review of Sociology*, 26: 611–639.

Betz, H. G. (1994) *Radical right-wing populism in Western Europe*, New York: St Martin's Press.

Betz, H. G. (1998) 'Introduction' in H. G. Betz and S. Immerfall (eds) *The politics of the right. neo-populist parties and movements in established democracies*, London: Macmillan.

Bigo, D. (2002) 'Security and immigration: toward a critique of the governmentality of unease', *Alternatives: Global, Local, Political*, 27: 63–92.

Bjørklund, T. (2011) 'The radical right in Norway: the development of the Progress Party' in N. Langenbacher and B. Schellenberg (eds) *Is Europe on the 'right' path?: right-wing extremism and right-wing populism in Europe*, http://library.fes.de/pdf-files/do/08338.pdf, accessed 11 March 2015.

Bjørklund, T. and Andersen, J. G. (1999) 'Anti immigration parties in Denmark and Norway. The progress parties and the Danish People's Party', working paper, Institut for Okonomi, Politik og Forvaltning, http://vbn.aau.dk/files/93212/35031999_4.pdf, accessed 11 March 2015.

Buzan, B., Wæver, O. and Wilde, J. D. (1998) *Security: a new framework for analysis*, Boulder, CO: Lynne Rienner.

Carter, E. (2005) *The extreme right in western Europe: success or failure?* Manchester: Manchester University Press.

CERD (2003) http://www.unhchr.ch/tbs/doc.nsf/(Symbol)/d6ddc0213d5edbebc1256e1c0036cc95?Opendocument, accessed 9 March 2015.

Coffi, H. (2004) 'Can extreme right voting be explained ideologically?', paper for ECPR Joint Sessions, Uppsala, http://ecpr.eu/Filestore/PaperProposal/82bf59be-4a49-426a-b9d4-4fb347e28475.pdf, accessed 11 March 2015.

Council of Europe and ECRI (European Commission against Racism and Intolerance) (2006) 'Third report on Denmark', http://ec.europa.eu/migrant-integration/, accessed 11 March 2015.

Crouch, D. (2014) 'The rise of the anti-immigrant Sweden Democrats: "We don't feel at home any more, and it's their fault"', *The Guardian*, 14 December, http://www.theguardian.com/world/2014/dec/14/sweden-democrats-flex-muscles-anti-immigrant-kristianstad, accessed 11 March 2015.

Dahlström, C. (2004) 'Rhetoric, practice and the dynamics of institutional change: immigrant policy in Sweden, 1964–2000', *Scandinavian Political Studies*, 27: 287–310.

Danskfolkeparti [DF] (2001) Manifesto, https://manifestoproject.wzb.eu/election_parties/407, accessed 11 March 2015.

Danskfolkeparti [DF] (2009) Arbejdsprogram, http://www.danskfolkeparti.dk/pictures_org/arbejdesprog-net(3).pdf, accessed 9 March 2015.

Danskfolkeparti [DF] (2015) http://www.danskfolkeparti.dk/Home, accessed 11 March 2015.

Davies, P. and Lynch, D. (2002) *The Routledge companion to fascism and the far right*, New York: Routledge.

Decker, F. (2004) *Der neue Rechtspopulismus*, Opladen: Leske und Budrich Verlag.

Druckman, J. N. (2001) 'On the limits of framing effects: who can frame?', *The Journal of Politics*, 63(4): 1041–1066.

Eatwell, R. (2000) 'The rebirth of the extreme right in Western Europe?, *Parliamentary Affairs*, 53(3): 407–425.

Entman, R. M. (1993) 'Framing: toward clarification of a fractured paradigm', *Journal of Communication*, 43: 51–58.

Fennema, M. (1997) 'Some conceptual issues and problems in the comparison of anti-immigrant parties in western Europe', *Party Politics*, 3(4): 473–92.

Fremskrittspartiet [FrP] (1985) Manifesto, https://visuals.manifesto-project.wzb.eu/mpdb-shiny/cmp_dashboard_dataset/, accessed 11 March 2015.

Fremskrittspartiet [FrP] (2001) Press releases archive, https://www.frp.no/, accessed 8 March 2015.

Fremskrittspartiet [FrP] (2015) http://www.frp.no/nor, accessed 11 March 2015.

Frontpage Magazine (2006) 'Europe's suicide?' http://archive.frontpagemag.com/readArticle.aspx?ARTID=4680, accessed 15 January 2015.

Georgiadou, V. (2008) *The far right and the consequences of consensus*, Athens: Kastaniotis Publications.

Golder, M. (2003) 'Explaining variation in the success of extreme right parties in western Europe', *Comparative Political Studies*, 36(4): 432–466.

Hagelund, A. (2003) ' A matter of decency? The progress party in Norwegian immigration politics', *Journal of Ethnic and Migration Studies*, 29(1): 47–65.

Hainsworth, P. (1992) *The extreme right in Europe and the USA*, New York: St Martin's Press.

Hainsworth, P. (2000) *The politics of the extreme right: from the margins to the mainstream*, London: Pinter.

Hainsworth, P. (2008) *The extreme right in Western Europe*, New York: Routledge.

Ignazi, P. (1996) *New challenges: post materialism and the extreme right*, Madrid: Instituto Juan March de Estudios e Investigaciones, Centro de Estudios Avanzados en Ciencias Sociales.

Ignazi, P. (1997) 'The extreme right in Europe: a survey' in P. Merkl and L. Weinberg (eds) *The revival of right-wing extremism in the nineties*, London: Frank Cass.

Ignazi, P. (2003) *Extreme right parties in Western Europe*, Oxford: Oxford University Press.

International Network Against Cyber Hate, Inach-Annual Repor(2005) http://www.inach.net/content/INACH-annual-report-2005.pdf, accessed 6 March 2015.

Isaksson, P. and Jokisalo, J. (1998) *Kallonmittaajia ja skinejä. Rasismin aatehistoriaa*, Helsinki: Like.

Ivarsflaten, E. (2003) 'The success of the populist right in Western Europe: Should mainstream parties be blamed?', paper for ECPR conference, Marburg, http://s3.amazonaws.com/zanran_storage/www.essex.ac.uk/Content Pages/165146510.pdf, accessed 11 March 2015.

Jyllands-Posten (2006) http://jyllands-posten.dk/international/ECE4771289/honourable-fellow-citizens-of-the-muslim-world/, accessed 9 March 2015.

Kamal Quereshi v. Denmark (2003) Communication No. 27/2002 U.N. Doc. CERD/C/63/D/27/2002 (2003), http://www1.umn.edu/humanrts/country/decisions/27-2002.html, accessed 11 March 2015.

Karyotis, G. (2007) 'European migration policy in the aftermath of September 11: the security–migration nexus. Innovation', *The European Journal of Social Science Research*, 20(1): 1–17.

Kestila, E. (2006) 'Is there demand for radical right populism in the Finnish electorate?', *Scandinavian Political Studies*, 29(3): 169–191.

Kitschelt, H. and McGann, A. J. (1995) *The radical right in Western Europe*, Ann Arbor: University of Michigan Press.

Korhonen, J. (2012) 'Ten paths to populism: how silent Finland became a playing field for loud populism' in C. Fienchi, M. Morris and L. Caballero (eds) *Populist fantasies: European revolts in context*, Counterpoint, http://counterpoint.uk.com/wp-content/uploads/2013/10/Populist-Fantasies-European-revolts-in-context.pdf, accessed 23 February 2015.

Lavenex, S. (2001) 'The Europeanization of refugee policies: normative challenges and Institutional legacies', *JCMS: Journal of Common Market Studies*, 39: 851–874.

Marcus, J. (2000) 'Exorcising Europe's Demons: A Far-Right Resurgence?', *The Washington Quarterly*, 23(4): 31–40.

McDonald, M. (2008) 'Securitisation and the construction of security', *European Journal of International Relations*, 14(4): 563–587.

Minkenberg, M. (1998) 'Context and consequence: the impact of the new radical right on the political process in France and Germany', *German Politics and Society*, 48: 1–23.

Minkenberg, M. (2004) 'Religious effects on the shaping of immigration policy in western democracies', paper for the ECPR Joint Session of Workshops, Uppsala, http://ecpr.eu/Filestore/PaperProposal/7392a0d4-d7bb-47c2-b917-ad433009f0be.pdf, accessed 11 March 2015.

Moller, F. (2007) 'Photographic interventions in post-9/11 security policy security', *Dialogue*, 38: 179–196.

Moufahim, M. (2007) *Interpreting discourse: a critical discourse analysis of the marketing of an extreme right party. The Vlaams Blok/Vlaams Belang*, PhD thesis submitted to the University of Nottingham, http://eprints.nottingham.ac.uk/11781/1/518835.pdf, accessed 11 March 2015.

Mudde, C. (2002) *The ideology of the extreme right*, Manchester: Manchester University Press.

Nelson, T. E., Clawson, R. A. and Oxley, Z. M. (1997) 'Media framing of a civil liberties conflict and its effect on tolerance', *American Political Science Review*, 91: 567–583.

Norris, P. (2004) 'The "new cleavage" thesis and the social basis of radical right support', paper for annual meeting of the American Political Science Association, Chicago, http://www.hks.harvard.edu/fs/pnorris/Acrobat/APSA%202004%20Radical%20Right.pdf, accessed 11 March 2015.

Pedersen, K. and Ringsmose, J. (2004) 'From the Progress Party to the Danish People's Party – from protest party to government supporting party', paper for Joint Session of Workshops, Uppsala, http://ecpr.eu/Filestore/PaperProposal/bfb7d87d-9ad0-47f0-ac00-a7977995cbb2.pdf, accessed 11 March 2015.

Pekonen, K., Hynynen, P. and Kalliala, M. (2001) 'The new radical right taking shape in Finland' in P. Perrineau (ed) *Les croisés de la société fermée. L' Europe des extrêmes droites*, Paris: Editions de l' Aube.

Perussuomalaiset [PS] (2011) Manifesto, https://www.perussuomalaiset.fi/, accessed 20 February 2015.

Perussuomalaiset [PS] (2015), https://www.perussuomalaiset.fi/, accessed 11 March 2015.

Pettersson, C. (2004) 'Right-wing politicians want to ban Islam', *Nettavisen*, 19 July, http://pub.nettavisen.no/254421.html, accessed 2 February 2015.

Rydgren, J. (2001) ' Why not in Sweden? Interpreting radical right populism in the light of a negative case', paper for ECPR Joint Sessions, Grenoble, http://ecpr.eu/Filestore/PaperProposal/f00035cd-d270-49b9-aad8-652b2aed53aa.pdf, accessed11 March 2015.

Rydgren, J. (2005) 'Is extreme right-wing populism contagious? Explaining the emergence of a new party family', *European Journal of Political Research*, 44: 413–437.

Scheufele, D. (1999) 'Framing as a theory of media effects', *Journal of Communication*, 49: 103–122.

Sverigedemokraterna [SD] (1999) Manifesto, https://sd.se/, accessed 11 March 2015.

Sverigedemokraterna [SD] (2005) Manifesto, https://sd.se/, accessed 11 March 2015.

Sverigedemokraterna [SD] (2011) Manifesto, https://sd.se/, accessed 11 March 2015.

Sverigedemokraterna [SD] (2014) Manifesto, https://sd.se/, accessed 11 March 2015.

Sverigedemokraterna [SD] (2015), http://sverigedemokraterna.se/, accessed 11 March 2015.

Taggart, P. (1996) *The new populism and the new politics: new protest parties in Sweden in a comparative perspective*, New York: St Martin's Press.

Van der Brug, W. and Fennema, M. (2006) 'The support base of radical right parties in the enlarged European Union', paper for EES, Lisbon, http://www.mzes.uni-mannheim.de/projekte/typo3/site/fileadmin/BookSeries/Volume_One/Ch10_chapter_final.pdf, accessed 11 March 2015.

Van Spanje, J. and Van der Brug, W. (2005) 'The immigration issue and anti-immigration party support in Western Europe', paper for ECPR general conference, Budapest, http://scholar.google.co.uk/citations?view_op=view_citation&hl=en&user=cJQGmHsAAAAJ&cstart=80&citation_for_view=cJQGmHsAAAAJ:TQgYirikUcIC, accessed January 2015.

Von Beyme, K. (1988) 'Right-wing extremism in post-war Europe', *West European Politics*, 11(2): 1–18.

Widfeldt, A. (2000) 'Scandinavia: mixed success for the populist right', *Parliamentary Affairs*, 53(3): 486–500.
Widfeldt, A. (2001) 'The democratic response to Swedish right-wing extremism', paper for the ECPR Joint Sessions of Workshops, Grenoble, http://ecpr.eu/Filestore/PaperProposal/48e6e67c-3a94-4ad6-a1ab-825a45467aa5.pdf, accessed 11 March 2015.
Widfeldt, A. (2015) *Extreme right parties in Scandinavia*, London: Routledge.
Wren, K. (2001) 'Cultural racism: something rotten in the state of Denmark?', *Social and Cultural Geography*, 2(2): 141–162.

Index

Notes are indicated by page number followed by 'n' and number of note, e.g. 204n21

Printed and bound by CPI Group (UK) Ltd, Croydon, CR0 4YY